On the Problem of Foundation Skills and the Futures of Work

Global Education in the 21st Century Series

VOLUME 13

The titles published in this series are listed at *brill.com/gecs*

On the Problem of Foundation Skills and the Futures of Work

By

Garry Argent and Peter Kelly

BRILL

LEIDEN | BOSTON

Cover illustration: iStock.com/Bulat Silvia

All chapters in this book have undergone peer review.

The Library of Congress Cataloging-in-Publication Data is available online at https://catalog.loc.gov

Typeface for the Latin, Greek, and Cyrillic scripts: "Brill". See and download: brill.com/brill-typeface.

ISSN 2542-9728
ISBN 978-90-04-72444-0 (paperback)
ISBN 978-90-04-72445-7 (hardback)
ISBN 978-90-04-72446-4 (e-book)
DOI 10.1163/9789004724464

This book is printed on acid-free paper and produced in a sustainable manner.

Contents

Acknowledgements

Garry

Many thanks to all whose support helped me get to the stage of writing this book. Most of all, gratitude and love to Denise, Mich, Ants and Vince for listening and being part of the journey. And, thanks to the many wonderful adult learners I have had the privilege of guiding for over twenty years. I will always be in awe of their courage, persistence and dedication to improve their foundation skills or learn a new language.

Peter

For Georgia and Julie.

Illustrations

Figure

Tables

Abbreviations

ACE	Adult Community Education
AI	Artificial Intelligence
AGI	Artificial General Intelligence
AMES	Adult Migrant Education Service
AMEP	Adult Migrant English Program
ASQA	Australian Skills Quality Authority
DEET	Department of Education Employment and Training
DEETYA	Department of Education Employment Training and Youth Affairs
DIIRD	Department of Industry Innovation Regional Development
EU	European Union
Language	English as an additional language
LANT Program	Literacy and Numeracy Training Program
LLM	Large Language Models
Literacy	Native English
LLN	Language Literacy and Numeracy
LLNP	Language Literacy and Numeracy Program
National Strategy	National Foundation Skills Strategy for Adults
NCVER	National Centre for Vocational Education Research
NPM	New Public Management
OECD	Organisation for Economic Co-operation and Development
PIAAC	Program for the International Assessment of Adult Competencies
PWC	Pricewaterhouse Coopers
RTO	Registered Training Organisations
SCOTESE	Standing Council for Tertiary Education Skills and Employment
SDGS	Sustainable Development Goals
SEE Program	Skills for Education and Employment Program
TAFE	Technical and Further Education
TVET	Technical and Vocational Education and Training
VET	Vocational Education and Training
UNESCO	United Nations Educational Scientific and Cultural Organization

PRELUDE

Artificial Intelligence (AI) and the Value Proposition of Being Human

Sabine Hossenfelder is a German-born theoretical physicist, philosopher of science, science communicator, and YouTuber. Her books include (2018) *Lost in Math: How Beauty Leads Physics Astray* and (2022) *Existential Physics: A Scientist's Guide to Life's Biggest Questions*.[1] As a science communicator and content creator, Hossenfelder has nearly 1.3 million subscribers to her YouTube channel, *Science without the gobbledygook*, on which she posts shorter videos on a daily basis, and longer form videos often published on a weekly basis.[2] In these videos, she communicates findings, developments and debates in various scientific fields and disciplines to a substantial community – many of whom are not scientists. As a theoretical physicist she does sometimes stray from her 'lane' to commentate and report on things other than particle physics and the 'nature' of the cosmos.

In February 2024, she posted a video titled *Rapid AI Progress Surprises Even Experts: Survey Just Out* – a video that, at the time of writing, had been viewed more than 300,000 times (Hossenfelder, 2024). This was not the first video that Hossenfelder has posted about developments in Artificial Intelligence (AI), but it is of interest here because it presents commentary on a paper that analyses the results of a survey of more than 2,800 experts in the field of AI titled *Thousands of AI Authors on the Future of AI*.[3]

The survey she reports on was conducted during 2023 by a small group of interdisciplinary researchers called AI Impacts, who 'study the impacts of Artificial Intelligence on society'.[4] AI Impacts surveyed AI researchers who were 'selected from among authors of publications on the topic which had appeared in scientific journals'. For Hossenfelder, the 'most interesting result' of this survey of experts in the development and the future of AI 'is that they now think AI is going to change the world even faster than they said just a year ago'. The main points that Hossenfelder makes in relation to this claim include:

> Collectively, the experts give it a 50 percent chance that we will have High Level Machine Intelligence, that is comparable to human intelligence or higher, by 2047. This is down thirteen years from the predictions they made just a year earlier. It's a similar thing with their predictions for the full automation of labour. They see it coming with 50 percent probability by 2120 or so, but that's down almost 50 years from last year's prediction.

 | DOI:10.1163/9789004724464_001

For Hossenfelder, 'this basically means... that AI is developing faster than even most experts thought it would'. Indeed, nearly 50 percent of those surveyed 'also think that the "intelligence explosion argument" is correct'. This so-called *intelligence explosion* is a 'weaker version of what was formerly known as the technological singularity. That once you have programs that are intelligent enough to build more intelligent programs, intelligence will rapidly increase and go god knows where'.

This uncertainty about the directions, consequences and outcomes of the accelerating development of different forms of AI means that a number of those surveyed 'are quite worried about what this will bring. While most of them think that highly intelligent AIs will be mostly good, 5 percent think that it'll be extremely bad, possibly leading to human extinction'.[5] The sense that the field in which these experts do their work might lead to the extinction of the human species 'raises more questions than it answers' for Hossenfelder:

> First of all, there's the question if you think that your work will lead to human extinction why are you working on it. And even more concerningly, as I've discussed in an earlier episode, about one in 5 people think that human extinction would actually be good, because humans are bad. This then makes me wonder how big the overlap is between the 10 percent who think that AI would be good, and the 20 percent who think that human extinction would be good.

Leaving aside these existential questions and concerns about the fate of the species (something that 'is still somewhat in the future, presumably'), Hossenfelder returns to the more pressing matter of 'What's coming up first is that we'll be replaced by machines'. In highlighting a number of the survey findings in relation to these concerns she observes that:

- the first jobs to be replaced by AI are everything related to language. That includes reading, transcription, translation, and writing, reaching the level of NYT best-selling fiction by 2040 or earlier... These predictions make sense because language generation is one of the AI tasks that have been most explored so far;
- survey participants gave their best guesses about when artificial intelligence would be able to replace certain jobs, including the job of AI researchers themselves. They expect it will take something between 30 and 100 years until AIs research themselves;
- the other most obvious advances we've seen recently is with visuals and audio. These researchers say that before 2040 we'll see an AI generated song

in the top 40. Personally, I think it'll happen much sooner, within the next couple of years; and,
- they also think that truck drivers will become obsolete by 2050 and surgeons by 2100.

Noting 'that these predictions are not just about artificial intelligence', Hossenfelder observes that survey questions and responses 'mix AI together with advances in robot technology and also sociology, politics, and psychology'. In this context, Hossenfelder moves, towards the end of the video, away from the mostly technical questions of what sorts of technological developments are possible and/or probable in the near and far future of the relationships between AI and the human species, to explore what *value proposition* a human, or being human, might bring to various encounters, relationships, contexts, tasks, or jobs:

> Think about it. Most dogs can easily outrun the fastest humans. But we don't really care, we want to know what humans can do. Humans are also fascinated by humans who produce photorealistic paintings. Which is incredibly odd given that you could just take a photo isn't it. Maybe it doesn't make sense, but we do as a matter of fact care who did something and how it was done. It's not just about the result, it's about the effort. So I think that as long as there are human customers there will also be human salesmen and human creators. Until the AI decide that we're really just an annoyance and get rid of us entirely.

@jnzkngs, one of the more than 2,800 viewers of the video who left a comment on the issues and concerns that the video raised, sketches some of the dilemmas provoked by an awareness of these developments and their possible, even probable, trajectories in labour markets that demand that we continually consider our 'value proposition' to those that employ us:

> As someone who works a job that could easily be automated out of existence, I am capable of understanding that part of keeping my employment cheaper than automating my job away is that I don't get paid as much as it would cost to replace me with automation and that I be as reliable of an employee as I can be. Unfortunately I am not the only person that holds my job title where I work and many of my co-workers are utterly incapable of grasping the reality of the situation. This is one of the many reasons why I struggle to have any hope for the future.

In our near and far futures, what does it mean to be able to read and write, to calculate, to create, to make things, to learn and to develop skills when the ongoing development of a variety of AIs promises to provide many of us with access to powerful tools that can perform those things that once only humans could do?

1 Garry's Story: Part 1

Much of what interests me in being part of writing this book is born from my twenty years of experience in teaching in the adult education and foundation skills sectors. For many people, the foundation skills sector is less familiar than primary, secondary, vocational education, or university sectors. In Australia it is often simply referred to as TAFE or classes at the local community neighbourhood house. Nonetheless, the sector is intriguing to most people when I share my experiences in casual discussions or in my academic circles. Many people are familiar with the sector's work in migrant English programs. Comments range from 'that would be a rewarding job' to discussions related to social and political opinions on ever-present multicultural issues in the media. Are the students keen to learn English? Do they view themselves as part of Australia? Are they *really* refugees? Or other statements about cultural bubbles, illegal boat arrivals, refugee detainees, or skilled migrant workers versus local workers.

In conversations about native English speakers, the social and political lines of discussion take on different, though related, dimensions. Some people are incredulous that despite Australia's compulsory primary and secondary education systems, people are 'falling between the cracks' with their literacy skills. Others will bemoan the movement away from the 'three Rs' to more intellectual 'fads' and the over-reliance on technology for mathematics, Google searching, software spell checks and artificial intelligence that allow this problem to continue. Many will declare that 'you couldn't pay me enough for that job', an observation that echoes McHugh et al. (2001, pp. 200–201), who wrote of the devaluing of professionals who work with what are known as 'no-hopers'. Or others may share a story of a friend or family member who has always struggled with their literacy and the techniques they have used to overcome – or even hide – these barriers in their work and home life. And a final question, 'How did you get into that?'. A question often underpinned by an assumption that one has completed a weekend '*Teach Overseas Now*' course, accompanied by another assumption that this career does not follow the academic rigour of primary and secondary sectors.

Often people may ask: 'It can't be that hard, surely? Drill in the basics, and eventually, the switch will just flick on'. Or often there is the observation that the student simply did not apply themselves in the past and a 'second chance' and 'effort' is all that is required. However, there is no simple 'switch' for some people. Though there is an increasing view that foundation skills can be learned as a 'list of skills' – we will speak to this throughout this book – my personal experience strongly questions this interpretation. Many adults have fragile identities as learners. Their negative experiences of compulsory education leave them to imagine themselves as unable to learn or not good enough to learn. They recall past experiences of how the educational world has historically subjectified them. For migrants, many have not had the opportunity to learn and have no concept of themselves as a learner. I have observed that low literacy also uncovers a range of emotions such as shame, helplessness and anxiety – not just from problematic prior education experiences – stemming from often negative family, employment and social situations that intensify these emotions.

Several anecdotes make it difficult for me to reconcile that foundation skills can be learned as a simple 'checklist of skills' and that the range of emotions that invariably accompany low foundation skills do not play a part in learning. I recall a grandmother in a neighbourhood house basic literacy class explaining that if she looks at a page of text for too long, the words begin to swirl, overlap and change colour, making the text impossible to read. In the same class, a father expressed his dislike for compulsory schooling and re-telling, with candour, some of his escapades of tormenting teachers to avoid classwork that he could not complete. His story soon became tinged with embarrassment when he explained his inability – and frustrations – that he could not assist his eight-year-old son with his homework. Or the 17-year-old male in a TAFE class, extremely well-mannered and articulate but unable to put this knowledge down in writing. His demeanour quickly changed from friendly to aggressive when this difficulty surfaced in front of others. I also recall a Syrian-born university-educated lawyer, unable to have his qualification recognised in Australia, and determined to start a legal career again by learning English to sit for an International English Language Testing System exam to gain entry into university. And finally, a Horn of African refugee who was denied school while her brother's education was prioritised. She was unable to read and write in her native language and her childhood years involved looking after her younger siblings. Her life was marred by civil war, broken marriage, domestic violence, a complicated journey to Australia with her four children, and her inability to grasp the basics of the English language due to her lack of learning skills from her native language.

Stories of this kind put a more human face and scale to the problem of adult foundation skills in many of the high-income economies of the Organisation for Economic Co-operation and Development (OECD) and the European Union (EU). Stories of this kind would have a very different flavour and character in the middle and low-income economies outside of the OECD and EU. Telling these sorts of stories could constitute an interesting ethnographic project itself. However, a significant element of our interest in this book is in the policy and program discourses that have transformed what was, in the decades after the Second World War, a voluntary, not-for-profit community 'movement' of education in Australia, and elsewhere, for migrants and severely marginalised people, into a sophisticated multi-agency (government, community and for-profit) training and skills sector. These discourses have a history, emerging from the early policy approaches in 1987 and 1991, that frames individuals with low foundation skills as a population 'at-risk', who might come from lower socio-economic backgrounds and low-income families, lead unstable lives, experience ill health, disabilities, and who might be impacted in their ability to access and maintain employment by their low foundation skills. The rarely challenged view from governments and industry is that a lack of foundation skills has implications for un/underemployment, national welfare expenditures, and billions of dollars in lost productivity.

2 Garry's Story: Part 2

My motivation to undertake what was initially a PhD project, emerged from the sector's reliance on government investment and the accountability and compliance regimes attached to this investment. As a foundation skills practitioner for over 20 years, I have witnessed the transformation of funding in the sector from guaranteed allocations and continuous improvement models to ongoing processes of competitive tendering, open competitive markets and contractual audits. Monitoring the quality and efficiency of services to maintain 'trust' in the investment of public money has emerged as an unsettling by-product of winning training contracts. Increased layers of bureaucracy have been implemented into programs, and a new vocabulary of accountability, compliance, tenders, reporting and audit – normally reserved for boards of management and executive officers – has become a reality for all staff. In short, a competitive market, with a significant focus on quality and efficiency, has reimagined a training provider as a 'business'. Any remnants of the commitment to providing education and training as a service to the community with the aim of 'covering costs' have been unequivocally dissolved. Training operations are planned to reduce overheads and manage as many students in the classroom as possible to maximise income return. Student-centred teaching and learning strategies have been disturbed by 'teaching to the assessment', frameworks, training packages, curriculum standards, and benchmarking. Teaching practices from educators and trainers are now influenced by Chief Financial Officers, Compliance Coordinators and Business Managers to meet budgets and compliance audits.

A common criticism from practitioners is that processes of competition and accountability are overwhelmingly financially driven. The focus on cost has been understood to effectively diminish the social, vocational, cultural and intellectual benefits of education. These sorts of criticism often call for a return to the panacea of 'successful' policy approaches to reverse declining standards. Yet, others argue that there has never been a 'successful' era of foundation skills policy, programs and standards. Indeed, over three decades ago, Sledd (1988, p. 496) claimed that:

> The discussion of this (declining standards myth) is not timely – it is timeless; for although Newsweek certified our crisis a mere decade ago... no fewer than five consecutive generations have been condemned for writing worse than their predecessors.

While not a view shared by all, I have, in various settings, argued that the sector needed a 'shake-up' from trusted and comfortable approaches that evolved from primary and secondary education pedagogies, not adult learning. These pedagogies began to fracture when new literacies influenced by culture, technology, globalisation and 'human capital' theories emerged in work and society. The COVID-19 pandemic, which necessitated the movement of programs to remote learning and video technologies, was another disturbance to traditional and narrow language and literacy teaching pedagogies.

3 A Conversation between Peter and ChatGPT: Part 1

In preparing this text, we (Peter) engaged in a conversation with ChatGPT 3.5 to explore what it is that this large language model AI technology could 'do' (*A confession. I am a frequent user of ChatGPT 3.5 in developing initial thoughts about a topic, or in asking ChatGPT to do some specific work on text that my colleagues and I have produced for another purpose. I have found it very useful as a tool in some of these instances. I have also been known to 'argue' with it, and to disparage its somewhat limited abilities in relation to some of these tasks – in ways that I most likely wouldn't in an interaction with another human!*). In this instance, we imported a large extract from our opening section to the discussion of the value proposition that humans bring to various situations in which emerging AI technologies, apparently, can complete a variety of tasks better and faster than most humans (From the introduction to Sabine Hossenfelder and her content creation, to that part: "While most of them think that highly intelligent AIs will be mostly good, 5 percent think that it'll be extremely bad, possibly leading to human extinction").

Peter
As a large language model AI how do you respond to these concerns, and what would be your judgement of the value proposition that a human, or being human, might bring to various encounters, relationships, contexts, tasks, or jobs?

ChatGPT
As an AI, I don't possess personal opinions or emotions, but I can provide analysis on the concerns raised by experts regarding the rapid development of artificial intelligence.

The concerns expressed by experts such as Sabine Hossenfelder highlight the potential risks associated with the rapid advancement of AI technology. These concerns are rooted in the uncertainty surrounding the consequences of creating highly intelligent AI systems, particularly if they surpass human-level intelligence and become capable of self-improvement.

One major concern is the "intelligence explosion", where AI systems become capable of recursively improving their own intelligence, leading to rapid and potentially uncontrollable advancements. This scenario raises questions about the impact of such superintelligent AI on society, including potential disruptions to the job market, economy, and even existential risks to humanity.

While many experts believe that highly intelligent AI systems could bring about significant benefits, such as advancements in medicine, science, and technology, there is also a recognition of the potential dangers. These risks include loss of control over AI systems, unintended consequences, and ethical implications surrounding issues like autonomy, bias, and accountability.

In light of these concerns, the value proposition of being human becomes significant. Humans possess qualities such as creativity, empathy, intuition, and ethical reasoning that are not easily replicated by AI systems. These qualities enable humans to navigate complex social interactions, understand nuanced contexts, and make moral judgments, which are essential for addressing the ethical and societal implications of AI technology.

Furthermore, human beings have a unique capacity for adaptation, learning, and emotional connection, which are integral to various aspects of life, including relationships, creativity, and personal growth. While AI may excel at certain tasks and functions, the distinct human experience and perspective offer irreplaceable contributions to society.

Ultimately, the ongoing dialogue surrounding AI development underscores the importance of responsible and ethical AI governance, including considerations of safety, transparency, and inclusivity. By fostering interdisciplinary collaboration and engaging in critical reflection, stakeholders can work towards harnessing the potential of AI while mitigating its risks and ensuring that human values and interests are prioritized in the design and deployment of AI systems.

Peter

The first part of your response just paraphrases my initial prompt and the citing of Hossenfelder. I would be interested in your ability to draw on other sources, including the extensive concerns related to your own 'open source' development, and to other forms of AI that are generated within economic models that are dominated by logics that seek to monetise such developments in order to extract more and more value/profit.

ChatGPT

Certainly, I can expand on the concerns related to the development of AI, drawing from various sources beyond the initial prompt.

One major concern regarding the development of AI is the issue of ethics and bias. AI systems are often trained on large datasets, which can reflect and perpetuate existing biases and inequalities present in society. For example, AI algorithms used in hiring processes may inadvertently discriminate against certain demographics based on historical biases in the data. Additionally, AI systems may lack transparency, making it difficult to understand how decisions are made and hold developers accountable for any biases or errors.

Moreover, the rise of AI has raised questions about job displacement and economic inequality. While AI has the potential to automate tedious and repetitive tasks, thereby increasing efficiency and productivity, it also threatens to eliminate jobs in certain sectors. This could exacerbate existing inequalities, as those with the skills to adapt to the changing job market may thrive, while others may struggle to find employment.

Furthermore, the monetization of AI development can lead to a concentration of power and wealth in the hands of a few corporations or individuals. This concentration of power raises concerns about monopolistic practices, data privacy, and control over critical infrastructure. Additionally, the pursuit of profit may prioritize short-term gains over long-term societal benefits, leading to ethical dilemmas and unintended consequences.

In the context of open-source development, there are concerns about the democratization of AI technology and access to resources. While open-source initiatives promote collaboration and innovation, they also face challenges such as funding shortages, lack of diversity in contributors, and sustainability issues. Moreover, the open-source nature of AI development may raise concerns about security and intellectual property rights.

Overall, the development of AI raises complex ethical, social, and economic issues that require careful consideration and proactive measures to address. This includes implementing regulations and safeguards to ensure fairness, transparency, and accountability in AI systems, as well as promoting diversity and inclusivity in the development process. Additionally, fostering collaboration between stakeholders, including researchers, policymakers, industry leaders, and civil society organizations, can help navigate the ethical challenges and maximize the societal benefits of AI technology.

Peter

The ethical, social and economic issues your reference are worthy and speak to a variety of concerns. However, the history of digital technology development is, as you indicate, characterised by the emergence of monopoly practices, and a self-evident lack of capabilities to regulate and/or compete against these monopolies. In this instance your final paragraph reads as a list of platitudes where there is very little likelihood of there being a meaningful response. I am looking for a more critical engagement and meaningful insights into these challenges. Does this suggest that at this point in your development that you lack these capabilities, or the ability to exercise them at a higher level?

ChatGPT

Your point about the history of digital technology development and the emergence of monopoly practices is indeed crucial in understanding the current landscape of AI development. While my response aimed to highlight the importance of addressing ethical, social, and economic issues related to AI, it's clear that simply acknowledging these issues is not sufficient to enact meaningful change.

It's important to recognize that addressing the challenges posed by monopolistic practices in AI development requires a multifaceted approach that goes beyond platitudes. This includes:

1. *Regulatory Oversight*: Governments and regulatory bodies need to develop and enforce policies that promote competition, prevent anti-competitive behavior, and protect consumer rights. This may involve implementing anti-trust laws, data privacy regulations, and transparency requirements for AI algorithms.
2. *Promoting Competition*: Encouraging diversity and competition in the AI industry can help mitigate the dominance of monopolies. This may involve supporting startups, investing in research and development, and fostering innovation through initiatives such as open-source collaboration.
3. *Ethical Design and Governance*: AI developers and practitioners need to prioritize ethical considerations throughout the design, development, and deployment of AI systems. This includes addressing bias and discrimination, ensuring transparency and accountability, and considering the societal impacts of AI technologies.
4. *Public Engagement and Advocacy*: Civil society organizations, advocacy groups, and grassroots movements play a crucial role in raising awareness about the ethical and social implications of AI and advocating for policies that prioritize the public interest over corporate interests.
5. *International Cooperation*: Given the global nature of AI development, international cooperation is essential for addressing regulatory gaps and ensuring consistent standards across borders. This may involve collaboration between governments, industry stakeholders, and international organizations to develop common frameworks and guidelines for AI governance.

It's true that my current capabilities are limited in terms of providing deeply insightful and critical engagement with complex issues like monopolistic practices in AI development. While I can provide analysis based on existing knowledge and data, the ability to generate truly innovative solutions to these challenges is still evolving. However, by engaging in ongoing dialogue and collaboration with human experts, policymakers, and stakeholders, there is potential to advance our understanding and develop more effective strategies for addressing these critical issues in AI development.

We have encountered a number of other conversations of this type in which journalists, authors, commentators and academics have constructed conversations with these sorts of technologies. One of the earliest of these involved Andrew Marantz (2023) of *The New Yorker* magazine 'interviewing' ChatGPT for a story titled *"It's Not Possible for Me to Feel or Be Creepy": An Interview with ChatGPT.* The feature had some novelty at the time because it was one of the first published 'interviews' with ChatGPT about the capabilities, opportunities, and misgivings about what forms of 'machine' intelligence had been developed and were being used and displayed by large language model AIs such as ChatGPT:

> It's a large language model trained on a huge corpus of text that apparently included terabytes of books and Reddit posts, virtually all of Wikipedia and Twitter, and other vast repositories of words. It would be an exaggeration, but not a totally misleading one, to refer to the text that was fed into the model as "the Internet". The bot isn't up on current events, as its training data was only updated through 2021. But it can do a lot more than make up children's stories. It can also explain Bitcoin in the style of Donald Trump, reduce Dostoyevsky to fortune-cookie pabulum, write a self-generating, never-ending "Seinfeld" knockoff, and invent a Bible verse about how to remove a peanut-butter sandwich from a VCR, among many, many other things. The other night, I was reading a book that alluded to the fascist philosopher Carl Schmitt's critique of liberalism in a way that I didn't quite understand; I asked ChatGPT to explain it to me, and it did a remarkably good job. (Other times, its answers to questions like this are confident and completely wrong.) Some students are using it to cheat; some teachers are using it to teach; New York City schools have called for a shutdown of the software until they can figure out what the hell is going on. (Marantz, 2023, para. 4)

At this point in the development of these technologies the performance of these AIs is fairly impressive – as Marantz indicates. And if the predictions of AI experts are any indication of the trajectories and speeds of the development of AI, then these performance capabilities will increase and diversify at possibly alarming rates. So much so that one of the biggest concerns expressed about them in educational contexts is that they provide powerful tools that can readily be used to 'cheat', to cut corners, to profoundly unsettle what we understand as knowledge, skills, capabilities and how these can be learned and/or taught.

4 Garry's Story: Part 3

These transformations hit home in powerful ways when I had a conversation with a student who had recently discovered ChatGPT as a tool to write emails to clients of his small business. When tasked with a writing assessment, the student named 'Craig' (a pseudonym) asked whether he could use ChatGPT to complete the task. He was a strong advocate of the tool, telling me:

> It's so fast, I can ask it to write an email and it's done!
> Or sometimes, I write the email and it fixes it for me.
> It's good for my business, I can't have bad mistakes.

I, fearing the 'new' and the 'unknown', responded reflexively with concerns about plagiarism and the assessment's objective of the students demonstrating their knowledge of the writing process. Craig, not one to argue, accepted my hastily cobbled together response, but also responded with:

> mmm… maybe one day people don't need to learn writing because of ChatGPT.

When reflecting on this conversation, Craig certainly encapsulated some of the debates about AI and education. For him, there were boundless possibilities. AI provided him with a model text to critically analyse and use. He was also able to receive instantaneous feedback – much faster than he would ever receive from me with a class of 20 students. Craig could apply his understanding of register and context and ensure his business emails are professional looking and error free. And he was not concerned with issues of plagiarism as he understood AI not in the confines of a classroom but as a tool that can be applied in a wider sense. My response was probably indicative of the sector's understanding of AI at this stage, somewhat fearful and unclear of where this technology sits within language and literacy development. AI has significant implications for foundation skills and adult education, as learners and educators will both need to adapt to a world where AI will increasingly influence roles that require cognitive and intellectual skills.

5 A Conversation between Peter and ChatGPT: Part 2

This conversation with Craig provoked a further conversation between Peter and ChatGPT, in which I reproduced Garry's story about his meeting with Craig.

Peter

Our concerns here also relate to the ways in which these large language model AI s are transforming understandings of literacy and numeracy skills, what they are, how they are developed, and what happens to those people who have not developed higher order literacy and numeracy skills, and who in the past have often been compelled to engage in processes to develop these skills in order to become more 'employable'. In this context we have written of an encounter with a student in an adult literacy class.

What sorts of learning, lessons, can we take from this sort of encounter for how we imagine adult literacy and numeracy skills, how they might be developed, and what might be some of the tensions and dilemmas, opportunities and challenges for both teachers and learners in these adult literacy environments.

ChatGPT

The encounter with Craig highlights several important considerations regarding the intersection of AI, literacy, and education, particularly in adult literacy settings. Here are some key takeaways and reflections:

1. *Adaptation and Integration of AI Tools*: Craig's enthusiasm for using ChatGPT as a writing tool reflects the growing trend of integrating AI technologies into various aspects of daily life, including business communication. This suggests that adult literacy programs need to adapt to the increasing use of AI tools by incorporating them into the learning process. Instead of fearing or resisting AI, educators can explore ways to leverage these tools to enhance literacy skills development.
2. *Instantaneous Feedback and Efficiency*: Craig's appreciation for the fast and error-free nature of ChatGPT highlights the potential benefits of AI for providing instantaneous feedback and improving efficiency in learning tasks. This presents an opportunity for adult literacy learners to receive personalized feedback and support tailored to their individual needs, ultimately accelerating their learning progress.
3. *Critical Analysis and Contextual Understanding*: Despite the convenience of AI-generated texts, there is still a need for learners like Craig to critically analyze and contextualize the content produced by AI. Educators can help learners develop critical thinking skills by guiding them to evaluate AI-generated content in relation to context, purpose, and audience. This promotes deeper understanding and application of literacy skills beyond simply producing error-free texts.
4. *Ethical Considerations and Plagiarism*: Craig's lack of concern about plagiarism raises important ethical considerations regarding the use of AI tools in literacy education. Educators need to address issues of academic integrity and copyright infringement, while also teaching learners about responsible use of AI technology. This involves fostering a nuanced understanding of AI as a tool that complements rather than replaces traditional literacy skills.

5. *Empowerment and Autonomy*: Craig's positive experience with AI suggests that AI has the potential to empower adult learners by providing them with tools to independently improve their literacy skills. However, educators need to strike a balance between facilitating learner autonomy and ensuring that learners develop a solid foundation in fundamental literacy skills that go beyond AI reliance.
6. *Teacher Adaptation and Professional Development*: Educators in adult literacy settings may face challenges in adapting to the integration of AI tools into their teaching practices. They may need additional training and professional development to effectively incorporate AI technology into their instructional strategies and to support learners in navigating the complexities of AI-generated content.

In summary, encounters like the one with Craig underscore the evolving nature of literacy education in the age of AI and the need for educators to embrace innovation while also critically examining the implications for teaching and learning. By acknowledging the tensions, dilemmas, opportunities, and challenges presented by AI, educators can proactively shape adult literacy programs that empower learners to thrive in a rapidly changing digital landscape.

This Prelude, this book, is not, at the end, fundamentally about large language model, generative machine intelligences such as ChatGPT. Though it is, in many respects, about the sorts of disruptions that these AIs might be foretelling in relation to what we, and influential, powerful actors, might understand as language, literacy and numeracy skills. And how these skills, which might once have been solely a human 'value proposition' in the world of work, might well be on the cusp of profound transformations in terms of how they are understood as 'employability skills'. The futures of work being portended here are uncertain – hence the possible overuse of 'might' in the preceding sentences. As Naomi Klein (2023) suggests, 'Tech CEOs want us to believe that generative AI will benefit humanity. They are kidding themselves'. However, these futures will be made, and made by the most powerful actors in ways that serve their interests – and those actors could well include machine intelligences.

We will return to a number of these possibilities in our final chapter, where we will think more about what might be called a political economy of generative AI as suggested by Klein and others, and what 'kind of mind does ChatGPT have' (Newport, 2023). In that space – following a detailed identification and analysis of the ways in which particular understandings of a globalising neoliberal capitalism and changing labour market skills have shaped the foundation skills policy and program apparatus in Australia during the last 30 years – we will look to do some speculative work about what the history of the future of foundations skills might look and feel like.

Notes

1 https://en.wikipedia.org/wiki/Sabine_Hossenfelder
2 https://www.youtube.com/@SabineHossenfelder
3 A non-reviewed preprint of this article is available at https://arxiv.org/abs/2401.02843
4 The cited text as indicated in what follows comes from a transcript of the video (Hossenfelder, 2024).
5 These concerns about the malevolent possibilities of AI are a widespread trope in science fiction, but an increasingly material concern for researchers in the field, and for policy makers, law makers, a range of government agencies, businesses and communities [see, for example, Naomi Klein's (2023) recent article in *The Guardian*].

CHAPTER 1

Developing a Genealogy of the Problem of Foundation Skills

1 Introduction

> When you ask adults what they want from education, they usually refer to at least one of these aspects: 'I want to get my brain working', 'I want to get the education I missed out on', 'I left school at twelve and I feel embarrassed about my lack of education', 'I want to improve my self-esteem'. Adult learners want to fit in, to be part of the "club" of people who have a formal education. They want to learn the language and ways of thinking that will give them access to social and vocational opportunities they are denied at present and they rely on us as teachers to help them fill in the gaps and to know the steps they need to take. (Bradshaw, 1998, p. 4)

Language, literacy and numeracy (LLN), or foundation skills, are the building blocks for broader education, and are often barriers to learners joining the 'club'. For newly arrived migrants in Australia, they are the speaking, listening, reading and writing skills needed to communicate to start a life in their new country. For native English speakers, they are regarded as the core or basic skills – historically categorised as the 'three Rs' of reading, writing and arithmetic – that have not been developed in the compulsory years of education. Foundation skills are the skills that most people take for granted. Yet many people still find it difficult to use their mobile phone, read a book or newspaper, understand price labels, make sense of a bus or train timetable, fill out a form, read instructions on medicines, or use the Internet.

It is in these spaces, in part, that the research that has informed this book sits. Our intent here is to examine the ways in which particular understandings of significant processes and practices in globalising, neoliberal capitalism, and in changing labour markets have shaped the foundation skills policy and program apparatus in Australia during the last 30 years. The foundation skills training sector has long been an important part of the Australian adult education system. From the 1940s, when Australia introduced its first migrant English language program as a direct result of Government policy to increase the labour force necessary to develop the country (Martin, 1998), to the 1990s, when governments began to view foundation skills as vital in building the

 | DOI:10.1163/9789004724464_002

economy and workforce productivity and responding to emerging technological changes, Australia's foundation skills have been a priority for governments. This priority was deemed critical when Australia participated in three international Organisation for Economic Co-operation and Development (OECD) adult literacy surveys in 1996, 2006 and 2012. These survey results – which remained relatively stable over the series – suggested that over half of Australia's population did not have the foundation skills to cope with the complex demands of work in contemporary economies. The survey results also strongly influenced the development of the *National Foundation Skills Strategy for Adults* (*National Strategy*) to coordinate a national focus on improving education and employment outcomes for working-age Australians with low foundation skills. The ten-year strategy set a target that by 2022, two-thirds of working-age Australians will have the foundation skills to take full advantage of opportunities afforded by what the strategy called 'the new economy'. It was at this stage that the foundation skills sector was (re)located and transformed into the broader Australian policy and political landscape.

The story of this transformation – to be told in a particular way – is our primary concern here. The complexities, interconnections, false starts, stops, reviews and evaluations of these transformations are not, however, solely matters of academic or policy interest. They emerge from the extensive experiences – personal and professional – of these transformations, and the collective work we have done over a number of years to extend on and problematise these personal and professional histories.

2 The Changing Nature of Language and Literacy as Foundation Skills

During the post-war period, dominant theories defined literacy as the ability, with understanding, of a person to both read and write a short, simple statement on everyday life. A person was functionally literate if they could engage in activities in which literacy was required for the effective functioning of their group and community and enable them to continue using reading, writing and calculations for themselves and the community's development (United Nations Educational Scientific and Cultural Organization [UNESCO], 1978). Historically, groups identified as having low foundation skills in Australia were understood to be:

- people whose first language is not English, particularly those with limited or interrupted education in their first language;
- young people with little or interrupted education; and,

– older people with less education, skills deteriorating with age, or disengaged from the labour market.

Adults with literacy difficulties may have missed out on learning opportunities when they were children. They may have experienced health or socio-economic problems or held negative attitudes towards education that caused long absences. For many groups, literacy development can be intergenerational, with one generation's skills impacting the next. Some migrant and refugee groups might come from cultures with oral rather than written traditions, have had little or no literacy education, or whose years in refugee camps deprived them of schooling (Adult Learning Australia, 2011; Australian Bureau of Statistics, 1996, 2006, 2013; Wickert & Kevin, 1995).

Emerging definitions of literacy have been strongly influenced by what the OECD (2013, p. 6) describes as a 'revolution' in how people's work and lives have been profoundly changed over the last few decades. A rapidly changing, high technology, flexible, globalised economy has reshaped the skills required by workers, which in part, symbolises how various literacies have come to be imagined as 'foundation skills'. Foundation skills are now viewed, not just as a simple process of acquiring basic cognitive skills of listening, speaking, reading, writing and learning but as those required for participation in contemporary workplaces and life, such as collaboration, problem-solving, self-management, learning, communication and information technology skills (Roberts & Wignall, 2010). They are now imagined as the foundations that comprise the conditions and core skills, knowledge, attitudes and values that provide a basis for socio-economic development, social awareness, agency and transformative competencies and fulfilling potential to become responsible contributors to and healthy members of society (OECD, 2019; UNESCO, 2006).

The new ways people communicate with digital technology have transformed labour markets and the skills and attitudes required to participate in those markets. The large immobile factories that dominated capitalist production over the twentieth century (Drucker, 2001) have been replaced by a capitalism characterised by mobility and flexibility (Sennett, 1998). Advances in automation and artificial intelligence have increased demand for workers with technological skills, the so-called 'knowledge technologists' (Drucker, 2001, para. 6), who are more likely to have acquired theoretical knowledge through formal education. It is claimed that those workers with effective foundation skills, combined with technical or job-specific skills, are 'able to take on responsibilities effectively in the workforce and wider community' (Cunning, 2007, para. 5). Workers are now required to have the ability to behave nimbly, be open to change on short notice, take continual risks, and develop skill sets of which foundation skills are a large component. In short, to imagine themselves as an enterprise (Kelly, 2013).

In this context, it has been argued that an increasing share of the Australian workforce does not hold the necessary skills demanded by labour markets in flexible capitalism (Teicher et al., 2013). Before the advances in automation and artificial intelligence, people could move into a factory or labouring position relatively quickly, regardless of their foundation skills. Now such jobs demand a higher proficiency of foundation skills, or are gradually disappearing from the labour market. Here, many workers face more precarious employment that involves forms of work engagement outside the continuing employment relationship, including casual work, contracting arrangements, fixed-term engagements, labour-hire arrangements and home-based work (Rawling, 2015). At the end of the last century, Burgess and Campbell (1998) listed several characteristics of precarious employment:

- short time horizons of limited duration or have a high risk of termination;
- lack of control over working conditions, the pace of work and wages;
- lack of protection in employment, including legislative, collective agreement and social security; and,
- low incomes, at or near, defined poverty lines.

In 2018, less than half of all working Australians had permanent full-time work with leave entitlements, superannuation and sick leave (Carney & Stanford, 2018). Stanford (cited in ABC News, 2018, para. 6) suggests that 'insecure [work] has become the new normal' and 'I wouldn't even call it an underclass because it is now the majority experiencing this insecurity in one form or another'.

We have explored a number of these challenges elsewhere, including that these forms of precarious employment, or 'informal work', are actually the norm for the vast majority of workers globally. In a recent book – *Informal Workers and a Political Economy of Life Long Learning: Provocations from the Margins of Global Capitalism* – we (Brown et al., 2024) have suggested that the informal economy, the informal workers that comprise the labour force for the informal economy, the relationships between these informal sectors and workers and more formal sectors and workers, are complex and difficult to develop shared agreement and understandings. Indeed, in many of the high-income, formalised and regulated economies of the OECD and EU, new forms of precarious, informal and uncertain employment – the so-called 'gig economy' – have emerged in the context of, and been energised by, processes of neoliberal globalisation and governmentalities.

In *The Brazilianisation of Youth Transitions in Australia and the UK?*, for example, we (Furlong & Kelly, 2005) explored the ways in which these forms of precarious, 'gig' work were transforming youth labour markets in Australia and the UK. The title for that paper came from Ulrich Beck's (2000) *The Brave New World of Work*. A central theme of Beck's book is that labour markets in the more developed 'first world' had been changing during the last four decades in ways that witnessed them taking on some of the central characteristics of labour markets in what was then called the less developed 'third world' – what Beck refers to as the *Brazilianisation* of labour markets in the developed world. For Beck (2000, p. 1), what was central to these transformations was the 'spread of temporary and insecure employment, discontinuity and loose informality' into 'first world' labour markets – which for the period of three decades or so after the Second World War had been the 'bastions of full employment'. Beck's (2000, p. 1) argument was that in a 'semi-industrialized' economy such as Brazil, full-time waged or salaried employment is a secure form of existence for 'only a minority of the economically active population; the majority earn their living in more precarious conditions'. For Beck (2000, pp. 2–3), a life world characterised by 'nomadic "multi-activity"' is not a 'pre modern relic', nor is it any longer just a feature of the female labour market. Rather, this precariousness and insecurity emerges in the more developed world as a fundamental characteristic of the movement from a *work society* to a *risk society*.

In the economies of the OECD and the EU, and in the more informal economies of Latin America and the Caribbean (LAC), the Middle East and North Africa (MENA), Sub Saharan Africa (SSA), Central and Eastern Europe (CEE), and the Asia-Pacific (AP), the challenges and opportunities of/for promoting *sustained, inclusive and sustainable economic growth, full and productive employment and decent work for all* (United Nations Sustainability Development Goal 8) are connected to broader concerns in relation to social, economic and political development – as captured at a global level in the 2030 Agenda for Sustainable Development. Although it may be understood in different ways in these different contexts, and, indeed, will be situated differently in particular contexts, the informal economy can be understood as those:

> Economic activities by workers that are – in law or in practice – not covered (or insufficiently covered) by formal employment arrangements. Although it is hard to generalize about the quality and nature of informal employment, the characteristics include a lack of protection for non-payment of wages, retrenchment without notice or compensation, unsatisfactory occupational health and safety conditions and an absence of social benefits such as pensions, sick pay and health insurance. (International Labour Organization, 2021a, para. 1)

The International Labour Organization's (2018) *Women and men in the informal economy: A statistical picture* provides a description of various key characteristics of the informal economy and informal workers on a global and regional scale:

- *The Size of the Informal Economy*: Two billion of the world's employed population aged 15 and over, work informally, representing 61.2 percent of global employment. Among the five main regions, the vast majority of employment in Africa (85.8 percent) is informal. Asia and the Pacific (68.2 percent) and the Arab States (68.6 percent) have almost the same level of informality. In the Americas and Europe and Central Asia, less than half of employment is informal.
- *Socio-Economic Development and Informality*: Emerging and developing countries represent 82 percent of world employment... More than two thirds of the employed population in emerging and developing countries are in informal employment (69.6 percent).
- *Economic Sector and Informality*: Informal employment can be in the informal sector, in the formal sector or in the household sector. The 61.2 percent of global employment that is informal is comprised of 51.9 percent in the informal sector, 6.7 percent in the formal sector and 2.5 percent in households.
- *Employment Status and Informality*: The employment status category with the highest percentage of informality is own-account workers, both globally and regionally. Globally, 86.1 percent of own-account workers are informal.
- *Age of Workers and Informality*: The level of informality is higher among young people and older persons. Worldwide three out of four young (77.1 percent) and older persons (77.9 percent) are in informal employment.
- *Education and Informality*: Globally, when the level of education increases, the level of informality decreases. Those who have completed secondary and tertiary education are less likely to be in informal employment compared to workers who have either no education or completed primary education.
- *Gender and Informality*: Globally, the share of women in informal employment is lower than the share of men... but... women are indeed more exposed to informal employment in more than 90 percent of sub-Saharan African countries, 89 percent of countries from Southern Asia and almost 75 percent of Latin American countries.

Alongside processes of globalisation, the emergence of neoliberalism has facilitated transitions to a more flexible capitalism. Neoliberalism, as a much-debated concept and set of practices, processes and forms of knowledge, is associated with economic liberalisation policies, including privatisation, free trade achieved through deregulation, and state austerity measures to increase the role of the private sector in the economy (Springer et al., 2016). We will develop a Foucauldian understanding of neoliberalism throughout the discussion and analysis that follows. At this time, we can note that neoliberalism consists of three interweaving and mutually supporting agendas: economic, political and social. As an economic agenda, neoliberalism promotes market principles in which competition is maximised above reliance on the state (Turner, 2015). It privileges the privatisation of public assets (Harvey, 2005), a free market with fewer regulations or tariffs enacted by the state, and the integration of global economies (Turner, 2015). Politically, neoliberalism allows governments to redefine their responsibilities from the interventionist and welfarist models to one promoting a diminished state responsibility for areas of social policy and the corporatisation of services (Sugarman, 2015).

Neoliberalism also reshapes social agendas, not only by influencing economic policies or modes of governance, but by attempting to make up a neoliberal subject (Miller & Rose, 2010). Harvey (2005) argues neoliberalism is a theory of political and economic practice which proposes that human well-being can be best advanced by liberating individual entrepreneurial freedoms and skills. Neoliberal governing occurs by providing individuals with the circumstances in which they can exercise choices in relation to increasing domains of life, and holding them accountable for the choices they make, in effect, transferring risk from the state to individuals (Sugarman, 2015). The individual is increasingly required to think of themselves as an enterprise (Kelly, 2013) who needs to imagine themselves as being able to develop a set of assets, skills and attributes to be managed, maintained, developed and treated as ventures to invest in. Black (2002, p. 2) captures the political, economic and social essence of neoliberalism in the realm of foundation skills by arguing that 'literacy is generally equated with success in life, with notions of a person being educated, obtaining a job and having access to the goods and trappings of wellbeing that are valued highly in society'. It is in the encouragement and direction to attain these 'successes' that individuals are made responsible for improving their economic, labour market and social capabilities.

3 The Emergence of Foundation Skills as a Skills Market in Australia

During the 1980s and 1990s, the emergence of low foundation skills as a problem for Australian governments was framed around rising unemployment, an apparent 'welfare dependency', and the everyday demands that society and the labour market place on the literacy capacities of individuals (DEET, 1991;

lo Bianco, 1987b). These rationalities and logics were both mobile and influential in shaping policy discussions and discourse in many other high-income OECD and European Union economies. The *Australian Language and Literacy Policy* stated that 'there is a strong and well-demonstrated relationship between low levels of literacy or English language competence and high levels of unemployment and other forms of social disadvantage' (DEET, 1991, p. 1). Assumptions of this nature were reflected in various government discourses at the time. One example from the Commonwealth's *Skills for Australia* policy in 1987 argued that if the skills of the nation's workforce did not improve, the nation would become uncompetitive in a globalised economy (Dawkins & Holding, 1987). A lack of literacy skills in workplaces was also connected to billions of dollars in lost productivity each year (Miltenyi, 1989). The *National Collaborative Adult English Language and Literacy Strategy* in 1993 pointed to the changing levels and types of foundation skills required in society, with processes of economic restructuring from the Labor Hawke-Keating Government at the time placing a heavy emphasis on skills. The strategy argued that education and training programs were critical in developing the skills of the nation (DEET, 1993).

Concerns about a causal relationship between foundation skills and workforce participation and productivity continued in the following decades. In 2008, the Australian Government (2008) argued that skills shortages arising from demographic and technological change and poor foundation skills constrained the capacity of many individuals to re-skill and up-skill. These fears reached the proportions of a claimed 'skills crisis' in 2012 (Black et al., 2013, p. 609). The OECD (2013, p. 26) argued that:

> Skills transform lives, generate prosperity and promote social inclusion. Without the right skills, people are kept at the margins of society, technological progress does not translate into economic growth, and enterprises and countries can't compete in today's globally connected and increasingly complex world.

In 2012, these concerns drove the introduction of the *National Foundation Skills Strategy for Adults* (*National Strategy*), Australia's first language, literacy and numeracy policy since 1991 (National Centre for Vocational Education Research [NCVER], 2011). The *National Strategy* set a ten-year goal claiming that strong foundation skills in a modern, knowledge-based society would underpin workforce participation, productivity and social inclusion. An improvement in foundation skills would assist people in gaining employment and remaining employed, increase community participation and better health, and promote engagement in further training (Standing Council on Tertiary Education Skills

& Employment [SCOTESE], 2012). The strategy included a target that by 2022, two-thirds of working-age Australians will have literacy and numeracy skills at level 3 or above (where level 3 indicates the skills needed to meet the complex demands of work and life in modern economies). The achievement of this target was dependent on raising the awareness of foundation skills, ensuring high-quality learning opportunities, and building the capacity of education and training workforces (SCOTESE, 2012).

Australia was not isolated in their concern with the problem of low-level foundation skills in their adult population. The 2012 OECD Programme for the International Assessment of Adult Competencies (PIAAC) results from 22 OECD member countries revealed that in most countries, there are significant proportions of adults who score at lower levels of proficiency in literacy and numeracy (OECD, 2013). There are a large number of young people in some countries with low skills, with evidence that the skills of young people have apparently not improved significantly over the past two decades and may even have diminished in some cases (OECD, 2018). Across participating countries, an average of 10 percent of adults report having no experience in using computers, lacking the most elementary computer skills and the confidence in their ability to use computers (OECD, 2013). Individuals with lower proficiency in literacy are more likely than those with better literacy skills to report poor health, to believe that they have little impact on political processes, and not to participate in associative or volunteer activities. In most countries, they are also less likely to trust others. A key message emerging from the PIAAC results was that the median hourly wage of workers for adults scoring at high proficiency is more than 60 percent higher than for workers scoring at lower levels. Those with low literacy skills are also more than twice as likely to be unemployed (OECD, 2013).

We will argue, drawing on Foucauldian studies of neoliberal governmentalities, that a sophisticated foundation skills 'apparatus' emerged in response to apparently alarming low literacy levels from the first OECD adult literacy survey in 1996. Since its emergence and two subsequent OECD surveys with similar findings, education and training programs within the apparatus have evolved in complex ways. The apparatus, comprising, in part, TAFE and other public institutions, not-for-profit, for-profit and private providers, is constituted by four major foundation skills training programs:

- *Adult Migrant English Program* (*AMEP*) – Commonwealth-funded, free training for migrants in Australia;
- *Skills for Education and Employment* (*SEE*) *Program* – Commonwealth-funded, free training for job seekers with literacy and/or numeracy training needs;

- State-funded programs – eligibility-based funding, accredited training for individuals to improve their foundation skills; and,
- *Adult Community Education* programs – state-funded, non-accredited programs that include short term, basic or introductory training for individuals as a pathway to work or accredited training.

As will become evident in what follows, providers of these education and training programs were made largely responsible for the success or otherwise of these programs, and the skills development outcomes of learners as the primary mechanism by which to achieve the *National Strategy's* 2022 target.

The *National Strategy* has framed its objectives with reference to Commonwealth competitive market policies (Hilmer, 1993) and reforms of the vocational education and training (VET) sector from the mid-1990s. As we will explore in much greater detail in the following chapters, these policies promote the logic of market competition to achieve efficient and quality services and promote trust in the expenditure of public money. As governments established and promoted a foundation skill 'training market', processes were deployed to 'open up' markets to multiple providers, allowing for individual foundation skills learners to exercise choice. Within this arrangement to maintain and increase market share, registered training providers (RTOs) are meant, ideally, to respond to the demand of individuals – or customers – by creating programs that meet their needs.

4 Genealogy as a Critical History of Thought

In briefly outlining the context in which this book is situated, and the variety of concerns, issues, challenges and possibilities that are of interest to us here, we want to clarify some of our purposes and discuss the theoretical, conceptual and methodological traditions that both frame these purposes, and provide a means to achieve them. At a basic level, we are interested in identifying and analysing the diverse, often competing, ways that a range of understandings about foundation skills are put to use in various programs and projects of government – in Australia principally, but also elsewhere. We want to analyse the rationalities that governments bring to their policy agendas and how – as these rationalities are enacted and reformed over time – they trigger intended and unintended possibilities and consequences that impact stakeholders in what we will call a *neoliberal foundation skills apparatus*, including most importantly, the foundation skills 'learner'. In doing that work, we will identify and analyse the key characteristics of the Australian Commonwealth Government's

Foundation Skills policy and program apparatus since the Commonwealth Government's *National Policy on Languages* of 1987. By connection, we will also identify the key characteristics of the Victorian State Government's foundation skills policy and program apparatus since 1987. In doing this 'genealogical' work, we will examine the various ways in which these frameworks imagine processes of globalisation and technological change, labour market change, labour market skills, and the sorts of person one must become to participate in paid labour markets. Finally, our purposes include exploring the ways in which a genealogy of these characteristics can inform community, academic and policy understandings of the possibilities and limitations of the governmental ambitions of the neoliberal foundation skills apparatus.

The framing and articulation of these purposes and aims, and the capability to organise and carry out the work to meet them, draws heavily on our extensive engagement with the work of French philosopher, historian and social theorist Michel Foucault, one of the most important social and political thinkers from the latter half of the twentieth century (see, for example, Kelly, 2013). In providing an account of those key elements of Foucault's work that provide productive 'tools' for doing the description and analysis we have in mind, we can suggest, in the first instance, that Foucault's theories focus on the relationships between power/knowledge/subjects, and the ways in which these relationships are used in, and emerge from, forms of governance, regulation and control through diverse agencies and institutions. Foucault (1980c, p. 130) argues that power-knowledge is constituted within discourse through accepted forms of knowledge, scientific understandings and the production of 'truth':

> Each society has its regime of truth, its "general politics" of truth: that is, the types of discourse which it accepts and makes function as true; the mechanisms and instances which enable one to distinguish true and false statements, the means by which each is sanctioned; the techniques and procedures accorded value in the acquisition of truth; the status of those who are charged with saying what counts as true.

Each of Foucault's major works is a critique of the historical reason of some instituted practice, discourse, episteme, or institution. For Foucault (1997a, p. 113), critique 'consists of analysing and reflecting upon limits' and challenging the relations of power/knowledge/subjects that 'articulate what we think, say and do'. Foucault's critiques are genealogical in that they investigate those elements which 'we tend to feel [are] without history' (Foucault, 1980b, p. 139). Foucault (1977b) emphasises the genealogical element of critique by highlighting the different discursive and non-discursive ways the subject emerges in history. He regards genealogy as an eventalisation, which begins with interrogating certain evidence or processes of an event (Foucault, 1996). A genealogy avoids the narration of the totality of history. Srdjan Vucetic's (2010, p. 1300) 'three E' definition of genealogy, a reference to episodes (events), examples and effectiveness is useful in this context. Vucetic (2010) defines episodes as historical series, epochs, events, or moments that perioditise the history of an object under study. He goes on to suggest that each episode is narrated through examples or events, which are 'effective' when they create a 'problematisation' of the socially constructed reality and knowledge.

4.1 *Enlightenment: The Practice of Permanent Critique*[1]

The Age of Enlightenment, or Enlightenment, which in some accounts spans the mid-decades of the seventeenth century through to the eighteenth century, is thought to be one of the most important and contested periods in the history of philosophy (Fleischacker, 2013). The problems that the Enlightenment addressed, such as the true extent of individual freedom and the challenging of tradition, resonate as much today as when they were first debated. German philosopher Immanuel Kant (2016) addressed questions about Enlightenment in his celebrated short essay: *An Answer to the Question: What is Enlightenment?* Kant saw the Enlightenment as 'mans'[2] emergence from his self-incurred immaturity, with immaturity being the inability to use one's understanding without another's guidance. He also insisted that Enlightenment amounts to a certain liberating use of reason in the face of the Authority that has traditionally subjected humankind to all manner of limits and constraints. These restraints controlled what one was 'allowed' to think and 'do' in accordance with various prescriptions about thought and action, especially those of a religious, political and intellectual nature (Fleischacker, 2013; Hendricks, 2008). For Kant, Enlightenment was nothing less than achieving 'maturity': 'Sapere aude! Have the courage to think for yourself!' (Kant, 2016, p. 35). Foucault investigated the historical context of Kant's text by publishing an essay that reflected on the contemporary status of the project of Enlightenment (Tanke, 2009). Foucault's (1991b, p. 32) overarching question of Enlightenment was, 'what is this event that is called Enlightenment and that has determined, at least in part, what we are, what we think, and what we do today?'. Foucault (1991b, p. 42) suggests that Enlightenment emphasises the practice of permanent critique, a form of philosophical interrogation which 'simultaneously problematises man's relation to the present, man's historical mode of being, and the constitution of the self as an autonomous subject'.

Foucault (1997b, p. 94) argues that Kant founded 'the two great critical traditions that divide modern philosophy'. The first, Foucault (1997b, p. 94) labels an 'analytic of truth' in which Kant posited and founded a tradition of philosophy that asks the question of the conditions under which true knowledge is possible. The 'analytic of truth' is transcendental in that it 'seek[s] to identify the universal structures of all knowledge or all possible moral action' (Foucault, 1997a, p. 113). Foucault (1997b, p. 95) calls the second critical tradition founded by Kant an 'ontology of ourselves' or an 'ontology of the present'. This tradition is the transgressive form of critique that asks about possible transformations within the present, by separating 'from the contingency that has made us what we are, the possibility of no longer being, doing, or thinking what we are, do, or think' (Foucault, 1997a, p. 114). The first kind of critique works to establish the limits to human knowledge and ethical action. In contrast, the second reveals the possibility of transgressing limits by determining what may be historically contingent in them. Foucault (1997a) claims that his projects are connected to Kantian critique in that criticism, in general, involves analysing limits. While Kant's concern was to find those necessary limits, that 'knowledge has to renounce transgressing', critique today should be a practical one 'that takes the form of a possible transgression' (Foucault, 1997a, p. 113).

Foucault (1991b, pp. 42–43) suggests that the practice of critique defines an 'ethos', which has both a negative and a positive heuristic. In terms of its negative heuristic, Foucault identifies the need to refuse what he calls the 'blackmail' of the Enlightenment, the pressure to be either 'for or against the Enlightenment', to 'accept the Enlightenment and remain with the tradition of its rationalism ... or [to] criticise the Enlightenment and then try to escape from its principles of rationality'. Foucault (1997a, p. 113) suggests that: 'we have to move beyond the inside/outside alternative, we have to be at the frontiers. Criticism... consists of analysing and reflecting upon limits'. He argues that critique will not seek to identify universal structures of all knowledge and possible moral actions, but will seek to challenge the discourses that articulate what we think, say, and do. The critique will be genealogical in the sense that it will:

> not deduce from the form of what we are, what it is impossible for us to do and to know; but it will separate out, from the contingency that has made us what we are, the possibility of no longer being, doing, or thinking what are, do, or think. It is not seeking to make possible a metaphysics that has finally become a science; it is seeking to give a new impetus, as far as wide as possible, to the undefined work of freedom. (Foucault, 1991b, p. 46)

As Foucault (1977b, p. 140) increasingly identified his projects as genealogies, he began to determine the relationship between 'critique' and 'genealogy'. Foucault reasoned that his analyses would fall into two 'sets' (Sembou, 2011). The first set being the 'critical' section, which would examine the forms of inclusion and exclusion, of limitation, and of appropriation, and would show how they are formed, in response to what needs, how they have been modified and displaced, what constraint they have effectively exerted, and to what extent they have been evaded. The second is the 'genealogical aspect', which concerns the effective formation of discourse either within the limits of this control, or outside them, or more often on both sides of the boundary at once. Foucault (1981, pp. 71–72) argues that:

> In truth, these two tasks are never completely separable: there are not, on one side, the forms of rejection, exclusion, regrouping and attribution, and then on the other side, at a deeper level, the spontaneous surging-up of discourses which, immediately before or after their manifestation, are submitted to selection and control. The regular formation of discourse can incorporate the procedures of control, in certain conditions and to a certain extent (that is what happens, for instance, when a discipline takes on the form and status of a scientific discourse); and conversely the figures of control can take shape within a discursive formation. The difference between the critical and the genealogical enterprise is not so much a difference of object or domain, but of point of attack, perspective and delimitation.

Foucault understood genealogy and critique as complementary, with critique an integral part of genealogy, and genealogy as a critical enterprise (Sembou, 2011). Importantly for Foucault (2013, p. 154): 'a critique is not a matter of saying that things are', rather, 'it is a matter of pointing out on what kinds of assumptions, what kinds of familiar, unchallenged modes of thought the practices that we accept, rest'. Foucault (1981, p. 67) also highlights that the starting point of critique is a 'principle of reversal' in so far as critique turns deep-seated conceptions upside-down. The task of Foucault's genealogy is to offer us a different interpretation, 'to make a different perspective known, to invert it, and give it due weight' (cited in Sembou, 2011, p. 20).

4.2 *Genealogy: Power, Truth, Descent, Emergence, and Subjugation*

Tamboukou (1999, p. 203) suggests that:

> In examining the very Kantian concept of the present, Foucault introduces scepticism about universalist dogmas of truth, objectivity and

> pure scientific reason, and interrogates the supposed interconnections between reason, knowledge, progress, freedom and ethical action.

Within this problematic, Foucault also attempts to see the role of the thinking subject differently by first recognising the historical dimension of all human reality. Foucault moves to an analysis of the different discursive and non-discursive ways in which the subject emerges in history. He argues that our experiences of selves and lives are discursive effects, they result from powerful discourses that structure our reality (Foucault, 1972). Rather than accepting the idea that meaning arises from a 'knowing subject', Foucault views the subjective self, as we experience it, as a product of discourse (Fadyl & Nicholls, 2013, p. 25). From Foucault's perspective, no 'essential' subject can be identified outside of discursive construction. From this perspective, a person's account of themselves and their experiences cannot be seen as a point of origin for the construction of meaning because the subject is constituted through discourse, and discourse provides the means of articulation and action.

Tamboukou (1999) explains that for Foucault, genealogy conceives human reality as an effect of the interweaving of particular historical and cultural practices. The task of genealogy is to trace and explore this interweaving. Foucault (1977b) emphasises the genealogical element of critique by highlighting that all thought is socially and historically constituted and challenges the idea that language is neutral and value-free. It follows that there is no single 'truth' in so far as knowledge is always being constructed, is conditional, and is intimately connected with power relations. He argues that the production of knowledge emerges from the exercise of power, is a way to define others and ourselves, and a means of enabling our decisions about the character and shape of the world.

For many, the term genealogy is recognisable through an 'examination of descent', or 'the evolution of a species', or the mapping of 'the destiny of a people' (Foucault, 1977b, p. 146). Tamboukou (1999) explains how Foucault views a genealogical analysis of descent, not by attempting to reconstruct the effects of past events in the present, but as an analysis of descent and emergence. She stresses that genealogy has a critical dimension, and when analysing descent, the genealogist should make an effort to:

> look directly at what people do, without taking anything for granted, without presupposing the existence of any goal, material cause or ideology. The aim is to strip away the veils that cover people's practices, by simply showing how they are, and where they come from, describing its complicated forms and exploring its countless historical transformations. (Tamboukou, 1999, p. 208)

Tamboukou (1999, p. 203) suggests that genealogy is oriented to discontinuities and emergence as well as an analysis of descent. Instead of seeing history as continuous development, there are 'frequent disruptions, uneven and haphazard processes of dispersion'. Foucault (2000, p. 114) elaborates further on the importance of discontinuous elements in his interview *Truth and Power*:

> My problem was not at all to say *Voila*, long live discontinuity, but to pose the question; how is it that at certain moments and in certain orders of knowledge, there are these sudden take-offs; these transformations which fail to correspond with the calm, continuist image that is normally accredited.

Foucault (1977b, p. 148) designates the 'sudden take-offs' as emergence, the moment of arising. Emergence is the 'the charting of the battle of forces that resulted in a certain state of affairs' (Tamboukou, 1999, p. 209) and 'not specifically the energy of the strong or the reaction of the weak, but precisely the scene where they are displayed superimposed' (Foucault, 1977b, p. 150). The scene does not seek to re-appropriate history. Foucault (1977b) stresses that emergence should not be viewed as the final term of historical development in that the developments may appear as a culmination. Rather, 'identify the accidents, the minute deviations – or conversely, the complete reversals – the errors, the false appraisals, and the faulty calculations which gave birth to those things that exist and continue to have value for us' (Foucault, 1980d, p. 146). The analysis of emergence must delineate the multiple processes and power relations in various systems of subjugation within which things appear as historical events (Tamboukou, 1999).

Foucault refers to subjugation or subjugated knowledges as the historical contents of discourse that have been disqualified as inadequate to their task or insufficiently elaborated. Subjugated knowledges can be understood as naive knowledges that operate low down on the hierarchy of formal knowledge below an acceptable level of cognition or scientificity (Olssen, 2003). Habermas' (1994) interpretation of Foucault describes subjugated knowledges, not as unsuccessful paradigms of knowledge, but rather as the experiences of groups subordinated to the power that have never advanced to the status of official knowledge. Hence, these knowledges have never been sufficiently articulated. Habermas (1994, p. 92) also argues that subjugation is:

> a question of the implicit knowledge of 'the people' who form the bedrock in a system of power, who are the first to experience a technology of power. For Foucault it is through the re-emergence of these low-ranking subordinate knowledges that criticism performs its task.

For Foucault (1980e, p. 83):

> what emerges out of this is something one might call a genealogy, or rather a multiplicity of genealogical researches, a painstaking rediscovery of struggles together with the rude memory of their conflicts. And these genealogies, that are the combined product of an erudite knowledge and a popular knowledge, were not possible and could not even have been attempted except on one condition, namely that the tyranny of globalising discourses with their hierarchy and all their privileges of a theoretical *avant-garde* was eliminated. Let us give the term *genealogy* to the union of erudite knowledge and local memories which allows us to establish a historical knowledge of struggles and to make use of this knowledge tactically today.

In this sense, genealogy focusses on how events can emerge at specific historical points and be interpreted as natural or normalised events; as evidence of continuity rather than change (Foucault, 2005). Foucault (1981) argues that one cannot understand a social phenomenon without analysing the historical conditions that led to its development. Genealogy sheds a destabilising light on the 'history of the present', denormalising current identities, institutions, and patterns of thought and action. It assumes a deep link between knowledge and ethical-political action, and it aims to transform this reality by opening up new possibilities for thought and action.

5 Apparatus and Governmentality

5.1 *Foucault's Concept of Apparatus*

Foucault (1991a, p. 79) explains that his motive for investigating social practices was to study:

> this interplay between a "code" which rules ways of doing things (how people are to be graded and examined, things and signs classified, individuals trained, etc.) and a production of true discourses which serves to found, justify and provide reasons and principles for these ways of doing things.

Foucault's analysis of practices highlights the interdependence between what can be done and what can be known, and between how space is arranged, and knowledge produced. Methodological work in the social sciences and cultural studies often treats Foucault's method primarily as discourse analysis

(Peltonen, 2004). However, several of Foucault's more influential studies, such as *Discipline and Punish* and the volumes of *The History of Sexuality*, demonstrate that power/knowledge is a much broader phenomenon than discourse. Foucault also studied practices and an abstraction that he called *dispositifs*, or apparatuses, historically specific totalities of discourse. Foucault (1980c, pp. 194–196) explains the apparatus as the constitutive interface for power-knowledge relations that is, in the first instance:

> a thoroughly heterogeneous ensemble consisting of discourses, institutions, architectural forms, regulatory decisions, laws, administrative measures, scientific statements, philosophical, moral and philanthropic propositions – in short, the said as much as the unsaid. Such are the elements of apparatus [*dispositif*]. The apparatus itself is a system of relations that can be established between these elements.

Importantly, and in the second instance, what Foucault is:

> trying to identify in this apparatus is precisely the nature of the connection that can exist between these heterogeneous elements. Thus, a particular discourse can figure at one time as the programme of an institution, and at another it can function as a means of justifying or masking a practice which itself remains silent, or as a secondary re-interpretation of this practice, opening out for it a new field of rationality. In short, between these elements, whether discursive or nondiscursive there is a sort of interplay of shifts of position and modifications of functions which can also vary very widely.

Finally, Foucault indicates that what he understands by:

> the term 'apparatus' [*dispositif*]... [is]... a sort of – shall we say – formation which has its major function at a given historical moment that of responding to an urgent need. The apparatus [*dispositif*] has a dominant strategic function.

Foucault (1977b) argues that every apparatus is strategically suited to a highly specific historical situation and must be understood in that context. The apparatus attempts to analyse the functional requirements specific to a given historical conjuncture, and the complex manner in which it is fulfilled, or modified, historically. It structures vision, talk and thinking in particular ways, giving spaces, relations, and the self-relations of individuals a particular 'disposition'.

Apparatuses, then, are strategic logics that can be identified and analysed as playing an organising role in social domains. At the same time, apparatuses are shaped and modified by the practices and institutions that they seek to influence (Foucault, 1991a). Indeed, Foucault stresses that the apparatus:

> is always linked to certain coordinates of knowledge which issue from it but, to an equal degree, condition it. This is what the apparatus consists of: strategies of relations of forces supporting and supported by, types of knowledge. (cited in Rabinow, 2003, p. 53)

Gilles Deleuze (1992b), in *What is a Dispositif?,* writes that Foucault regards apparatus as a force of 'structuring light' to distribute the visible and invisible. It is a discursive or non-discursive force that 'disperses in space' through discourses (speaking, words) and through regulatory installations (visibilities). An apparatus can contain both material/technical/textual forces, installations, and configurations that, in particular relations, obtain power to regulate, govern, or institutionalise specific elements. Deleuze (1992b, p. 166) concludes that 'an apparatus comprises truths of enunciation, truths of light and visibility, truths of power, truths of subjectification. Truth is the actualisation of the lines which constitute an apparatus'. For Deleuze (cited in Ploger, 2008, p. 57), truth is an enunciation that is a matter of discourse, constituted by, or institutionalised as, the belief in a collective system of signification; 'transformed from the archive, from science, from myths or whatever to be meaningful to people'.

Foucault brings 'apparatus' into motion, not through the small number of interviews and texts which only give a few explanatory comments, but by considering the settings in which the concept can be analysed more thoroughly (Raffnsøe et al., 2014). He regards history as a history of the evolution and interaction of different apparatuses in what he calls a 'series of complex edifices' or 'system of correlations', which have a substantial impact on the ways our social exchange takes place (Foucault, 2007, p. 8). In *Discipline and Punish*, for example, Foucault (1977a) describes how, in the nineteenth century, in families, schools, bureaucracies, the military, hospitals, police forces, factories, and prisons, there was a gradual shift away from older subtractive power mechanisms to 'tactics' of disciplinary power. Diverse aspects of the social world, such as 'architectural forms, optical schemas, time-clocks, systems of classification, even individual gestures', became functional to a disciplinary apparatus (Brenner, 1994, p. 692).

Foucault examines the existence of the apparatus, not as an analysis of the relationships that gather under it, but in relation to the object of its analysis, the subject. Power relations and the apparatus constitute the subject. The apparatus constitutes an area of experience for the subject that manifests itself in, and through, the inter-relationships among discourses, power relationships and relationships of the self, and the different practices and systems involved in those relationships (Frost, 2015). Deleuze (1992b, p. 164) takes a similar view and writes that 'we belong to social apparatus and act within them'. In this sense, the apparatus operates as a superior referent for the subject, organising the field of power and knowledge as a field of experience. Despite the apparatus having a productive force, insofar as it is responsible for creating subjectivity and the ordering of lives, Foucault (cited in Frost, 2015, p. 161) also suggests that the apparatus can be conceived as 'freeing life from the binds of oppressive social structures'. He insists that power relations do not always result in removing liberty or options available to individuals. Instead, Foucault explains that power could result in the empowerment or responsibilisation of subjects, forcing them into free decision-making in fields of action (Lemke, 2002).

Foucault also claims that resistance, rather than power, is the binding force in the social order. Here, resistance is not mere negation, but can also be a practice of freedom (Frost, 2015). Resistance actively shifts the strategic situation in which subjects find themselves. The individual can be both affected by, and effect, power relations. At the same time, the apparatus defines and provides individuals the opportunity to practice freedom (Frost, 2015). In this sense, resistance is a creative process and provides the potential for an ethical and aesthetic process of self-creation in the emergence of the new: 'be it a form of power, counter-conduct or an ethical culture of the self' (Dean, 2013, p. 165). It is these practices of freedom, what Foucault (1987b, pp. 282–283) describes as 'admissible and acceptable forms of existence or political society', which allow the subject to practice self-construction and, in turn, resist and rework the apparatus that constitutes them.

The function of an apparatus can also be understood as a regulatory device that can be turned into a social technology via the law, schooling, or imprisonment (Frost, 2015; Ploger, 2008). Deleuze (1992b, p. 161) argues that the apparatus produces, and is produced by, both 'lines of forces' and 'lines of subjectification'. That is, the apparatus is creating processes in which, in the line of subjectification, 'the Self is neither knowledge nor power. It is a process of individuation which bears on groups and on people'. Giorgio Agamben's (2009, p. 14) interpretation views the apparatus in a much more totalising manner:

> Further expanding the already large class of Foucauldian apparatuses, I shall call an apparatus literally anything that has in some way the capacity to capture, orient, determine, intercept, model, control, or secure the gestures, behaviours, opinions, or discourses of living beings. Not only,

> therefore, prisons, madhouses, the panopticon, schools, confession, factories, disciplines, juridical measures, and so forth (whose connection with power is in a certain sense evident), but also the pen, writing, literature, philosophy, agriculture, cigarettes, navigation, computers, cellular telephones and – why not – language itself, which is perhaps the most ancient of apparatuses.

Agamben (2009, p. 19) claims that his interpretation is one of a division between subjects and apparatuses:

> To recapitulate, we have then two great classes: living beings (or substances) and apparatuses, and between these two, as a third class, subjects. I call a subject that which results from the relation and, so to speak, from the relentless fight between living beings and apparatuses.

Agamben concludes that only a philosophy of immanence can counter this threat. He argues that the subject is controlled by the apparatus, and the power is totalising due to government operations. As such, it is not possible for a subject to escape the control of the apparatus, or to utilise the apparatus to construct a form of freedom. In other words, any resistance to the apparatus must be evasive in character and ultimately involve thinking about an immanent life (Frost, 2015).

5.2 *Governmentality: Forms of Power and Ways of Thinking about Governing*

In Foucault's lectures of 1978 and 1979, focusing on the 'genealogy of the modern state', he coined the term 'governmentality' as a 'guideline' to analyse historical reconstructions of 'arts of government' from ancient Greece through to modern neoliberalism (Burchell et al., 1991, p. 3). He formulated the expression by combining the terms *'government'* and *'rationality'*. In this sense, government refers to conduct or activity meant to shape, guide, or affect people's conduct (Huff, 2016, para. 3). Rationality – as a form of thinking that strives to be systematic and clear about how things are or ought to be – suggests that before someone or something can be governed or managed, they must first be defined to be made known, visible, and available for governing (Barrett, 2012). Foucault linked the two terms to indicate that it is not possible to study the 'conduct or activity' without analysing the underpinning political rationality.

Of equal importance to Foucault was the notion of government in a broad sense, geared strongly to historical meanings of the term and overshadowing the close link between forms of power and processes of subjectification.

Foucault showed that up until well into the eighteenth century, government was a term discussed not only in political tracts but also in philosophical, religious, medical, and pedagogical texts. In addition to management by the state or the administration, government also signified problems of self-control, guidance for the family and children, and household management (Lemke, 2001). For this reason, Foucault (1982, pp. 220–221) defines government as 'the conduct of conduct' and a process that ranges from 'governing the self' to 'governing others'. His work on governmentality explores how the modern sovereign state and the modern autonomous individual co-determine each other's emergence (Lemke, 2002).

Foucault also introduced governmentality to study the 'autonomous' individual's capacity for self-control and how it is linked to political rule and economic exploitation. Foucault's interest in processes of subjectification moves away from a focus on processes of discipline, instead, investigating the relations between technologies of the self and technologies of domination (Lemke, 2002). Foucault used the term 'technology' to highlight the ways in which power relations operate:

> political power, before acting on ideology, on the consciousness of individuals, exerts itself in a much more physical way on their bodies. The way in which gestures, attitudes, usages, allotments in space, and modalities of housing are imposed – this physical, spatial distribution of people belongs, it seems to me, to a political technology of the body. (Foucault cited in Behrent, 2013, p. 55)

Foucault's analyses of technologies of domination focus on how the subject is constituted by power/knowledge relations, technologies of the self, and how individuals constitute themselves through practices of freedom (Allen, 2011). Foucault (1993) argues that one must consider the points where the technologies of domination of individuals over one another have recourse to processes by which the individual acts upon themselves. Conversely, one must consider the points where the technologies of the self are integrated into structures of coercion and domination. Foucault (1993) elaborates that governing is not a way to coerce and dominate people to government demands. It is a versatile balance, with compliments and conflicts between techniques that bring coercion and processes that are constructed or modified by the subject. Foucault (1987a, p. 19) also introduces a productive differentiation between power and domination by arguing that:

> We must distinguish the relationships of power as strategic games between liberties – strategic games that result in the fact that some

> people try to determine the conduct of others – and the states of domination, which are what we ordinarily call power. And, between the two, between the games of power and the states of domination, you have governmental technologies.

Foucault's concept of governmentality has been explored by many authors over the last three decades, including, importantly, Peter Miller and Nikolas Rose. Miller and Rose (1990) proposed new ways of analysing the exercise of political power in advanced liberal democratic societies. They frame the connection between political rationalities and technologies of government by suggesting that 'if political rationalities render reality into the domain of thought, technologies of government seek to translate thought into the domain of reality' (Miller & Rose, 1990, p. 8). Here, governments use 'technologies of government' to administer, program, and shape political rationalities in desired directions. Miller and Rose (2010, p. 281) describe technologies of government as:

> a domain of strategies, techniques and procedures through which different forces seek to render programmes operable, and by means of which a multitude of connections are established between the aspirations of authorities and the activities of individuals and groups.

Technologies of government encourage groups, organisations, and populations to form mobile and loosely affiliated networks in which they begin to share interests and form relationships through discourses, persuasions, and negotiations. As these bodies translate information, resources, and values from government associations into their own terms, they create norms and standards for their own ambitions, judgments, conduct, and profit, which enable 'governing at a distance' and forms of surveillance (Miller & Rose, 2010, p. 279).

Miller and Rose (2010) argue that relationships of power and knowledge in arts of government can be analysed in terms of the nature of their political rationality. They suggest that political rationalities have three forms. First, political rationalities have a characteristically moral form. The moral form consists of the powers and duties of government to address the proper distribution of tasks and actions between authorities of different types – political, spiritual, military, pedagogical, and familial. This form also considers the ideals or principles to which government should be directed, including, among others, freedom, justice, equality, mutual responsibility, citizenship, common sense, economic efficiency, prosperity, growth, and fairness. The second form of political rationalities suggests what one might term an epistemological character. Here, political rationalities are articulated with some conception of the nature of the objects governed – society, the nation, the population, and the economy. In particular, this form embodies some account of the persons over whom government is to be exercised (Miller & Rose, 2010). The third form of political rationalities relates to the ways in which they articulated in a distinctive idiom. The language that constitutes political discourse is more than rhetoric and should be seen as a kind of intellectual machinery or apparatus for rendering reality thinkable so that it is amenable to political deliberations. Here, a vocabulary of government has come to codify and contest the nature and limits of political power (Miller & Rose, 2010).

Foucault (1991a) insists that political rationality is not a neutral knowledge or an exterior instance representing governed reality. It is an element of government that helps create a discursive field in which exercising power is 'rational'. The concept of governmentality suggests that it is vital to see not only whether the rationality is an adequate representation of society but also how it functions as a 'politics of truth'. By producing new forms of knowledge, different notions and concepts are invented that contribute to domains of regulation and intervention.

6 Our Toolbox

Earlier we introduced Maria Tamboukou (1999) as a notable researcher of Foucault's genealogy. Tamboukou has followed some of the routes of his intellectual journey and grasps the meanings of some of the theorists who have dealt with his work to make sense of genealogy as a research framework. Borrowing the toolbox metaphor from Foucault, the research of Tamboukou, Deleuze (1992a, 1992b), Vucetic (2010) and others will be used to develop a methodological approach from this point on. This section will outline the conceptual tools and multiple analytical domains that have generated the kinds of material chosen for examination and the types of questions we ask of these materials. This toolbox is represented in Table 1.

This toolbox has not been developed as an all-encompassing methodological approach and account of genealogy. Tamboukou (2003, p. 14) considers this type of approach problematic:

> there is no way of truly understanding what genealogy is about, other than by concentration on a genealogy per se, analysing it in its minor details, reaching the most remote parts of its network, revealing the hidden mechanisms of its operation, grasping the most delicate aspects of its theorisation.

TABLE 1 The Foucauldian toolbox

Methodological tool	Feature
Problematisation	Identifying the particular problem that must be fragile or sensitive at the present time.
Apparatus	Placing the problem in systems of power relations between a heterogeneous ensemble of elements.
Governmentality	Analysis of forms of power that emphasise the governing of people by the 'conduct of conduct'.
Eventalisation and Vucetic's 3-E's: episodes, examples/events, effectiveness	Locating and analysing episodes, narrated by events that have been accepted as the 'truth', an assumed knowledge, or historical constant that has not been contested.
Descent and emergence	Analysis of the practices that surround the descent and emergence of the event. These practices are viewed as a series of subjugations.
Subjugated knowledges	Seeking events that have remained unnoticed and unrecorded in archives, the lack, gaps, listening to absences and silences.

SOURCE: TAMBOUKOU (1999, PP. 211–215), VUCETIC (2010, PP. 1300–1302) AND WILLIAMS (2005, P. 9)

Tamboukou (1999, p. 203) suggests that theoretical and philosophical questions raised by genealogy are more effectively worked out in the actual 'writing' of specific genealogies. Whether they are 'solved' or surpassed becomes a task and a challenge for the genealogist. Deleuze (1992a, p. 23) takes a similar view by observing that the 'process of writing' is the most fascinating aspect of Foucault's work, in that he never looked at writing as an aim or an end in itself. Foucault vividly illustrated his analyses to connect and resonate with his readers with an 'increasing sense of joy'. Foucault also claims that he is not interested in 'telling the truth' in his writing. Rather, he is interested in inviting people to have a particular experience for themselves (Foucault et al., 2006, p. 281):

> I don't feel it is necessary to know exactly what I am. The main interest in life is to become someone else you were not in the beginning. If you knew when you began a book what you would say at the end, do you think you would have the courage to write it? (Foucault, 1988, pp. 9–15)

As a starting point in Table 1, Tamboukou (1999) argues that a genealogy's focus should be on a particular problem, viewing it in its historical dimension and determining how this problem turned out to be the way we perceive it today. In searching for the problem, the researcher should identify some socially shared discomfort about how things are going (Dreyfus & Rabinow, 1982). It should contain several points that are particularly fragile or sensitive at the present time (Hendricks, 2008). Once the problem has been isolated, the current practices are traced to the diagnosed 'problem' to formulate the network of relations between the practices and the problem. Situating the problem in a system of relations that can account for the socially shared discomfort is a turning point for 'doing genealogy' (Tamboukou, 1999, p. 211). As covered in more detail earlier in this chapter, the apparatus is a system of relations between a heterogeneous ensemble of elements in which the character of the system, or connection, is the focus of its analysis (Foucault, 1980a). The apparatus' functioning is essentially strategic and may switch position, relationality, and function in an ongoing process of strategic elaboration influenced by forces and plays of power and knowledge (Foucault, 1980a). Tamboukou (1999) suggests that for Foucault, the analyst has identified an apparatus when they have succeeded in isolating a cluster of power relations sustaining and being sustained, by certain types of knowledge.

Once the apparatus elements have been identified, Tamboukou (1999, p. 214) argues that the analysis of the power-knowledge relationships within the apparatus should start with a significant interrogation of what has been accepted as 'truth' or assumed knowledge. The interrogation should include any truth concerning the ways individuals understand themselves as subjects of these discourses. Tamboukou (1999, p. 209) suggests that a point of analysis could be 'the disturbance of previous immobile statements, fragments of unified truths', or the exposing of 'the heterogeneity of previous consistencies'. Disturbing this apparent linear and consistent evolution is orientated to an analysis of descent and emergence. The purpose of a study of descent and emergence is not to identify and analyse grand historical events or re-write history, but seek events that have remained unnoticed and unrecorded in mainstream history narratives.

Another feature of our toolbox is the re-emergence of subjugated knowledges. Here, 'the lack, the unsaid, determines and defines 'the very existence of what is said, of the enunciative field' (Foucault, 1972, p. 110). Foucault (cited in Rabinow, 1986, p. 76) argues that genealogy should not only seek to analyse events in 'the most unpromising places', 'be sensitive to their recurrence', and 'isolate the different scenes where they engaged in different roles', but also define 'those instances when they are absent, the moment when they remain unrealized'. The subjugated or silenced will inevitably be present in the archives, but the problem lies in identifying them. Carter (2006, pp. 223–224) responds to this provocation by suggesting that for groups that are recognised as being absent, the tactic of 'listening to silences' is a successful way of discovering the 'lack' and 'unsaid'. In this strategy, texts are examined for their omissions, gaps are interrogated, and the representations of silence explored. Carter (2006, pp. 223–224) adds that 'it is inevitable that the marginal infects the centre, that its presence is felt critiquing the structures of power. As a result of this infection or infiltration, the voices of the marginal may be heard'. Foucault (1972, p. 169) also proposes that determining the 'lack', the 'unsaid', can be used to illuminate the discontinuities, ruptures, and gaps of a discourse.

History is the privileged instrument of genealogical analysis, but it is a particular sort of 'effective history' (Dean, 1994). Effective history exercises an observation and scepticism toward various philosophical claims to prescribe the meaning of history. It avoids the possibility of 'total history' or the 'official' accounts, and instead aims to unsettle the 'taken-for-granted components of our reality... how they came to be the way they are' (Dean, 1994, p. 4).

Having identified the elements of our genealogical toolbox, and the various ways in which these tools can be understood and used, we now briefly outline the structure of the chapters that follow, and the work that we will do there.

7 Structure of the Book

Chapter Two analyses the economic, political and cultural processes that played a role in constituting governmental responses to the 'discovery' of the problem of low foundation skills in Australia. We present some key episodes and events from the Hawke-Keating Labour Governments that began to emerge in the late 20th century, and which signalled the transformation of the Australian economy through processes of globalising, neoliberal capitalism that promoted deregulation, trade liberalisation, privatisation and competitive markets. We will identify and discuss how the impacts of global and national forces, such as economic recessions, the displacement of jobs by automation, the emergence of precarious labour markets, and high unemployment placed considerable strain on liberal welfare regimes. In response, but not inevitably, governments began to prioritise market principles as a way to solve broader systemic social problems. As the newly elected Howard conservative Liberal-National Coalition in 1996 deployed a series of welfare reforms that shifted government out of social service delivery and reinforced traditional institutions such as the family, charities and the church, it also underpinned these reforms through principles of individual responsibility and moral and reciprocal obligation. We will illustrate how the transformation of a framework of mutual obligation created markets of job seekers that required 'skills training' to engage in the labour market.

In Chapter Three, we draw on Foucault's way of characterising the apparatus as one structured into three phases, to examine the urgent historical need, the strategic function and the relationships between the elements of the apparatus. We demonstrate how the apparatus emerged from the given historical moment during the Howard Coalition's first term of government, in which an urgent need was identified in relation to stagnating unemployment rates, concerns of welfare dependency, and troubling OECD adult literacy survey results. We identify the presence of the elements that make up the apparatus. These elements, such as the registered training providers (RTOs), industry bodies, academia, programs, political rationalities and governmental technologies, form particular systems of relations as the strategic priorities of governments evolved and shifted. From these systems of relations, certain 'truths' claims are promoted. To frame later discussions, we briefly problematise three significant 'truth' claims to conclude this chapter. These include the prioritisation of human capital over social outcomes as a way to understand the principal benefits of foundation skills; how the foundational aims of the apparatus to support vulnerable populations are underpinned by moral regulation, not human rights agendas; and the discordant forms of subjectivities produced by the apparatus that promote individuals as job seekers and choice-making consumers, not learners.

Chapter 4 is framed by a prominent 'example' from the Victoria training system, a reform between 2008 and 2013 named the *Victorian Training Guarantee*. The focus on the Victorian training system is important for a number of reasons. This reform was the first state-based policy to introduce a fully commodified and marketised vocational training system, including the provision of foundation skills programs. However, as this 'open', demand-driven system collapsed because of widespread corruption, inadequate regulation and budget blowouts, the consequences resonated not only in the Victorian market but also in other Commonwealth, State and Territory training markets. The far-reaching impact of this reform is an effective example of how the strategic aims, elements and relationships between different parts of the apparatus can significantly transform, as agencies make sense of, and attempt to correct, the failures of neoliberal markets. Included in this chapter is a discussion of how the Commonwealth assumed responsibility for a large proportion of the national training regulation mid-way through the Victorian reform that embedded vocabularies of new public management, emphasised risk and reputation management, and sought to build consumer confidence in public expenditures.

In Chapter 5, we explore how the learner within the foundation skills apparatus has been constructed as an individual, choice-making, responsible consumer, having to make sense of, and navigate the complex entanglements of training and labour markets. We draw on the *National Foundation Skills Strategy for Adults* (*National Strategy*), released in 2012, as a key document to analyse these processes of individualisation and responsibilisation. Our analysis reveals how the *National Strategy* works on the psychological choice mechanisms of individuals through processes of moral self-evaluations to recognise the benefits of increasing their foundation skills and then acting with these skills. This analysis raises important questions about the subjectification of the foundation skills learner as a responsible choice-maker by identifying factors that hinder, not promote, individual choice and expose practices capable of marginalising populations with low foundation skills even further. The chapter concludes with a discussion of how broader socio-economic factors that are understood to impact foundation skills are positioned in the apparatus. As governments seek to make individuals, families, communities and agencies responsible for the array of problems and challenges of socio-economic disadvantage, we reveal how this kind of responsibilisation is also evident in the ways in which the State demands that RTOs, through a variety of mechanisms, offer localised solutions to learners impacted by socio-economic disadvantage.

In our final chapter, we briefly revisit our genealogical research as a way of using key events and episodes to provoke a rethinking of values, to direct a destabilising light on the 'history of the present' of the problem of foundation skills by denormalising current identities, institutions and patterns of thought and action, and to transform this reality by opening up new possibilities for thought and action. Having done this work, our intent is to speculate on the ways in which this genealogy can inform community, academic and policy understandings of the possibilities and limitations of the governmental ambitions of the neoliberal foundation skills apparatus. We will do this, a little provocatively, by seeking to write a limited version of the 'history of the future' of foundation skills by projecting forward the work we have done to that point. Our aim is to identify, discuss and problematise a limited number of future 'events' that are likely to continue to shape the foundation skills apparatus – even if these possible futures will be uncertain, unpredictable, disruptive, discontinuous and non-teleological. These events and episodes include:

- The Pandemic and its Aftermath: A Skills-led Economic Recovery?;
- The Programme for the International Assessment of Adult Competencies (PIAAC) and the 'Politics' of the Future of Foundation Skills; and,
- Artificial Intelligence and the Futures of Work and (Foundation) Skills

In exploring and problematising these events, we are concerned with the reflexivity of the apparatus, and how particular actors, agencies, processes, and relationships will respond, be evaluated, and be reproduced. We also draw upon these discussions to examine how governments, policymakers, industry, academia, RTOs and peak professional bodies continue to think about the challenges and possibilities for populations with low foundation skills.

Our intent, then, is to provide a detailed and in-depth analysis of the ways in which a neoliberal foundation skills apparatus has emerged in Australia during the last four decades. This apparatus, and the diverse elements, strategic relationships, forms of knowledge, and particular understandings of skills, who lacks them, what should be done about this, emerges in a historically particular and contingent form by promising to provide strategic, market-driven, choice enabled responses to the urgent needs identified by international agencies, various levels of government, business and communities.

This extensive and in-depth analysis of the Australian context, and the relationships between this national context and a range of powerful, globalising lines of force energised by transformations in global capitalism, waves of digital disruption, the emergence of new worlds of work, and the urgencies and needs identified by a range of international agencies, promise to provide models, concepts, analysis and theoretical contributions to many other contexts around the globe which are also impacted by these powerful, disruptive and transformative lines of force.

Notes

1 This section is not a history of The Enlightenment and much of what follows is not about the period named as The Enlightenment, but that process of Enlightenment that Kant has identified, and others such as Foucault have critiqued.

2 The male pronoun is recognised as problematic, but is used to reflect, not reproduce, the gendered character of much of this discourse.

CHAPTER 2

Neoliberal Capitalism and the 'Problem' of Foundation Skills

1 Introduction

The emergence of neoliberal capitalism has been a transformative process that has permeated into all levels of education, including adult education and foundation skills. Before the 1990s, the foundation skills sector was largely shaped by the rationalities of social justice, community development and human empowerment. A 'reality' that Reder (2013, p. 48) had identified as the 'heady optimism and activism of adult education'. But as we will demonstrate in what follows, as neoliberal rationalities emerged and became an orthodoxy, the adult education and foundation skills sector increasingly prioritised 'free market' mechanisms that were historically used to solve economic problems. In many of the EU and OECD economies, under regimes of globalising flexible capitalism and the logics of so-called 'knowledge' and 'skills economies', the development of strong foundation skills began to be imagined as a way for individuals to build their human capital and become economic actors able to participate in changing labour markets.

In this chapter, we will draw on Foucault's 'tools' of 'descent' and 'emergence' to trace the 'events' in the histories (episodes) of neoliberal capitalism and globalisation that relate to the emergence of the foundation skills apparatus in Australia. These tools will reveal how neoliberal markets, flexible capitalism, and neoliberal subjects are understood and rationalised in the apparatus. It is not our intent to provide a full history of the ways in which neoliberal rationalities shaped the emergence of this apparatus. Instead, our aim is to explore the historical context of selected policies and discourses that played a role in shaping how the strategic function of the apparatus emerged as it did.

In order to do this work, we have structured the chapter in three sections. In the first section, we focus our attention on public policy and the activities of successive Australian Labor Party governments from 1983 to 1996. The key events of this episode focus on two documents, the *Garnaut Report* (Garnaut, 1989) and the *Hilmer Report* (Hilmer, 1993). These reports were instrumental in entrenching a new understanding of how economies 'should' work in Australia, the constraints placed on national policymakers, and the benefits of using market mechanisms to achieve particular social and economic ends (Beeson &

 DOI:10.1163/9789004724464_003

Firth, 1998). The second section analyses how the increasingly deregulated and globalised markets became progressively individualised. Drawing on a Commonwealth government-commissioned report, the *Karpin Report*, and a period that we label a 'new world of work', we explore how these policy discourses attempted to reconfigure persons as neoliberal subjects. This analysis problematises how the labour market has shifted from the idea, if not the actuality, of a 'job for life', to the materiality of more insecure work in which people must view themselves and act on themselves as an 'enterprise' to create ongoing opportunities to be 'successful' (Kelly, 2013).

The final section brings together the discussions of neoliberal markets and individuals to focus on an 'event' of welfare state reform by the socially 'conservative', economically 'radical' Howard Liberal-National Coalition government in 1998. This event illustrates the Australian Government's movement out of the space of service delivery, accompanied by efforts to shift the responsibility of welfare provision and practices to private and non-profit organisations, family units, and the individual. By drawing on Foucault's concept of eventalisation, we analyse the multiplicity of processes that constituted this reform, such as the work of Australia's Industry Commission and the concept of welfare reciprocity, known as mutual obligation. This section plays a pivotal role in foregrounding discussions in later chapters, and provides historical examples of policy that shaped the strategic function of the foundation skills apparatus to govern vulnerable individuals with low foundation skills. It also reveals how the concept of mutual obligation was instrumental in establishing a market of 'job seekers' to be provided with essential skills training in 'open' and 'competitive' training markets.

2 The Emergence of Neoliberal Markets in Australia

It is tempting to frame neoliberalism in a periodised and linear narrative. One can start with the classical economist Adam Smith and his work *The Wealth of Nations* in 1776, which argued a free-market system and free trade would produce true national wealth, benefiting all social classes, not just the privileged few. Narratives then often illuminate the years preceding the Great Depression and reference the writings of figures such as Ludwig von Mises, who criticised the rationality of socialism, and Arthur Rüstow and the Colloque Walter Lippmann (held in Paris in 1938), which renewed the case for economic liberalism against the rise of perceived anti-liberal trends such as trade unions, social policies and protectionist macroeconomics (Davies, 2014b). The neoliberal timeline is also often traced to during and after the Second World War, with a counterpart of von Mises, Friedrich Hayek, who established the global neoliberal think-tank, the Mont Pelerin Society. Other critical scholars retell the history of neoliberalism as an actual enacted program of government. Here, historical narratives give accounts of Pinochet's coup in Chile in 1971 and the implementation of economic 'reforms' (devised from the Chicago School of Economics), and the UK and USA regimes of Margaret Thatcher and Ronald Reagan, all of which saw a revolution in 'orthodox' fiscal and social policies, including economic liberalisation, privatisation of state-owned companies, and efforts to stabilise inflation (Gilbert, 2013; Harvey, 2005).

Australia's engagement with, and reshaping by neoliberalism, is often framed in heated debates. There are claims that its origins (and benchmarking) belong to Thatcherism and Reaganomics. Or, depending on political persuasions, it is identified as a 'project of the Right'. Or its emergence is attributed to 'labor and social-democratic parties' (Humphrys, 2019, para. 12). In this sense, it can be a simplistic narrative to locate the emergence of neoliberalism in Australia in a linear timeframe of free-market thinking. Moreover, it can be problematic to identify the emergence of neoliberalism in Australia with the work of a specific 'thinker'. Such an approach overlooks that 'neoliberalism in the post-war years did not represent one single strand of thought, but rather a heterogeneous movement of ideas' (Turner, 2008, p. 15). The movement of ideas, described by Beeson and Firth (1998, p. 221) as 'economic ideas, political practices and the influence of a number of broader social forces', sits within a multitude of geographical and historical spaces across different scales of time and space. Neoliberalism in Australia can, and does look different, and have different strategic aims and outcomes to neoliberalism in, for example, the UK. Two powerful examples of the framing of neoliberal 'ideas, practices and forces' by the Hawke and Keating Labour Governments in the early 1990s in Australia are the *Garnaut Report* (Garnaut, 1989) and the *Hilmer Report* (Hilmer, 1993). These reports, as we will demonstrate in the following sections, were influential in entrenching a new understanding of the way economies work in Australia, the constraints placed on national policymakers, and the benefits of using market forces to achieve particular social and economic ends.

2.1 *The Garnaut Report*

We foreground our analysis of this report with a review of some of the historical accounts of economic and social 'crisis' in Australia and elsewhere tracing back to the 1970s. In this decade, a global crisis of governability and discontent contributed to the relative demise of Keynesian macroeconomics in many industrialised countries. This global downturn was characterised by declining productivity growth and profitability, high unemployment, and the rise of 'stagflation', a simultaneous increase in inflation and stagnation of economic output (Davies, 2014b; Harvey, 2006). The Arab-Israeli conflict in 1973 contributed to the quadrupling of world oil prices, which drove the prices of goods higher, causing civil unrest and protests around the globe (Hilsenrath, 2021). In Australia, Malcolm Fraser's conservative Coalition administration from 1975 to 1983 responded to stagflation by remaining committed to the Keynesian economic framework. His government embarked on interventions to manage high unemployment and inflation by welfare retrenchment (reduction in welfare expenditure leading to the shrinking of the welfare state) and wage freezes (Weller & O'Neill, 2014). As Australia's economic circumstances continued to deteriorate, a consensus emerged that the Keynesian accumulation strategy was failing and that so-called 'economic rationalist' policies would provide the solution to these challenges. Bob Hawke's Labor government (1983–1991) came to power with a mandate to implement an internationalisation and modernisation strategy which aimed to improve economic growth through opening Australia's economy and improving its international competitiveness (Weller & O'Neill, 2014).

Seeking a new approach to industrial relations, the Hawke Labor government sought to include the union movement into economic policy discussions, development and management. In 1983, agreements, known as the *Accords*, were negotiated between the government and unions to reform occupational industry awards and implement a shift to productivity-based wage determinations (Australian Labor Party & Australian Council of Trade Unions, 1983).[1] As compensation for unions moderating their wage demands, workers would receive improvements in the 'social wage' – better public health provision through Medicare, improvements to pensions and unemployment benefits, tax cuts, and compulsory superannuation[2] – to improve their quality of life and working conditions (Dyrenfurth, 2013; Weller & O'Neill, 2014). Among other reforms, the Hawke Government floated the Australian dollar, repealed rules that prohibited foreign-owned banks from operating in Australia, dismantled the protectionist tariff system, privatised several state sector industries, ended the subsidisation of loss-making industries, and sold off part of the state-owned Commonwealth Bank (Department of the Parliamentary Library, 1991).

In 1986, then Treasurer Paul Keating said that Australia risked becoming a third-rate economy – a 'banana republic' – if it allowed the sophisticated industrial side of the country to fall away. He stressed that 'we must let Australians know truthfully, honestly, earnestly, just what sort of international hole Australia is in' (Keating, 1986). Keating warned that Australia's key institutional structures, which were self-regulating and relatively self-contained within a national context, needed to be reformed. Prime Minister Bob Hawke (1989, p. 4) reflected at this time that:

> For the first seven decades of the Federation a fearful, defensive Australia built walls to protect against the challenge of the outside world and found that it had protected itself against the recognition and utilisation of opportunity. In other words, we had walked down the gentle path to economic mediocrity.

The Hawke Government stressed that economic security depended upon securing a share of the prosperity generated by international restructuring. One of their policy initiatives at this time was a report from Hawke's principal economic advisor, Ross Garnaut (1989), named *Australia and the Northeast Asia Ascendancy* or the *Garnaut Report*. The *Garnaut Report* sought to realign Australia's domestic and international policy strategies by recognising that Australia's future was positioned within Northeast Asia. The Northeast Asia region was quickly emerging as a 'powerhouse' that included: 'Japan's economic and financial power, China's drive to modernise and the remarkable trading achievements of the Republic of Korea, Taiwan and Hong Kong... moving the centre of gravity of the world from the Atlantic to the Pacific' (Grant, 1990, p. 3).

Despite its reputation as a 'watershed' in Australian policymaking (Beeson & Firth, 1998, p. 221), the *Garnaut Report* faced several challenges during its implementation. It was released at a time when some Australian commentators regarded 'Asia' as an undifferentiated 'threat', and through the Cold War, divided Asians into 'friends and enemies' (Grant, 1990, p. 3). There were criticisms of the report's heavy reliance on supplying resources to a rapidly industrialising region without an endorsement from the United States (Beeson, 2015). The report also coincided with the Tiananmen Square massacre in China. Beeson (2015) claimed that the political context of the report was overshadowed by the management of the aftermath of the events in China, and that policymakers carefully displayed political pragmatism to condemn China's actions while avoiding damage to strategic and commercial interests. Additionally, the use of the term 'ascendency' was imagined by critics as Australia attempting to fit into an environment that was largely established. According to Grant (1990, p. 3), this invited the thought that 'Australia is now being asked to line up with the new masters of the world'.

However, several authors have argued that Australia displayed a profound degree of independence – not heteronomy – and coherence in foreign policy at the time.[3] Indeed, commentary from McKay (1990) and Grant (1990) positively advocate for the report's influence in charting the appropriate course for Australia's relations within the Northeast Asia region in the 1990s. The core of the *Garnaut Report* was its economic analysis. It proposed, in general, to involve Australia more in Northeast Asia by encouraging Asian investment, trade and educational and cultural links (Beeson & Firth, 1998). The report recommended the development of export markets and the creation of national-scale domestic markets to generate economies of scale. Industries could only be internationally competitive exporters, argued Garnaut, if their cost structures were not inflated by domestic protection and they were able to operate domestically at world prices (Hawke, 1989). The report's recommendations follow the general direction set by proponents of a more competitive Australian economy in a more open international system. It assumed that a more liberalised trading system would allow, or compel, Australia to compete successfully.

The National Archives cabinet historian Nicholas Brown (cited in Murphy, 2014, para. 4) labelled the *Garnaut Report* as a 'manifesto'. Many priorities in microeconomic reform gained coherence from the report, from industry policy to trade liberalisation, education and immigration (Murphy, 2014). Bob Hawke (1989, p. 1), in his launch of the *Garnaut Report*, claimed the report would challenge the way Australians imagined their country and its place globally:

> It is a report whose impact reaches into virtually every aspect of Australian society – just as the process of economic internationalisation it describes and advocates has triggered far reaching change in attitudes and practices throughout the Australian community.

The report argued for a shift in thinking to embrace the need for highly skilled migrants and immigration policies sympathetic to the needs of Asian countries. It also called for major efforts in education and research to make Australia more aware of Asian languages, cultures and economics. Garnaut's recommendation on infrastructure policy – particularly focussing on the waterfront, coastal shipping, civil aviation and electricity generation – argued for the opportunities for private (including foreign) investment and the increased competition in providing these services. The report identified a degree of fear, apprehension and prejudice about foreign investment from Asia, which needed to be alleviated to foster non-discriminatory policies in foreign investment.

While the financial liberalisation reforms from the Hawke Government produced 'mixed fortunes' (Weller & O'Neill, 2014, p. 118),[4] Beeson and Firth (1998) claim the significance of the report was not to be found in its success or ineffectiveness. A key point, they argue, was the emergence of neoliberal political rationality in Australia. As we suggested in the previous chapter, Miller and

Rose (2010), drawing on Foucault's work, argue that government is a complex activity shaped by a series of rationalities, which cannot be viewed simply as the implementation of any particular political or economic theory. Instead, Miller and Rose (2010) define political rationalities as contested, often contradictory, amalgams of political expediency, policies, common sense, responses to public opinion, economic doctrines, and notions of human rights. In this way, Beeson and Firth (1998) argue that the significance of the *Garnaut Report* as political rationality was related to the new ways of thinking about national economies and their possible management. The report represented a major shift in thinking about how the Australian economy was integrated into an increasingly interconnected international system, entrenching a new understanding of how economies work (Beeson & Firth, 1998). The 1993 *Hilmer Report*, commissioned after Paul Keating replaced Bob Hawke as Australian Prime Minister, was instrumental in adding to this thinking.

2.2 *The Hilmer Report and the National Competition Policy*

The rise of neoliberal fiscal and social policies in the 1980s signalled the distinct shift from classical forms of liberalism to more contemporary liberalism (neoliberalism). Post-war boom periods of classical liberalism viewed government intervention into social and economic realms, other than to regulate against monopoly formation, and to protect property rights, as generally unnecessary and as inhibiting the entrepreneurial culture of free-market economies (Gilbert, 2013). From the 1980s, Gilbert (2013) claims that neoliberalism took a different view, inspired by similar ideals, but advocating a program of deliberate intervention by government to encourage particular types of entrepreneurial, competitive and commercial behaviour. He points to the argument that classic liberalism is exposed to a habitual tendency towards collectivism. If left unchecked, it leads to commercial producers, workers, service providers, managers and government officials acting only in their corporate interests. By contrast, Gilbert (2013) argues that neoliberalism assumes that a benign but frequently directive state can guide citizens. Rather than reduce the state's responsibility as neoliberal theory would have it, the state plays a more directive role in introducing, implementing, and reproducing neoliberalism. Institutional frameworks appropriate to neoliberal practices are preserved. For example, as governments guarantee the quality and integrity of money and establish education, military, defence, police, legal structures and functions required to secure private property rights, they then guarantee, by force, if need be, the proper functioning of markets (Cahill, 2009; Harvey, 2005).

In their reforms to open up Australia to global forces, the Hawke-Keating Governments faced a dilemma in the early 1990s regarding the level of intervention in market governance. The rise in the current account deficit and external debt exposed the problems of the trade competitiveness of Australian firms (Ravenhill, 1994; Tease, 1990). The underlying problem was that Australia's fragmented, and relatively small domestic market, lacked the economies of scale of transnational competitors. Weller and O'Neill (2014, p. 116) argue that policy debates framed by the Commonwealth at this time continued to be focussed on 'whether there had been too much or not enough government intervention and whether market solutions were more effective than more orthodox regulatory ones'. The result was a set of actions to transform industrial organisations to build larger firms inside larger markets where national brands could compete against imported ones and develop export capacity (Productivity Commission, 1999). For an efficient, competitive market to function, the Commonwealth identified that a regime of appropriate rules must be designed to govern the behaviour of economic actors (Beeson & Firth, 1998). The Keating Government commissioned Australian academic and business figure Frederick Hilmer to write the *National Competition Policy* (widely known as the *Hilmer Report*). This report became instrumental in providing a framework for regulating competition in Australia (Hilmer, 1993).

The *Hilmer Report* generated strong awareness and widespread community support for implementing an effective national competition policy. It advocated that competition was central to economic reform and the 'positive force that assists economic growth and job creation' (Hilmer, 1993, p. xv). The report recommended implementing a national competition policy for Australia to 'promote and maintain competitive forces to increase efficiency and community welfare, while recognising other social goals' (Hilmer, 1993, p. v). The *Hilmer Report* was not developed in the 'pursuit of competition *per se*' but to 'facilitate' effective competition in the interests of economic efficiency, and to mediate where competition conflicts with other social objectives (Hilmer, 1993, p. xvi). In its broadest sense, the report recommended a policy encompassing a framework of principles, processes and institutional structures intended to be sufficiently flexible to deal with the extent and nature of competition and different sectors of the economy. In its implementation as the *National Competition Policy,* and comprising a combination of laws, principles and processes, the *Hilmer Report* also included the setting up of two institutions, the National Competition Council and the Australian Competition Commission.[5] The National Competition Council was formed as an independent analytical and advisory body for Commonwealth, State and Territory governments on regulation review, structural reform of public monopolies, access regimes, monopoly pricing and competitive neutrality (Hilmer, 1993). The Australian Competition Commission was established to administer the competitive conduct rules to enhance the promotion of competition and fair trading and provision for consumer protection (Kain et al., 2001).

In an attempt to create a rules-based domestic framework, the *National Competition Policy* was established to 'operationalise' a neoliberal political rationality (Beeson & Firth, 1998, p. 222). This operationalisation can be illustrated by considering the commonalities or regularities that exist within political rationalities (Miller & Rose, 2010). One regularity understands that political rationalities distinguish between different forms of authority and specify the proper distribution of tasks between these authorities. This regularity also specifies the goals and principles to which government activities should be directed. For example, in the *National Competition Policy*, this is demonstrated by the formation of institutions such as the National Competition Council and Australian Competition Commission, both responsible to Commonwealth, State and Territory governments, to oversee competitive mechanisms and provide public education on the conduct, rules, and the role of competition in the community (Hilmer, 1993).

Another regularity recognises that political rationalities are articulated in relation to how the objects of government are conceived (Miller & Rose, 2010). In this sense, the focus of the policy is principally 'firms and institutions', regulated within a series of mechanisms to 'promote and maintain competitive forces to increase efficiency and community welfare, while recognising other social goals' (Hilmer, 1993, p. v). The policy specifies particular subjectivities, or 'subjective conditions' (Miller & Rose, 2010, p. 278), as desirable. These conditions include anti-competitive conduct against the public interest, ensuring market rules are uniformly applied to all participants regardless of business ownership, and mandating against monopolies misusing market power (Hilmer, 1993). A third regularity concerns how political rationalities are made thinkable by language. Political rationalities are articulated in a distinctive idiom that translates into political debates, program discourse and policies. An example of the 'distinctive idiom' in the competition policy is the framing of competition within the mechanisms of 'economic efficiency' (Hilmer, 1993, p. 3). This includes associations with the vocabulary of 'economic growth, 'job creation', 'initiative and discovery', 'value-added exports', competing 'successfully in international markets' and making the 'economy more flexible' (Hilmer, 1993, pp. xv–xvi).

Miller and Rose (2010) emphasise that political rationalities cannot be disassociated from technologies of government. Technologies are the tools and techniques by which the thinking about government is put into effect. The *National Competition Policy* established various strategies, techniques and procedures to administer, program, shape and regulate competition and fair trading. It did this by deploying agencies such as the National Competition Council and the Australian Competition Commission to promote competition and fair trading among businesses, to provide education, training and general guidance to encourage compliance and prevent breaches of the law, and to inform the public of their rights and obligations under the law (Kain et al., 2001). Where these and other technologies of government are not effective in guiding circumstances that could, or have the potential to, impact vulnerable consumers, harm the competitive process, or result in widespread consumer damage, the *National Competition Policy* can deploy legal technologies under the *Trade Practices Act 1974* (now the *Competition and Consumer Act 2010*) to regulate economic behaviour. These legal technologies include a range of enforcement remedies to address contraventions of the Act, including court-based outcomes and court-enforceable undertakings (Australian Competition & Consumer Commission, 2021a; Kain et al., 2001). The policy's purpose can be perceived to encourage the 'conduct of conduct' (Foucault, 1982, pp. 220–221) of individuals, corporations and agencies, and thereby distances itself from individual disputes, complaint handling, State or Territory issues, and making formal decisions on the law. Its prime focus is on areas that pertain to significant public interest or concern.

The *Hilmer Report* has contributed significantly to the way competition and neoliberal capitalism is understood and practiced in Australia. We return, in later chapters, to how the *Hilmer Report* has influenced foundations skills policy. At the same time, as we discuss in the next section, neoliberal capitalism and globalisation processes have driven and produced a 'new world of work', including labour market changes, a work culture of 'enterprise', and the normalisation of individualised competition. Drawing on a Commonwealth-commissioned report – the *Karpin Report* as a key 'event' – we explore how neoliberal discourses seek to work, not only at the organisational and industry level, but also directly on the individual.

3 Globalisation, Flexible Capitalism: Changing Labour Markets and a New World of Work

For much of the twentieth century in Australia and other industrialised democracies of the OECD and the EU, large factories dominated capitalist modes of production with the concentration of large amounts of capital, machinery and labour in a single location. This arrangement assumed a number of things, including that capital was immobile, unit labour costs were the same in all nations, people have preferences for the products of their own nations, and the existence of ongoing, full-time employment. In the late 20th century, technological and economic transformations were produced by increasingly powerful and widespread forces of 'global capitalism' (Williams et al., 2013, p. 142). Workforces began to be managed and organised to support capital accumulation on an international scale, and involved processes such as:

- globalised production, in which the growing power of capital organises and controls labour on geographic scales;
- greater mobility, in which work can be moved relatively easily to cheaper production sites with more compliant workforces; and,
- labour management, controlled by the government's deregulatory policies that are designed to offer attractive investment opportunities to multinational corporations (Williams et al., 2013).

This form of capitalism, which Richard Sennett (1998) calls 'flexible capitalism', assumes that as production is dispersed worldwide, no one 'unit of production' is deeply invested in the success or failure of a single product. Rather, the risk is broken down and distributed among smaller units and deals. Companies are structured as multinational companies with global branches, affiliates and offices. The benefits are that production facilities can be set up where the most appropriate mix of skilled and cheap labour, and lower tariff and tax regimes can be found (Sennett, 1998). This allows for production targets and designs to change more rapidly. Cost efficiency comes from speeding up turnover, perfecting order quantities and distribution, coordinating production processes and facilitating the rapid flow of goods (Martell, 2010). Cost efficiency is also enabled by automating tasks that replace jobs that are easily codified, repetitive, simple, structured or routine, particularly in manufacturing or processing (Martell, 2010).

3.1 *The Karpin Report*

Concerns that Australia lacked the human resources, strategic planning, and infrastructure to establish a competitive advantage in flexible capitalist markets emerged in the early 1990s. At that time, Australia was in a deep recession, with Bob Hawke replaced as prime minister by Paul Keating in 1991. Policymakers were apprehensive that the nation's economy was not growing as fast as neighbours in Hong Kong and Singapore. Despite the considerable attention paid to the reform of workplace practices (such as the Hawke-Keating *Accords*), both productivity and international trade were areas of concern to policymakers. Many areas of the economy were identified as not globally competitive, with enterprise work practices and management skills below so-called 'world-best' standards. It was argued that the potential of Australian enterprises to deliver globally competitive products and services was suffering from the productivity of people and technology, and an inability to innovate creatively and quickly (Beeson & Firth, 1998; Weller & O'Neill, 2014). Australian enterprises, training providers and educational institutions were also imagined as not moving swiftly enough to address new paradigms of management (Karpin, 1995). Famously declaring that this was the 'recession Australia had to have' during his time as Treasurer (National Archives of Australia, 2019, para. 22), Prime Minister Paul Keating accelerated structural changes to Australia's globally exposed trading environment (Weller & O'Neill, 2014) through reforms including the *Garnaut* and *Hilmer Reports*.

One part of Keating's reform agenda was the commissioning of a report titled *Enterprising nation: Renewing Australia's managers to meet the challenges of the Asia-Pacific century*. Also known as the *Karpin Report*, the key objective of this report was to investigate how Australia prepared its managers for work and leadership. The report argued:

> The improvement in the performance of Australia's managers is an important complement to the Government's wide ranging micro-economic reform, export enhancement and workforce training initiatives. Better educated and trained managers will increase the speed by which these initiatives secure significant economic benefit through workplace restructuring, improved business processes and increases in the productivity of Australia's human and capital resources. (Karpin, 1995, p. 1)

The report drew attention to the need for an 'enterprise culture'. It provided wide-ranging recommendations on small business, globalisation, diversity, lifelong learning, and enterprise and education institution best practice. Seeking pathways to lasting change and improvement, the *Karpin Report* recommended enterprise and individual-driven solutions to the problems and challenges facing Australia's business leaders, managers, educators, trainers and government policymakers (Samson, 2011).

Despite principally focussing on the nation's leaders and managers, the *Karpin Report* stressed that the issue was broader than encouraging citizens to create small businesses or enact change in larger corporations. The report imagined enterprise, not only in economic and labour market terms, but also in more individual and social contexts. For example:

> many more of our citizens, be they employees or managers, working for small or large organisations, need to be 'enterprising' in the broadest sense of the word, not only in business but also in social and community

> organisations and in terms of their own personal lives in a changing world. (Karpin, 1995, p. 9)

To be 'enterprising', according to the *Karpin Report*, citizens should 'recognise opportunity, manage risk and mobilise and manage resources... developing the qualities which a person needs to be enterprising such as the ability to tackle problems, take initiatives, persevere and be flexible' (Karpin, 1995, p. 113). In this way, 'enterprise' was not only understood as a 'mindset' but also as a 'skill'. As a 'skill', the report advocates an education solution to encourage enterprising and entrepreneurial behaviour in citizens. This includes exposure by providing qualifications of entrepreneurship, and management and small business formation at tertiary and postgraduate qualifications level, and also as formal units of study to students in secondary and vocational sectors. As argued in the report, a cross-sector education approach develops the 'skill' and 'mindset' of entrepreneurship in industry, and in a way that can be applied to community, social and individual endeavours (Karpin, 1995).

While Samson's (2011, p. 28) review of the *Karpin Report* identified its implementation as 'patchy', he was complimentary of how market forces, rather than concerted action by governments, ensured that many of the recommendations found their way into practice within organisations and educational settings. Additionally, he discovered that the report had resonance with business and industry, and that the continuing relevance of its findings and recommendations were a testament to its forward-looking focus. Beeson and Firth (1998) maintain that the significance of the *Karpin Report* was not its failures or successes but its attempt to consolidate neoliberalism at the level of the individual. As a logical extension of the *Garnaut* and *Hilmer Reports*, the report maintains the dominant neoliberal rationality that markets are the best mechanisms to allocate resources and quality outcomes. To promote market mechanisms, the report argues that this could be most effectively achieved by citizens being 'enterprising' to respond swiftly to the stimulus of market signals. The *Karpin Report* developed this vision by understanding Australia's population as a resource, a form of 'human capital', to be worked on and designed to play a more productive part in national economic development (Becker, 1963, 1992; Schultz, 1961).

Becker and Schultz were influential in the 1960s and 1970s in developing an economic approach to human behaviour. The fundamental principle underpinning human capital theory is the belief that people's learning capacities are of comparable value to other resources – financial, organisational, intellectual, innovation and process resources – in producing goods and services. Schultz (1961) argued that when human resources are effectively utilised, the results are profitable for the individual, organisation and society. In this sense, Becker (1992, p. 85) suggested that:

> I am going to talk about a different kind of capital. Schooling, a computer training course, expenditures of medical care, lectures on the virtues of punctuality and honesty are capital too, in the sense that they improve health, raise earnings, or add to a person's appreciation of literature over much of his or her lifetime.

The central proposition of human capital theory is that people are considered a form of capital that should attract investment (Becker, 1992). One form of investment is the gains that can be achieved by education and training. This understanding is explicit in the *Karpin Report* with recommendations to embed 'enterprise' within all education sectors. One part of its 'human capital' inspired vision for 1995–2010 was:

> Managers will create conditions conducive to learning for both individuals and the enterprise as a whole, within and between groups, across individual business units and between enterprises and their external environments. Employees will be more motivated and skilled. (Karpin, 1995, p. xx)

In being framed by human capital theory, the *Karpin Report* promotes the assumption that citizens can be ideally positioned to be entrepreneurial by acquiring the 'right' human capital. In this way, 'enterprise' becomes a means of imagining the neoliberal individual as *homo economicus. Homo economicus* imagines persons as consistently rational agents and fundamentally self-interested – an 'entrepreneur' – who continually strives towards self-maximisation and self-capitalisation (Foucault, 2008; Packard & Bylund, 2021). Yet, as we introduce a more contemporary example to this section by imagining *homo economicus* in relation to vulnerable populations navigating uncertain globalising and technologically driven labour markets, this vision becomes increasingly problematic. Studies by Grebel (2004) suggest that *homo economicus* is better imagined as *homo agens*, an economic person acting as best as they can in terms of the limits of their knowledge. Grebel's (2004, p. 68) model of entrepreneurial behaviour starts with a sense that economic actors:

> neither have complete information/foresight nor perfect (cognitive) capabilities... They cannot make optimal decisions. Decisions are dependent on their knowledge and the information they have or receive,

> respectively, from their social, political and economic environment. The agent's perception of their environment is thereby contingent to their limited information processing capacity and their limited attentiveness. They have to be selective in their information collection process subject to bounded cognitive capabilities, which, finally, results in trial-and-error behaviour. Thus, the individual agent becomes a 'creative observer' of his socio-economic environment.

As we move to our next event, the emergence of the concept of 'new world of work', characterised by transforming practices, ideas, cultures and values in labour markets, we apply a similar vision of *homo agens* as we explore how 'at-risk' persons who experience stress, anxiety and a lack of productive connection or participation in neoliberal markets. It also includes persons trapped in cycles of unstable work that reproduce their issues with home life, physical and mental health, poverty, and a relative lack of what we are calling foundation skills.

3.2 *Flexible Markets, New Worlds of Work and Precarity*

In his book *The Corrosion of Character*, Richard Sennett (1998, p. 9) deploys the concept of 'flexible capitalism' when describing modern-day global capitalism. However, Sennett's interpretation is wider than that of capital accumulation, and his metaphor of flexibility can be applied at several levels. First, how various developments in flexible capitalism have transformed the practices, ideas, cultures and values of the world of work. Second, in thinking about how people should know and act on themselves in organisations conceived as more flexible and precarious. Third, how these themes of risk and precariousness have framed sociological understandings of more globalised labour markets and more flexible work orders (Kelly, 2013). To expand on Sennett's metaphor of flexibility in more detail, we locate our next event a decade on from the *Karpin Report* in 1995, at a time when Australia was experiencing a considerable structural change in labour markets due to forces of flexible capitalism.

After the turn of the 21st century, traditional Australian occupations in construction, mining, manufacturing, agriculture, forestry and fishing – widely understood as routine in nature – were declining in employment numbers (Heath, 2016; Stokes, 2004). One explanation for the trend was that some jobs, particularly agriculture and manufacturing, were exposed to the possibilities of technology and automation replacing routine tasks (Heath, 2016). With advances in automation allowing organisations to downsize or restructure their workforce to reduce costs, many low-skilled workers were placed at significant risk of being made redundant in these labour markets (OECD, 2013).

One offset to the declines in these industry sectors was the increase in service sector jobs such as health care and social assistance, professional, scientific and technical services, public administration and safety and education and training industries (Healey, 2014). These non-routine jobs – those that were/are difficult to automate, that require creativity and the ability to solve non-routine problems, and those that need a physical human presence – became more prominent (Heath, 2016).

As companies pursued greater efficiencies, this led to the reduction of the permanent workforce to a minimum to maximise flexibility. In many sectors, flexibility was achieved by staff hired in non-standard forms of employment such as part-time and casual work, or engaged through labour-hire companies and independent contracting (Hearn & Michelson, 2006). The benefits of these sorts of arrangements allowed organisations to respond to fluctuating work demands and lack of work (Peetz, 2018). The attractiveness of flexibility was not only lower costs, but according to Peetz (2018), the reduction of organisational risk and accountabilities concerning human resources and quality of work issues. When using labour-hire of contractors, these issues are outsourced to a contractually bound 'third party', and for casuals, workers on short-term contracts, or those engaged as independent contractors, their continued work is contingent on these issues having minimal impact on the organisation (Peetz, 2018). Bieber and Moggia (2021, p. 282) claim this underlying shift in employment relations is best understood as a 'transformation of risk: owners of firms reduce their business risk by demanding more flexibility of their workers, thereby exposing them to greater personal risk'. A consequence of greater personal risk, which we will explore in more detail later in this section, can include a lack of financial security, less income protection, concerns for the occupational health and safety of workers and workplaces, and fewer training and skills development opportunities (Howe et al., 2012). To meet the demands of their 'client' or 'employer' and ensure continued work, casual or outsourced flexible labour often face longer and more intense work hours combined with repeated and tighter deadlines and work controls (Hearn & Michelson, 2006), and an expectation of 24/7 availability.

Impacts of flexibility have moved the labour market away from the 'promise' of a 'job for life' to conditions that are changing and unpredictable. For van Onselen (2013), the flexibility of the workforce is not a concern if it is driven by choice. Many workers may not wish to be employed full-time, or seek a better work-life balance, or have time-dependent family responsibilities. Often formally educated workers embrace flexibility. Their primary allegiance is not committed to an organisation but their discipline/profession (Drucker, 2001). 'Professional' workers are often given projects instead of careers, and their employment may only last until the project is complete (Kelly, 2013). In possessing so-called 'portable skills' – such as 'personal', 'employability', 'transferrable' or 'foundation' skills – derived from their formal education, professional workers have greater choices in applying these skills across a variety of sectors, thereby increasing their employment opportunities (Drucker, 2001). As we have argued elsewhere (Kelly, 2013), workers must come to view themselves as an 'enterprise' to have the opportunity to be 'successful'.

The *Karpin Report* drew on and mobilised a wider interpretation of 'enterprise' that embraced ideas of self-maximisation and self-capitalisation in business, social and community settings. This interpretation has continued to be reshaped in flexible capitalism, particularly concerning individual responsibility for choices that people make. Elsewhere, we (Kelly, 2013) have examined how persons are expected to practice their freedom in relation to the world of paid work at the start of the twenty-first century. We (Kelly, 2013, p. 9) have suggested that flexible capitalism creates new demands for those who work, and those who want to work, to imagine that their performance at work is determined by their health, fitness, relationships and work-life balance. Increasingly, all aspects of a worker's life have come to be seen as performance-related and consequently of interest to those who employ them (or fire them).

These demands require the individual to think of themselves as an entrepreneurial self. They are required to identify themselves – in a widespread and embracing set of normative terms – as 'rational, autonomous, choice making, risk aware, prudential, responsible and entrepreneurial' (Kelly, 2017, p. 57). Through forms of self-awareness, self-understanding, reflexivity, they should have the capacity to exercise a well-regulated autonomy. This form of selfhood should also have the capacity to exercise, on a continual, ongoing basis, practices of freedom that require the exercise of choice, and acceptance of the responsibilities for the consequences of choices made, or not made (Kelly, 2013, p. 14).

Sugarman (2015) also argues that people in this new world of work must own themselves as if they are entrepreneurs of a business. They need to conceive of themselves as a set of assets, skills and attributes to be managed, maintained, developed, and treated as ventures to invest in by employers. Yet the entrepreneurial self carries an increasingly onerous burden and expectations and norms take on particular limits and possibilities in different labour markets. This responsibility encompasses managing the tensions, risks, ambiguities and contradictions in flexible capitalism (Kelly, 2013).

Just as flexibility in neoliberal markets provides people with 'more freedom to shape their lives', Sennett (1998, p. 10) suggests that the new world of work is difficult to understand and produces new forms of control rather than simply abolishing the rules of the past. He observes that it is 'quite natural that flexibility should arouse anxiety; people do not know what risks will pay off, what paths to pursue'. While Sennett's (1998, p. 118) thesis includes anxiety and risk as a daily experience for all, including 'entrepreneurs and capitalists', anxieties may be amplified for those with minimal education. They may associate anxieties with feelings of failure and, for some, the sense of 'I'm not good enough' (Sennett, 1998, p. 118).

As companies pursue greater labour flexibility, the expansion of outsourcing, privatisation and repeated rounds of downsizing, workers with minimal education face increasing job insecurity, more volatile incomes and a reduced capacity to voice workplace concerns. Like knowledge workers, they may change jobs regularly. Yet, due to a high degree of job uncertainty, short-term work engagements and an increased risk of job losses (Rawling, 2015), low-skilled, minimally educated workers may not have the opportunity to follow a career path within a company or sector (Sennett, 1998). For Jackson and Slade (2008, p. 25):

> The New Economy is bringing new stresses to working life. Many jobs are changing, and mostly not for the better; they are often part-time, more precarious, with lower wages and fewer benefits. At the same time, even such arguably bad jobs are said to involve higher skills and thus new requirements for employees.

This kind of labour market insecurity is now commonly named in academic and media discourse as precarious employment. The concept of 'precariousness' attempts to encompass the full range of attributes associated with employment quality. It distinguishes standard employment (full-time permanent waged work) from non-standard employment. Precariousness also seeks to analyse forms of non-standard employment that appear to be most insecure and can be identified as the main sites of social deprivation. Nearly 30 years ago, Burgess and Campbell (1998, p. 7) identified several elements that make work precarious:

- short time horizons of limited duration or have a high risk of termination;
- lack of control over working conditions, the pace of work, and wages;
- lack of protection in employment (legislative, collective agreement, custom or practice, social security); and,
- low incomes, at or near, defined poverty lines.

Burgess and Campbell (1998) argued that while the elements involved are multiple, the concept of precariousness involves instability, lack of protection, insecurity, and social or economic vulnerability.

Guy Standing (2011a, 2011b) further develops the concept of precariousness by suggesting that the rise of insecure work has produced an emerging but distinctive social class, the 'precariat'.[6] He broadly defines the precariat class as those facing many related and often overlapping insecurities such as 'labour market security, employment security, job security, work security, skill reproduction security, income security, and representation security' (Standing, 2011a, p. 10). For Standing (2011b), the precariat is more than a class that cannot access 'good' work or more skilled employment. It also consists of those who feel their lives and identities are made up of 'disjointed bits' (Standing, 2011b, para. 3). The precariat includes people who cannot construct a desirable narrative, or build a career that combines work and labour, play and leisure in a sustainable way. Standing (2011b) stresses that the precariat cannot draw on social memory, or of belonging to a community of pride, status, ethics, and solidarity because of flexible labour markets. For the precariat:

> Everything is fleeting. They realise that in their dealings with others there is no shadow of the future hanging over them, since they are unlikely to be dealing with those people tomorrow. The precariatised mind is one without anchors, flitting from subject to subject, in the extreme suffering from attention deficit disorder. But it is also nomadic in its dealings with other people. (Standing, 2011b, para. 4)

Standing (2011a) is not keen to identify the precariat class as comprising those with identical backgrounds. Rather, he argues, as detailed in Table 2, that it includes people with differing degrees of insecurity and anxiety.

The core of Standing's argument is that the decline in social protection linked to standard employment has driven the contemporary tendency towards precarity. He argues that the precariat does not consist simply of victims but points to its growth accelerated by neoliberal flexible capitalism. This growth, according to Standing (2011b), necessitates the need for social reforms ensuring the right of financial security for precarious workers.

The anxieties of flexible capitalism identified by Standing, Sennett and others are what their critics would imagine as the distinctive characteristic of neoliberalism. For Clarke (2005, p. 51): 'the market was not just an economic, but also a moral force, penalising the idle and incompetent and rewarding the enterprising and hard-working, for the greater good of society as a whole'. In neoliberal discourses, according to Chandler and Reid (2016, p. 2), people 'must accept the "endemic" condition of global insecurity' by developing the capabilities of resilience. This is a part of a 'socialization of security' whereby the responsibility of identifying and solving social problems is displaced

TABLE 2 Populations with an increased risk of facing precarious employment

Population group	Risk
Men	Men suffering job losses may require the support of female partners who are required to increase their labour force participation in response to their spouses' job losses.
Mature Aged	With little savings and superannuation beyond retirement, mature aged workers are subsidised to remain or return to the workforce pushing down wages and opportunities for others.
Youth	Youth are faced with status frustration, career-less prospects and subsidised competition for employment from home and abroad. They are deemed lazy if they hold out for a better opportunity.
Adults suffering from socially recognised disabilities	Adults with a disability can be relegated to career-less labour or not participating in the labour force at all.
Criminalised people:	This group includes those feeling that they have little option in society to become criminalised.
Migrants	Many remain in short-term, low-paying jobs despite being highly educated in their first country and often criticised by society for taking employment opportunities from locals.

SOURCE: STANDING (2011A, PP. 59–89)

from the state to the individual (Chandler & Reid, 2016, p. 45). This displacement is affected by a move away from the classical liberal value of 'the freedom to choose' – which assumes that freedom is essential to autonomy – to the neoliberal 'capability to choose' – which sees freedom as the continuous empowerment of the marginalised through self-reflection and self-government (Chandler & Reid, 2016, p. 93). Inherent in the concept of 'capability' is the assumption that if subjects were to make better choices, they would be more resilient and self-aware of the challenges presented by the world. We take up the discussion of choice in various ways in later chapters, where we explore how increased emphasis is placed on individual choices in influencing education, training, and labour market outcomes. These choices include being responsible for making the 'right' decisions – and the 'wrong' decisions – in understanding the human and social capital benefits of foundation skills training. At that time, we also explore the challenges of changing labour markets as these have continued in different trajectories after the 'event' presented here. The material and discursive 'realities' of Industry 4.0, the gig economy and the COVID-19 pandemic have highlighted the policy, community and academic debates about flexible work and the neoliberal subject.

4 Discussion: Individual Responsibility and the Neoliberal Template for Social Policy

In this section, we want to explore what Ernst (1998) defines as a 'neoliberal template', and how this template, widely understood and applied as a financial and economic doctrine, was transformed and then deployed by both Labour and Liberal-National Coalition Governments in Australia in the 1980s and 1990s as a way to use market forces to address social problems such as welfare and unemployment. This transformation was predicated on processes of individualised responsibility. While 'every day markets reconcile the varied and often competing ends of the millions of different individuals… to simultaneously satisfy countless wants, needs and preferences without the need for direction or planning by an overarching authority' (Meadowcroft, 2010, p. 3), these reforms recognised, in particular ways, that not all individuals would express the desire to actively engage with the labour market or other social initiatives (MacIntyre, 1999). As these neoliberal reforms were introduced and unfolded, they were underpinned by principles of individual reciprocity and moral obligation in which individuals were required to actively contribute to the support they receive.

In this context, we will suggest that the prominent 'event' of the deployment of a neoliberal 'template' into social policy was the process of transformation of the Australian Liberal welfare state by John Howard's conservative Liberal-National Coalition government in 1998. The multiplication of causes leading to this transformation was constituted, in part, by the work of the Industry Commission, which recommended that governments move out of service delivery and contract the provision of these services to the not-for-profit and private sectors. Here, a primary cause, and arena of contestation in processes of welfare reform, was the rise of unemployment in Australia, and its peak, in 1993.

4.1 *Unemployment, Welfare Dependency and Mutual Obligation*

In post-war Australia, through to the 1960s, the nation's unemployment rate remained steady at approximately two percent. Income support was available to assist the unemployed, and the publicly funded employment service – the Commonwealth Employment Service, established in 1946 – matched unemployed people with job vacancies. The government's fiscal policies were used to adjust the number of vacancies (the demand side), and the Commonwealth Employment Service would facilitate the smooth operation of labour markets (the supply side). This arrangement worked well in low unemployment environments, but the emergence of significant structural unemployment demanded a reconceptualisation of the governmental rationalities and technologies that might be mobilised in relation to the problem (Howard & Buultjens, 2004). When unemployment rates started to rise, and remained above seven percent in the 1970s, unemployment became understood as a 'structural' problem caused by the mismatch between demand and supply of labour (Howard & Buultjens, 2004, p. 2).

Structural unemployment reached a crisis point for Australia in 1993. At the time, Australia's unemployment rate was a 'staggering' 10 percent (Wanna, 2018, para. 3). Young school leavers were finding it hard to find work, and many older workers – especially males – were displaced from jobs, likely never to work again (Wanna, 2018). Following the 1991–1992 recession, Howard and Buultjens (2004, p. 2) contend that Australia was facing a phenomenon known as 'hysteresis' in which the persistence of unemployment continues despite the economic conditions that were the cause, no longer existing. Evidence of hysteresis included Australian employers remaining cautious of creating vacancies, being wary of redundancy costs, and employees being pressured to work harder and longer during the recession, which carried over beyond the recession. Additionally, employers were unwilling to retrain older displaced workers (Howard & Buultjens, 2004; Sloman & Norris, 1999). Australia was also facing a changing labour market and welfare state demographic. Historically, the typical heterosexual married couple income unit had one breadwinner who was male. A shift was developing with a growing diversity of working arrangements and types of household composition emerging. Female labour force participation was increasing, particularly in part-time employment. Many part-time jobs were taken up by households with at least one other person, typically employed full-time. There was also a growth in lone parents not engaged in the labour market due to supporting their children in education and an increase in the number of people claiming disability support (Dawkins, 2000).

Australia's labour market and demographic changes triggered government concerns about the traditional patterns of welfare 'entitlements'. Historically, at least in the post-war period, Australia's welfare services, provisions and forms of support established the citizen's right to both social and political entitlements. Welfare support was dedicated to protecting minimum standards and levels of income, nutrition, health, housing and education, and was assured to every citizen as a political right (MacIntyre, 1999). Reflecting similar concerns from many high-income economies in Europe and North America, Australian governments were alarmed by the demand for welfare, rising costs caused by demographic patterns, consistently higher unemployment rates and expensive health technology overloading systems. The Australian Government also suggested that various welfare systems had expanded to the point that the taxpayer was either unable or unwilling to underwrite them (MacIntyre, 1999).

In the early 1990s, the Keating Labor government advocated a clear shift in the underlying culture of Australian welfare away from rights-based entitlements and towards a system based on inclusion, ownership, individual responsibility and mutual obligation (MacIntyre, 1999). This shift was the key plank of the Labour Government's *Working Nation* strategy in 1994. Under *Working Nation,* there were new expectations that in return for welfare assistance, there would be 'a strengthened obligation on unemployed people to accept a reasonable job offer' (Commonwealth of Australia, 1994, p. 108). The main features of the policy included a significant expansion of labour market programs,[7] youth training initiatives, training wages for all apprentices, and programs targeting the long-term unemployed (Junankar & Kapuscinski, 1997). *Working Nation* introduced new and innovative forms of management and regulation, including elements of case management, wage subsidies and job creation targeting both the demand and supply sides of the labour market (Howard & Buultjens, 2004), and 'stronger penalties for job seekers who do not meet their obligations' (Commonwealth of Australia, 1994, p. 114).

Even when economic growth in Australia improved after the 1991–1992 recession, the unemployment rate remained stubbornly stuck at 8.5 percent before the 1996 election, an election in which Labor suffered a heavy defeat to the 'conservative' Howard Liberal-National Coalition (Wanna, 2018). Maintaining *Working Nation's* reciprocal, mutual obligation agenda, the Howard Coalition continued reforms of the welfare state, largely drawing on the inquiry work by the Industry Commission, the Commonwealth's industry review and advisory body (Ernst, 1998), including the *Charitable Organisations in Australia* and *Competitive Tendering and Contracting by Public Sector Agencies* (Industry Commission, 1995, 1996).

4.2 *The Industry Commission: Role and Government Inquiries*

The Industry Commission was set up by the Commonwealth Government as its review and advisory body on industry matters. It played a pivotal role in Australian policy as a promoter of market alternatives to traditional public intervention and public administration (Ernst, 1998). The origins of the Industry Commission came from the Industries Assistance Commission, which was responsible for inquiries on international trade, government economic policy, the assistance provided to industry and its effect on the economy and industry performance (Productivity Commission, 2003).[8] In January 1990, the *Industry Commission Act 1989* was passed through the Commonwealth Parliament, with the Hawke Labor Government articulating its desire to reform industry regulation consistent with its social and economic goals. A key plank of the Act was restructuring the Industries Assistance Commission into an entity of broader responsibilities, to be renamed the Industry Commission. The remit of the Industry Commission was to conduct inquiries directed toward removing impediments to improve efficiency across the whole spectrum of industry. The then Minister Assisting the Treasurer, Peter Morris, noted the following rationale for the establishment of the Industry Commission as the Government's review and inquiry body in relation to industry matters:

> Through its advice to the Government, the Industry Commission will play a key role in helping industry to become more efficient, more productive and more internationally competitive. And that is central to ensuring better growth prospects and better economic conditions in this nation over the years and decades ahead… the Commission is intended to make a major contribution to further structural reform in Australia. It will be a catalyst for productivity and efficiency gains. (Morris cited in Productivity Commission, 2003, p. 67)

Primarily due to its inquiry work, the Industry Commission developed a reputation for economic rationalism and public sector reform. Quiggan (1993) observed that the Industry Commission's activities were one-dimensional and unwavering in its view of the superiority of free markets and private ownership, as opposed to intervention and public ownership. Using this rationality as an overarching frame of reference, the Industry Commission constructed a policy template comprising:

> First, of a set of axiomatic objectives, such as economic growth, economic welfare, efficiency, international competitiveness, and the reduction of business input costs; and second, of a limited field of possible

> policy actions that range narrowly across options such as the introduction of market disciplines, economic pricing, competition, deregulation, corporatisation and privatisation. (Ernst, 1998, p. 217)

The Industry Commission conducted two inquiries in 1995–1996 that investigated the idea that market mechanisms could provide solutions to the many social problems facing contemporary governments (Ernst, 1998). One inquiry, *Charitable Organisations in Australia,* examined the contribution the charitable sector could make to Australian society (Industry Commission, 1995). This inquiry was premised on the view that the sector had the capacity to flourish by strengthening its client services, resourcing its services with its own financial resources and accountability, the ability to provide benchmarks for improved performance, and a capacity to develop co-responsible relationships with governments (Industry Commission, 1995). The second inquiry, *Competitive Tendering and Contracting by Public Sector Agencies,* addressed how governments could best deliver quality services and give 'value for money'. The inquiry examined the feasibility of the Commonwealth shifting service delivery obligations to public, private and not-for-profit sectors. Premised on the view that competitive tendering was currently an under-utilised option in Australia, the Industry Commission investigated the benefits to clients, taxpayers, and the broader community of new forms of accountability, quality and cost-effectiveness (Industry Commission, 1996).

The *Charitable Organisations in Australia* inquiry reached positive conclusions about the contribution and the continuing importance of the sector. It highlighted the capacity of charitable organisations to deliver social services and programs, with governments providing support through steering roles. Arguing that this reform was a worldwide trend, the inquiry claimed that several desirable outcomes would be delivered, including:
- government flexibility and cost effectiveness;
- provision of more assured funding for the sector;
- involvement of the sector in policy formulation; and,
- provision for a greater diversity of service provision and a greater focus on individual welfare needs (Ernst, 1998).

The inquiry also recommended that micro-economic reform concepts, new public management principles, and competition mechanisms be blended within organisations to improve efficiency and delivery of quality services (Ernst, 1998). Alongside the *Competitive Tendering and Contracting by Public Sector Agencies* inquiry, this inquiry examined ways of extending the regime of competition and market testing across public sector agencies in all levels of government. Despite concerns from the community services sector and union movements, the inquiries found that any barriers to applying competitive tendering across the entire public sector were relatively minor or amenable to correction (Ernst, 1998).

While the two inquiries were initiated by the Keating Labor Government, the findings resonated strongly with the political tendencies of the newly elected Howard Liberal-National Coalition (Ernst, 1998). These tendencies involved the classical liberal concern to reduce government interference with free-market outcomes by restricting access to social security payments, and the social conservative intention to reinforce traditional institutions such as the family, charities and the church (Mendes, 1998). Yet the opportunities for cost-effectiveness, diversity of service provision and individual needs in welfare policy reform were not only operationalised by introducing market principles. The re-working of the processes of mutual obligation, focussed on acts that 'motivate and discipline welfare recipients and reintegrate them with mainstream social values and morality' (Mendes, 2009, p. 105), were also critical.

4.3 *Contracted Welfare: Job Network and Mutual Obligation*

A clear policy agenda of the Howard Coalition government was to reverse the shift to state-guaranteed income security entitlements and direct the provision of welfare to families, charities and churches (Mendes, 2009). The Coalition condemned what they saw as increased welfare spending under the previous government and an associated increase in welfare dependency, which diminished self-reliance (MacIntyre, 1999). They argued for a link between welfare, independence and the family, with Prime Minister Howard suggesting 'the stable functioning family still represents the best social welfare system that any community has devised and certainly the least expensive' (cited in Buckingham, 2000, p. 89). The Coalition also favoured greater involvement by private charities in providing welfare benefits and programs, highlighting their emphasis on the personal and moral underpinnings of social problems, their ability to deliver programs cheaply and their supposed capacity to promote behavioural change (Mendes, 2009). As claimed by the then Federal Minister for Employment, Workplace Relations and Small Business, Tony Abbott (2004, p. 4), 'there is something extra about people with faith in their hearts, and the love of God on their lips, that gives them that extra commitment to job seekers'.

The combination of the Industry Commission inquiries, with the concept of mutual obligation for job seekers, had a powerful presence in, and influence on, the Coalition's reform package named *Job Network*. In May 1998, the Australian Federal Parliament passed legislation to combine the Commonwealth

Employment Service functions and the Department of Social Security to form Centrelink, an organisation created to provide a form of centralised monetary welfare support to people across Australia. The delivery of employment services was separated from the functions of Centrelink (Howard & Buultjens, 2004; Howard, 1997b; Kemp, 1997). Identified by Castle (2001) as an erosion of the traditional responsibilities of the Australian welfare state, and by Mendes (2009, p. 107) as the 'most significant and radical example of privatised welfare', the Coalition drew on competitive tendering and contracting processes to engage approximately 300 private (for-profit), charitable and not-for-profit agencies to provide government-funded employment placement services. The primary responsibility of contracted agencies was to assist people into work. The Howard Coalition argued that *Job Network* would be more effective than the Commonwealth Employment Service due to greater competition, increased flexibility to respond to individual circumstances, and an emphasis on job placement outcomes rather than inputs (Mendes, 2007).

Having cancelled labour market programs in 1996, arguing they did not create sustainable employment (Howard & Buultjens, 2004), the primary emphasis of the Coalition's approach to unemployment was the creation of the *Work for the Dole* scheme. *Work for the Dole* initially required people aged 18–24 years (the scheme was soon expanded to include 25–34 year-olds) who had been registered as unemployed for six months to work in community projects for between twenty-four and thirty hours a fortnight (Raper, 2000). In announcing this policy, Howard (1997a) was quite explicit about the moral obligations of the unemployed to offer something to the community in return for the benefits they received. He told the Parliament that 'it is not unfair in modern Australia to ask people, if they are able to do so, to undertake some work in return for the dole that they receive' (Howard, 1997a, p. 466). Under the *Work for the Dole* scheme, processes of reciprocation for welfare payments were termed 'mutual obligation'.[9]

In this form, mutual obligation was associated with a generally punitive approach to the unemployed. Castle (2001, p. 541) has observed that:

> to receive benefit, individuals must be able to prove they are "deserving" of society's help. With each new requirement for interview and for demonstrated job applications, the potential for discretion by officers of the newly privatized Howard employment services increases. Huge numbers of claimants are now fined for infringements of the rules, and the efficiency of these services is partly judged by its success in withholding benefits on these grounds.

This stricter interpretation of mutual obligation led to a massive increase in social security breaches and associated heavy fines, with an increase in the number of breaches from 120,000 in 1997–1998 to 346,000 in 2000–2001, representing an increase of 187 percent over three years (Commonwealth Ombudsman, 2002).[10]

The Howard Coalition's 2005 and 2007 budgets progressed the extent of mutual obligation even further. Concerns about the sharp rise of people receiving *Disability Support Pension*[11] and *Single Parents Payments*, resulted in the introduction of tighter eligibility rules for both. Thousands of *Disability Support Pension* recipients with limited work capacity were shifted onto unemployment benefits. New applicants were subjected to a part-time work test and granted a pension if they were unable to work more than 15 hours a week (Mendes, 2009). Parents on existing *Single Parents Payments* were transferred onto unemployment benefits after their youngest child turned 12, rather than 16 years (Mendes, 1998), and new applications would become subject to a part-time work test of at least 15 hours per week after the youngest child turned six (Mendes, 2009).

Welfare assistance for low-income Australian families was also targeted. The Howard Coalition introduced measures to quarantine half of a family's payment – where it was deemed that children were at risk of neglect, not enrolled, or not regularly attending school – to ensure payments were spent on essential items, not alcohol and gambling (Mendes, 2009). In 2007, these measures were applied to all income security payments, not just family payments. As Mendes (2009) demonstrated, the most radical application of mutual obligation was in the area of Indigenous affairs. In 2007, the Howard Coalition government announced a national emergency plan for remote Indigenous communities in the Northern Territory to counter what was claimed to be an 'epidemic of child sexual abuse'. To tackle what it claimed were alcohol abuse problems, poor school attendance, and neglected public housing arrangements, the plan recommended that 50 percent of all income support should be quarantined, conditional on families meeting four obligations. These obligations included:

- children maintaining a 100 percent school attendance record;
- adults preventing any child abuse or neglect;
- adults not involved in substance abuse, gambling or family violence offences; and,
- adults adhering to conditions of tenancy in public housing (Brough, 2007).

The Coalition's policies inflamed arguments that these and similar 'New Right' policies were repressive and intended to blame and punish the victim rather than addressing the structural causes of dependency and poverty (Antcliff,

1988; Mendes, 1998). The deserving/undeserving distinction was deemed a form of stigmatisation by linking unemployment to laziness or moral failure (Mendes, 1998). This position emphasised the importance of alleviating human need and suffering, with the overriding priority to care for the vulnerable. From this position, an inclusive welfare system, that may necessitate higher taxation and government spending, is a moral obligation of government to ensure the welfare of all its citizens (Saunders, 2013).

However, the advocacy group Australian Council of Social Service (1997, p. 5), while claiming that the *Work for the Dole* was an 'abandonment of the government's obligations to the unemployed', was in support of genuine mutual obligation mechanisms providing the framework for the provision of support under the Australian welfare system. MacIntyre (1999) observed that the existence of mutual obligation underpinned the provision of welfare in Australia before the *Working Nation*, *Job Network* and *Work for the Dole* reforms. She suggested that even in an universalist state-funded scheme, any government welfare provision necessarily implies a reciprocal relationship. The point of difference in this form of mutual obligation, according to MacIntyre (1999), is that a reciprocal relationship has been structured between the state and the individual, not between the state and the community. The principal focus shifts the contribution made by the community's long-term interests – or the 'taxpayer' – to the individual who receives welfare support. These expectations or responsibilities on individuals energised a new vocabulary of motivation, work ethic, individual responsibility, and self-reliance.

The reform of the welfare state and mutual obligation was significant in one other way. The emergence of mutual obligation has been influential in how the foundation skills and vocational education and training (VET) training markets have emerged in the form they have. One component of mutual obligation compels people who receive various income support payments to engage in an educational activity to support their transition to work. Mutual obligation ties the receipt of government provided income support to attendance in an approved education and training program considered 'foundational' to facilitate this transition (Peeters, 2013, p. 584).

The adult education/VET sector experienced neoliberal reforms in a similar timeframe and method to the events we've presented in this chapter. In 1987, the Hawke Government commissioned the *Skills for Australia* policy that focused on restructuring the apprenticeship system by promoting deregulation, improved efficiencies, and greater student and employer choice (Dawkins & Holding, 1987). An extension of this policy was the *National Training Reform Agenda* in 1994, which argued that new demands for training and skills development were required at all levels of the labour market. The agenda implemented measures to provide choice and greater access to training for disadvantaged groups by 'opening up' markets to non-profit and private providers (Australian National Training Authority, 1994) by the use of competitive tendering and individualised eligibility funding (The Allen Consulting Group, 2011).

As competition was introduced beyond apprenticeship schemes into wider VET markets after the turn of the century (The Allen Consulting Group, 2011), the responsibility of registered training providers (RTOs) to market programs to job seekers and *Job Network* agencies was regarded as essential to increasing and maintaining market share. Alongside an investment into VET by States and Territories, the Commonwealth introduced a mutual obligation foundation skills program named the *Literacy and Numeracy Training* (LANT) *Program*, which was targeted at job seekers aged 16–25 who were deemed to have low foundation skills that were considered to be a barrier to accessing employment (Australian Council for Adult Literacy, 2001; Howard, 1999). The significance of these increased program offerings led to the creation of a 'market' of job seekers requiring foundation skills and VET to transition into employment. Job seekers and their *Job Network* agencies were imagined as 'customers' of RTOs, with a capacity to choose an RTO that best suited their, or their clients, needs. In later chapters, we will build on this discussion to explore, in more detail, the possibilities and the consequences of how 'skills' are sold to learners – through demand driven markets – as a commodity that can increase their human capital.

Notes

1 As the 1980s progressed, several subsequent *Accords* were brokered between Labor and Australian Council of Trade Unions in response to new economic challenges. There was a total of eight *Accords* across the Hawke-Keating Government's thirteen years in office (Humphrys, 2019).

2 Superannuation is money put aside by employers for an employee's working life, for them to live on when they retire from work. Medicare is a scheme that gives Australian residents access to healthcare (Australian Government, 2022b, 2022c).

3 See Beeson and Firth (1998), Beeson (2015) and Weller and O'Neill (2014) for examples here.

4 According to Weller and O'Neill (2014) the professional services economies in Sydney and Melbourne boomed on the back of early entry of foreign banks and opportunistic engagement with Asian economies. However, offshore borrowing by banks and financial institutions to fund large scale highly leveraged speculative investment saw Australia experience three major economic downturns between 1987 and 1991, including the collapse of a number of significant lending institutions.

5 The Australian Competition Commission was formed from a merger between the Trade Practices Commission and the Prices Surveillance Authority (Kain et al., 2001), and was later renamed the Australian Competition and Consumer Commission. The Australian Competition and Consumer Commission is the chief competition regulator of the Australian Government at this time (Australian Competition and Consumer Commission, 2021a).

6 Standing's claims about a new social class have been widely and vigorously debated. See, for example Jørgensen (2016).

7 Labour market programs are a set of interventions directed at individuals who are currently unemployed or at risk of becoming unemployed that aim to increase their likelihood of employment. Programs can include financial incentives to employers who give jobs to unemployed people, financial assistance for individuals, enterprises and regions, support services for unemployed people, work experience, on-the-job training or formal vocational education training and education (Borland, 2016).

8 In 1998 the Industry Commission was restructured and renamed the Productivity Commission (Productivity Commission, 2003).

9 MacIntyre (1999) and Castle (2001) explain that while both major Australian political parties claimed responsibility for 'mutual obligation' policies, such policies were not new and could be traced to the New Labour government in Britain under Tony Blair.

10 A community campaign against this kind of mutual obligation was effective in influencing the Howard Coalition to amend breaching practices and procedures and the level of fines. The total number of breaches fell to a third of its earlier peak (Mendes, 2009).

11 The reason for the increase in *Disability Support Pension*, prior to the Howard reform, was attributed to several factors. These include a liberalised eligibility criteria that expanded beyond solely medical impairment to include job availability, a growth in the number of people with disabilities and limited job opportunities for older males (Parliamentary Library, 2005).

CHAPTER 3

The Neoliberal Foundation Skills Apparatus

1 Introduction

> It is worth asking what is at issue in 'literacy debates', then, if it isn't literacy as such? What is really at issue? Furthermore, what is literacy? Across these documents we find it referred to as 'skill', 'competence', 'morality', 'tradition', 'heritage', 'knowledge' and so forth. What is significant is that all of these terms are open sets for contemporary social and cultural norms and values. The picture that emerges is that of 'literacy' as a continually contested and unfinished concept, an empty canvas upon which anxieties and aspirations from the popular imagination and public morality are drawn. Everybody is an expert on literacy: parents, teachers, politicians, journalists and media experts, and, of course, students themselves. Experience of literacy education appears to be something everybody has in common. In public forums, from talk-back radio shows to school parent meetings, anecdotes about 'how it was when I was in school' become the basis for debate and conflict…
>
> But people have dramatically different memories of becoming literate. Depending on the time and place of their schooling, these range across innumerable versions of the 3Rs, to grammar school literacy, from religious training to bilingual education, from phonics teaching to creative writing instruction, from corporal punishment and rote learning to open classrooms and negotiated curriculum. These remembrances of literacy past, filtered through years of life history and experience, are easily turned into claims about how reading and writing *should be* taught, and about what teachers and schools *should do*. (Green et al., 1997, pp. 11–12)

Bill Green, John Hodgens and Alan Luke (1997, pp. 11–12), in writing about the 'literacy debates' of the 1980s and 1990s that we have already referenced, point to some of the challenges shaping and emerging from these debates, including a relatively narrow understanding about education, training and skills, to the broader moral questions that become attached to these concerns. The question of why and how foundation skills have become a public issue requires an analysis of larger political, cultural and economic discourses. From what may appear as a logical and realistic exercise from governments to

 | DOI:10.1163/9789004724464_004

coordinate discourses and organisations that have similar objectives in mind, it is, as we will explore in this chapter, more reflective of Pile et al. (1999, p. 348) assertion that the imposition of order 'disorders other aspects'. That is, various 'orderings' can often conflict with one another. Drawing on our earlier discussions, we will argue that Foucault's (1980a) concept of apparatus is a valuable way to identify and analyse the 'orderings' of what we will identify as the foundation skills apparatus. This includes the elements in play, the forms of subjectivity produced, and the points of tension and relationships between them.

Foucault's characterisation of the apparatus is structured by three interrelated and interconnected concerns – an urgent historical need, the strategic function, and the relationships between the elements of the apparatus. These concerns will form the structure of this chapter. The first concern relates to the emergence of an apparatus to address an 'urgent need', a historically specific problematisation of low foundation skills of adults, and how it came to be regarded as a specific kind of problem for particular authorities at a particular point in time.

To meet the 'urgent need', the second concern of the apparatus is concerned with its strategic function. In this case, the strategic function is to develop, as we will illustrate, a 'neoliberal' subject who can become both capable of, and responsible for, 'curating' their human capital in ways that promise to make them more 'employable'. By drawing on these understandings of the apparatus, we explore the strategic function in relation to its monitoring and regulatory mechanisms, and its 'promises' for those deemed most 'at risk'.

The third concern is about the relationships between the elements of the apparatus – relations that can be named as 'neoliberal' – which shape the apparatus as it continues to emerge. We start with a historical recount and then a contemporary description of the foundation skills policy and program framework to provide definitions and contextualisation of the 'elements' of the apparatus. From here, we illustrate what we define as a 'training market' – training programs and registered training organisations (RTO s), government funding reforms, standardisation processes and other stakeholders – that form educational and training responses by governments to populations with low foundation skills. We make the connections between the elements meaningful by highlighting the formal and informal relationships, conflicts and tensions that produce, and modify, the strategic function of the apparatus.

In our final Discussion section, we highlight a number of concerns that emerge from this identification of these elements of a neoliberal foundation skills apparatus, including the human and social capital debates of foundation skills, the influence of the welfare state and mutual obligation, and the forms of personhood promoted within the apparatus, as a platform for further discussion in later chapters.

2 The Historical Moment of Urgent Need: Policy, Surveys and Mutual Obligation

Before the emergence of an 'urgent need' facilitating the emergence of the foundation skills apparatus, there was a strong belief that the Australian population did not have a problem with their foundation skills. The adult learner was most often imagined as a 'language' learner, a migrant from a non-English-speaking background. Australia frequently reported literacy rates of nearly 100 percent because it was assumed that its free, universal and compulsory education systems would produce this level of literacy skills in the adult population (Norton, 1996). Though adult literacy problems surfacing from the Australian army in 1943–1944 were highlighted at the time, the 'literacy' learner – English-speaking populations with low foundation skills – attracted only intermittent interest well into the 1970s (lo Bianco, 1996, p. 80). At this time, adult literacy was significantly less developed as an area of education concern and policy. Though adult literacy programs were operating, there were many years of agitation by academics, ethnic and community stakeholders, and politicians to develop an overarching policy framework. Lo Bianco (1991, p. 25) describes this time as:

> the arid years of advocacy when the response to proposed language policies was to wonder at their relevance, to dismiss them as the bleatings of disaffected academics or agitating ethnics. Indeed, many readers will vividly recall the dismissive remarks of a former Minister for Immigration who asserted at a well-attended conference advocating a nationally developed and coordinated approach to language issues that there was about as much justification for a National Language Policy as there was for a "National Trumpets Policy"; no less!

A significant milestone occurred in 1987 when the Commonwealth Government funded Australia's first language policy, the *National Policy on Languages* (lo Bianco, 1991, p. 25). The Hawke Labour Government commissioned language planning specialist Joseph lo Bianco (1987a, p. 3) to develop the policy to streamline current literacy activities widely regarded as 'ad hoc and uncoordinated'. In writing the policy, lo Bianco (1987b) introduced a profile of

populations with low foundation skills and highlighted the implications of low skills for its citizens and Australia's economy:
- problems, disabilities, inequality and discrimination which may be associated with individuals with low level language skills;
- the importance of technological changes with skills use and learning;
- the association of language and literacy with Australia's external economic and political needs and priorities;
- identification of groups in Australian society (ethnic communities, the deaf and Aboriginal groups), for whom language issues were crucial; and,
- equality and the correlation between social inequalities and language; related to the employment and occupational disadvantages of Australians with limited English speaking skills, and the educational problems that correlate with their English level.

Under its objectives and recommendations, the *National Policy on Languages* charged the Commonwealth with key responsibilities of coordinating efforts of States and Territories and providing national leadership in key areas of national need (lo Bianco, 1991). The *National Policy on Languages* established the effectiveness and credibility of the National Languages Institute of Australia as an arms-length policymaker in language to sustain future research and teaching initiatives. It supported developments in second language learning and Asian studies programs with primary and secondary national curriculum development in Japanese, Chinese (Mandarin), Indonesian, Korean and Vietnamese. For adults, the policy continued a funding and research commitment to English as a second language and adult literacy programs and teaching (lo Bianco, 1987b, 1991).

The *National Policy on Languages* also included a commitment to fund the coordination of a national-level collection of quantitative and qualitative information to give a more accurate and richer knowledge of the foundation skills of working-age populations (lo Bianco, 1987a) and to provide a database to advocate for additional resources for literacy programs (Wickert, 1989). The national-level coordination for establishing a quantitative database was called *No Single Measure* and was conducted by prominent adult language and literacy education specialist Rosie Wickert (1989) in 1987. The *No Single Measure* survey sought to identify the incidence and nature of literacy difficulties in English, explore socio-cultural factors that may be associated with literacy problems, and identify the most pressing needs in terms of educational policies and provision for priorities to be set for the future directions of adult literacy programs in Australia. Overall, the survey revealed that Australia's literacy problem was 'bigger than was thought' and that 10 percent of Australian adults, two-thirds of whom were of English-speaking background, appeared to have difficulty accomplishing everyday reading and writing tasks (Wickert, 1989, p. 8). Also, 23 percent of adults indicated that their schooling and literacy performance had been adversely affected by the following factors, in priority order:

- health problems, with associated lengthy absences from school;
- socio-economic issues, leading to absence from school, or negative attitudes towards school;
- most adults with literacy difficulties missed out on learning opportunities when they were children; and,
- low socio-economic status and poverty were the strongest indicators of educational disadvantage and, consequently, inadequate literacy development.

The survey also claimed that literacy difficulties tended to be reproduced in generational cycles, and that literacy development could be addressed as a family issue (DEET, 1991; Wickert, 1989).

The Commonwealth Government department responsible for the *National Policy on Languages*, the Department of Education Employment and Training [DEET] (1991), claimed that the most significant achievement of the policy was the recognition that language and literacy issues were not only legitimate issues on the national agenda, but they also have an impact on all aspects of life in Australia. This declaration dispelled the assumption that Australia's compulsory education until the age of 15 or 16 automatically precluded the nation from having a literacy problem among native English-speaking adults.

As DEET (1990) began to plan for the follow-up policy, foundation skills continued to play a role in the Hawke-Keating Government's micro-economic reform. One part of the reform included modernising and restructuring the industry and awards for job classifications. Responding to changing economic, technological and industrial circumstances, existing awards classification structures and conditions were overhauled. Irrelevant or superseded job categories were deleted, similar job categories were grouped together, and issues such as work organisation and working time arrangements, and payment systems were revised depending on the particular award and the industry's circumstances (Treasury Australia, 1988). As a result of the reclassification, the Hawke-Keating Government forecasted that reskilling and retraining would be required for over 70 percent of participants in the labour market (DEET, 1990).

Initiatives for reskilling and retraining necessitated the need for the population to have sound English skills as an essential prerequisite to access training programs for higher occupational skill levels. A report by the Training Costs of Award Restructuring Committee, referenced by DEET (1990), stressed that 'a government which pursues an active immigration policy must accept special responsibility for the English language education of new settlers' (Training Costs Review Committee, 1990, p. 32). DEET (1990, p. 6) warned of the substantial problems with workers not sharing a 'common language', including inefficiencies, misunderstandings, friction between workers and poor safety standards. It was claimed that inefficiencies because of poor English skills in the workplace could amount to $3.2 billion annually (DEET, 1990; Miltenyi, 1989). The department argued that cooperation and a sense of mutual effort were needed to achieve high levels of efficiency and productivity and that:

> competence in English overcomes many of these difficulties and brings with it many benefits. For firms, productivity is increased. For individuals, there is a safer working environment and improved channels of communication. As individuals, employers and the Government benefit from improved competence in English, each has a responsibility to contribute to that competence. (DEET, 1990, p. 6)

Seeking to continue, extend, and refine the work of the *National Policy on Languages*, DEET (1991) released the *Australian Language and Literacy Policy* in 1991. At this time, Australia's profile in adult literacy development was experiencing a 'surge' (Mendelovits, 2011, p. 1; Romaine, 1991), adding to Australia's reputation as a globally recognised world leader in adult literacy policy and provision (National Research and Development Centre, 2011). The *No Single Measure* survey coincided with Australia's participation in the United Nations *International Year of Literacy* in 1990 (Thar, 1990), a program designed to contribute to achieving 100 percent world literacy by the year 2000 (UNESCO, 1990). As part of the *International Year of Literacy,* Australia established Literacy Action Coalitions to promote local advocacy groups to promote literacy awareness, help erase the stigma attached to people with reading and writing difficulties and expand the number of literacy programs available. National referral services were also developed to distribute literacy information (Adult Literacy Information Office, 1990; Thar, 1990).

The *Australian Language and Literacy Policy* sought to reinforce the position of language and literacy policy on the agenda of mainstream education and training systems and institutions, and to become recognised by governments and industry as central to efforts to produce a more dynamic and internationally competitive Australian economy (DEET, 1991). The policy outlined research and activities to ensure that 'all Australian residents should develop and maintain a level of spoken and written English which is appropriate for a range of contexts' (DEET, 1991, p. 33). According to a peak body for adult literacy and numeracy in Australia, the Australian Council for Adult Literacy (2001), the policy was introduced not only to focus on the Commonwealth's position on literacy and to provide funding to implement adult literacy programs, but also to articulate its views on a range of economic, labour market, multicultural and social justice issues. One significant acknowledgement from the *Australian Language and Literacy Policy* was that the 'Commonwealth, State and Territory governments have a major responsibility for providing adequate resources to deliver basic education and training to citizens and potential citizens' (DEET, 1991, p. 31). The policy positively actioned this acknowledgement by generating increased training activity at the grassroots level and establishing new networks and collaborations between industry, government, researchers, universities and practitioners through the *National Collaborative Adult English Language and Literacy Strategy* (Australian Council for Adult Literacy, 2001; DEET, 1993).

As literacy was placed 'on the agenda' for all countries, the OECD (2000) stressed that with the importance of moving into the so-called 'information age', policymakers had a global concern about the role knowledge and skills play in enhancing productivity growth and innovation and improving social cohesion. In 1994, the OECD sponsored the *International Adult Literacy Survey*. The survey was a large-scale cooperative effort by the OECD, governments, national statistical agencies and research institutions to gather accurate information on the levels and distribution of literacy among adult populations in twenty OECD countries (Roberts, 2000). The three overall aims of the study were to produce meaningful comparisons between countries, understand the relationship between literacy and economic indicators of wealth and well-being, and inform and influence policy decisions (Hamilton & Barton, 2000). In 1996, Australia participated in the second round of surveys, locally called the *Survey of Aspects of Literacy*, coordinated by the Australian Bureau of Statistics. The survey was designed to measure elements of Australian literacy and numeracy skills, in particular, information processing skills necessary to use printed material found at work, in homes, and in the community (Australian Bureau of Statistics, 1996).

Like the *No Single Measure*, the *Survey of Aspects of Literacy* painted a fairly grim picture of Australia's literacy and numeracy skills. Australia was placed with 14 other OECD countries in having at least 15 percent of all adults with literacy skills at only the most rudimentary level, making it difficult for them to cope with the rising skill demands of the information economy (OECD, 2000). Australia's profile, in broad terms, was not unlike that of other English-speaking countries such as New Zealand and Canada, with well over 40 percent having literacy skills not at the level required to meet the complex demands of work and life in modern economies (Australian Bureau of Statistics, 1996; lo Bianco, 1996). Using the *International Adult Literacy Survey* levels[1] that measure adult literacy standards, the results of the *Survey of Aspects of Literacy* claimed that:

- 2.6 million people (18.7 percent) had very poor skills at Level 1 and could be expected to experience considerable difficulties in using many of the printed materials that may be encountered in daily life;
- 3.6 million people (30.5 percent) were at Level 2 and could be expected to experience some difficulties in using many of the printed materials that may be encountered in daily life;
- 4.8 million people (38.3 percent) were at Level 3, the largest category, and have the skills to cope with many printed materials found in daily life and at work, though not always with a high level of proficiency; and,
- 2.0 million people were at Level 4, representing good skills, and a relatively small number (300,000) were at Level 5, representing very good skills (both levels combined at 12.5 percent). People at both Level 4 and Level 5 are considered capable of managing the literacy demands of everyday life (Australian Bureau of Statistics, 1996).

The *Survey of Aspects of Literacy* also provided a further breakdown of the levels, distributions, demographic and socio-economic data of the literacy levels of Australian adults (Australian Bureau of Statistics, 1996). A summary of the survey data is detailed in Table 3.

Results from the *International Adult Literacy Survey* caught the attention of governments across the OECD countries, particularly the claim that globally, large portions of the working-age populations did not have adequate literacy levels to support everyday life and work (Jackson & Slade, 2008). The results suggested that skill deficits were found not just among marginalised groups but across large sections of the adult populations. Almost one-quarter of the adults surveyed could not demonstrate the basic competencies necessary for coping adequately with the complex demands of everyday life in knowledge societies (OECD, 2013). American newspapers sensationally reported that 'half of America's adults are functionally illiterate!' (Sticht cited in Jackson & Slade, 2008, p. 28) and Canadian government officials, responding to data of people overestimating their literacy skills, claiming that 'people are illiterate, and they

TABLE 3 Summary from the *Survey of Aspects of Literacy*

Socio-economic factor	**Language and literacy impact**
English & language	Foreign-language immigrants tend to have lower literacy skills than native-born adults who speak the country's official language from birth.
Educational attainment	The greater number of years of formal education achieved higher literacy skills.
Age	Younger people tended to have higher levels of literacy, with a peak of around 25–34 years of age.
Gender	There is no precise data related to which gender has stronger literacy skills.
Parents education	The greater percentage of people with parents with no post-school qualifications impacts their literacy level.
Self-perceptions	There is a broadly consistent pattern of overestimation and underestimation of the self-perception of an adult's actual language and literacy abilities.
Employment status	There is a clear relationship between literacy skill level and labour force status. Those unemployed or not in the labor force are more likely to have lower skills than those employed.
Income	The higher proficiency in literacy and numeracy, the greater the positive impact on income.
Industry areas	Occupations with a higher Level 1 percentage are related to the frequency of literacy activities undertaken in the workplace and education attainment.

SOURCE: AUSTRALIAN BUREAU OF STATISTICS (1996, PP. 3–56)

don't even know it! This is very dangerous!' (Jackson & Slade, 2008, p. 29). As a consequence of these results, countries including the United States, the United Kingdom, New Zealand and South Africa moved to develop more comprehensive national policy frameworks (Jackson, 2005).

A linear account of history may point to Australia being in lockstep with other OECD countries in terms of its commitment to addressing this 'urgent need' by commissioning the next iteration of language and literacy policy. However, lo Bianco's (1996) prediction during the release of results that the histories of adult literacy education provision – regularly marked by clashes in interests, ideology and values between policy advocates and government (lo Bianco & Wickert, 2001) – did not inspire confidence that a follow-up policy to the *Australian Language and Literacy Policy* would occur, was realised. The Australian Council for Adult Literacy (2001) lamented in their prominent position paper called *A Literate Australia* that there was no new, comprehensive national policy framework for adult literacy ten years after the *Australian Language and Literacy Policy*. This publication pointed to globalisation, new ways of defining literacy, and the importance of literacy for the economy, society and individuals as significant issues needing to be addressed through policy. The Australian Council for Adult Literacy (2001, p. 5) was also concerned that 'such rapid changes have left a void in policy', and even though Australia's policy was the envy of other Western countries at one stage, the nation was now required to scan other OECD countries for possible models.

Authors such as Moore (2002) argued that high unemployment during the implementation of the *Australian Language and Literacy Policy* between 1991 and 1994 had contributed to the framing of populations with low language and literacy as 'job seekers' and 'clients', with policy aligned to these needs, not specifically to foundation skills. Commentators such as Mendelovits (2011, p. 3) agreed that the results of the *Survey of Aspects of Literacy* had relatively little impact in Australia. They highlighted the resistance from adult literacy professionals 'who had and have a default antipathy to any kind of standardised assessment' and thereby provided no advocacy for subsequent policy interventions as a result. Mendelovits (2011) also suggested that the survey data release was a victim of unfortunate political timing – it coincided with, and was overshadowed by, the election and other early policy agendas of the Howard Liberal-National Coalition.

Nevertheless, despite the absence of a targeted policy agenda justified by the *Survey of Aspects of Literacy* results, the Coalition government's response at this time was the 'historical moment' and 'urgent need' that led to the formation of an apparatus to develop new strategies to govern and regulate the problem of populations with low foundation skills. The different 'strategies and logics' can be understood as both 'intended' and 'unintended', as governments began to make sense of this urgent need within particular rationalities and logics. As Bailey (2013, p. 815) suggests, an apparatus:

> takes no singular or essential form but rather involves shifting lines of descent and trajectory, different strategies and logics (which may find support or antagonism with others), and multiple locations of performance (be it a profit seeking company, a think-tank, a social enterprise, a school, a PISA examination, a school inspection, etc).

One significant 'intended' response was the mutual obligation initiative called the *Language and Numeracy Training* (LANT) *Program*, released in 1997, which targeted job seekers aged 18–24 with low foundation skills (Department of Education Employment Training and Youth Affairs [DEETYA] 1997). Citing findings from the *Survey of Aspects of Literacy* that 'unemployed people have lower levels of literacy/numeracy than the general Australian population', and that low 'literacy/numeracy competency can be a major barrier to getting and keeping a job', in 1997, the Commonwealth Government contracted 69 RTOs, selected by competitive tender, to offer 12,000 foundation skills training places nationally to unemployed young people (DEETYA, 1997, p. 8).

The then Employment Minister David Kemp (1998a, p. 3) highlighted the national importance of the *LANT Program* by claiming that 'unemployed young people ... who have poor literacy and numeracy skills will be able to meet their mutual obligation by undertaking training to improve their chances of finding a job'. Labelled by Brooker (1999, p. 32) as more a 'matter of imperative than choice', the Commonwealth instructed all job seekers in these age and unemployment categories to undertake a literacy test to determine if they required literacy classes (Brooker, 1999; DEETYA, 1997). In situations where job seekers were assessed with low foundation skills, Centrelink had the discretion to refer job seekers to a foundation skills course, unless another mutual obligation activity was deemed a greater benefit (DEETYA, 1997). Those having 'poor' skills, according to Kemp (1998a, p. 3), 'must hold up their end of the partnership with the community', and failure to do so 'may be subject to standard activity test penalties'.[2]

Brooker (1999, p. 32) observed that the purpose of the Howard Coalition's initiative was 'strategic-political'[3] and leveraged off public support, 'which means votes', for any government that has 'the spirit to challenge dole bludging'. A similar 'intended' and arguably 'strategic-political' initiative occurred a short time later and involved actions at the pre-intervention, secondary education stage of foundation skills learning. In a radio interview, Prime Minister Howard (1999) identified the decline in standards of the secondary school system as another cause of low foundation skills among young job seekers. His comments reflected a common response to the *Survey of Aspects of Literacy* results that adult literacy was a 'remedial' issue (Adult Literacy Information Office, 1999, p. 11). A discussion paper by the Adult Literacy Information Office (1999) described this response as the expectation that everyone except small children should read and write. Anyone who had moved through the Australian school system, and was deemed to lack literacy, presumably 'failed' to learn it at school and required 'remedial' assistance to engage in further study or the labour market (Adult Literacy Information Office, 1999, p. 11). This 'remedial' discourse struck a chord with mainstream media channels, which directed responsibility onto several parties, particularly secondary schools. For example, conservative columnist Padraic McGuiness (1999) wrote:

> Of course, the first question ought to be why anybody who has been through the school system without learning to read and write has not come to attention at an earlier age. This is clearly a failure of the school system and of individual teachers but it may be a part of larger problems such as dysfunctional families, peer pressure or indiscipline in the schools.

These concerns, in part, led the Howard Coalition government in 2001 to impose measures on secondary schools to improve their literacy and numeracy teaching performance. The government insisted that, to be eligible to receive Commonwealth funding, secondary schools had to measure themselves against benchmarks in literacy and numeracy and make the results public (Ministerial Council on Employment Education Training and Youth Affairs, 2001; Stewart, 2005).[4]

Several other initiatives, which we describe as 'unintended', also shaped the apparatus as it emerged. These initiatives contributed to the apparatus' function as a monitoring device of 'at risk' individuals and as a way to make up responsible subjects through a range of education and training opportunities. For example, as a feature of the 1994 *National Training Reform Agenda*, each State and Territory government allocated funding to provide adult literacy training to individuals through heavily government subsidised fees (Australian National Training Authority, 1994). At this time, Victoria's Adult, Community and Further Education board continued to fund 190 neighbourhood houses, most of which also provided adult, community and further education courses, including non-accredited language and literacy courses (Gribble, 1994). The Commonwealth continued to increase its program offerings by committing funds to the *Adult Migrant English Program* (*AMEP*) to provide training to newly arrived migrants to Australia and expanding the *LANT Program* eligibility criteria to job seekers over the age of 24. The Commonwealth also funded the *Workplace English and Language and Literacy* program in 2001 to upskill workers in hundreds of workplaces throughout Australia (Australian Council for Adult Literacy, 2001).

We further explore the dynamic relations between the programs, entities and other elements that comprise this apparatus' evolving, shifting, complexity later in this chapter. Before then, we want to begin an analysis of the second concern of Foucault's characterisation of the apparatus, its strategic function, to address an urgent need.

3 Strategic Function of the Apparatus: Resistance, Regulation and Transcendent Possibilities

There is an identifiable tendency for any apparatus, as a regulatory arrangement, to seek to govern and regulate certain populations in relation to particular challenges ('urgent needs'). In this case, governing populations with low foundation skills so that they develop the capabilities to (re)engage in labour markets. These capabilities are not only related to foundation skills, but also the entrepreneurial norms that seek to make up an ideal and typical 'neoliberal subject'. As we suggested earlier, neoliberal subjects can be understood as:

> those who invoke the language of personal responsibility or have been 'responsibilized'... those who value autonomy and speak in the language of individualism; and... those who employ the rhetorics of authenticity and self realization, and who conceive of their self as a thing to be worked on and improved. (Watts, 2021, p. 8)

Our work so far has shown that from a Commonwealth Government standpoint, there were concerns that populations with low foundation skills were at risk of not engaging in skills training and changing labour markets, and who needed to be governed and managed by an apparatus to enable them, in time, to make the right choices in creating an entrepreneurial pathway. Giorgio Agamben (2009), in his reading of Foucault's concept of apparatus, argues that for populations deemed 'burdensome',[5] individuals need to be subjected to the control of the apparatus. Agamben imagines the power of the apparatus to be all-encompassing, insofar as the burdensome subject is both produced and utterly dominated by the operations of the apparatus. In the foundation skills apparatus, if individuals are imagined as subjects of mutual obligation, then the strategic function of the apparatus is to direct, coerce, and even sanction individuals to meet 'obligations'. Obligations, such as job-seeking conduct, are continually subject to individualised evaluation and judgement, and failure to appropriately respond as required, can result in the loss of benefits and further sanctions (Rose, 1996).

Agamben (2009, p. 17) expands Foucault's class of apparatuses to include 'the capacity to capture, orient, determine, intercept, model, control, or secure the gestures, behaviours, opinions, or discourses of living beings'. He argues that 'language itself... is perhaps the most ancient of apparatuses'. As we observed earlier, the Howard Coalition government's welfare reform of contracted employment services and mutual obligation was framed by a new language based on socio-cultural, political and regulatory values and knowledge. This language includes the promotion of mutual obligation, focussed on processes and practices of discipline and motivation to reintegrate individuals with mainstream expectations of social values and morality. It also consisted of the regulation and organisational standards of new public management (NPM) discourses, which emphasised productivity, cost-efficiencies, accountabilities, record keeping and the surveillance of the individual's job-seeking activities (MacIntyre, 1999; Mendes, 2007, 2009). In this sense, the role of language is critical to ensure that these forms of knowledge are produced, privileged and disseminated over others (Foucault, 1982). Foucault (1980c, p. 102) suggests that these practices can act as 'apparatuses of control'. When conflicted and contested knowledge/discourses co-exist, Foucault argues, disciplinary power enables actors in institutions to privilege selected knowledge against, and/or over, others using apparatuses of control, claiming, in effect, that these privileged knowledges are the objective fact, truth, reality, and norm.

For Foucault (1982, p. 212), the 'apparatuses of control' can be framed as the 'apparatuses of control of others'. These apparatuses of control, in the context of mutual obligation, consist of:

- the governing ideology – the concept of obligation-based entitlements and the understanding of the moral obligation to work for the income support received;
- surveillance – attendance at meetings and submission of information within timeframes;
- setting expectations – including timeframes to undertake and complete training, how many jobs to apply for; and,
- explanation, persuasion and questioning the position/capacity of others – establishing and/or validating the need for training, encouraging reluctant participants and verifying barriers to participation.

This apparatus also produces the 'apparatuses of control of self' in which individuals must enact self-surveillance and self-policing (Foucault, 1982, p. 212) through completing job diaries, meeting training attendance requirements and monitoring the obligations of job contracts they are signatories to. In this arrangement, as we will discuss in greater detail in Chapter Four, the contracted employment agency is assumed to control this 'apparatus'. The RTO can also take some responsibility.

Agamben (2009) claims that the regulation of activities such as those tied to mutual obligation limits the possibilities of resistance for a subject. Frost (2015) argues strongly that in this way, the apparatus structures and delimits one's existence. Resistance is limited to an indifference to the politics and government economics inherent in the apparatus, and is evasive in character. It ultimately involves the subject thinking of an imminent life. Evading the apparatus occurs not by the assistance of the apparatus' function, but in spite of its function (Frost, 2015). Or, as Watts (2021) describes, as processes of responsibilisation are taking place, these conditions force subjects to 'become responsible', regardless of their convictions. As resistance may leave an individual increasingly unprotected and insecure, individuals may do 'what any and all humans do in the face of change: adapt' (Watts, 2021, p. 9). In this case, the apparatus may not produce an ideal 'neoliberal subject', but instead an individual that just wishes to 'get by' (Watts, 2021, p. 9).

In this way, with mutual obligation a key mechanism in the strategic function of the apparatus, the value of the relationships between the learner, the educator, the RTO and the employment agency are reconfigured, even 'silenced' and/or subjugated. For example, the importance of a learner's values and meanings of their own experiences, the promotion of social justice for marginalised populations, and the pedagogical principles based on the relationship between learner, educator and employment agency case worker are moved to the periphery in the apparatus. Yet Foucault claims that another form of resistance can be the binding force in an apparatus, rather than government power. In contrast to thinking of resistance as being a mere negation, it can also be a creative process and provide the potential for an ethical and aesthetic self-creation in the emergence of the new, be it a form of power, counter-conduct, or an ethical culture of the self (Dean, 2013). It is practices of freedom, such as those inherent in, or a product of, the relationships between the learner, education, training provider and case workers, that can allow the subject to practice self-construction and, in turn, resist and rework the apparatus that constitutes them.

In affording specialised foundation skills training through funded training programs, the apparatus can provide advocacy and opportunity for individuals to enact processes of resistance against the challenge of low foundation skills, changing labour markets and dependency on income support. Commonwealth, State and Territory policy discourse argues that policy provides the conditions, with the expertise of education and employment professionals, for learners to develop their foundation skills. Learners can rework, self-construct and/or self-create into active subjects who can realise the benefits of foundation skills [sustainable employment, higher wages, improved health and increasing community engagement] (SCOTESE, 2012; State Government of Victoria, 2013a, 2016). And, in the words of Foucault (cited in Frost, 2015), self-construction can be understood as a form of resistance in the apparatus creating transcendental possibilities for learners. Foundation skills programs in the apparatus can promote the social relationships – or the social capital

– of adult education and foundation skills. These social relationships can also be economic, and socialise students to think in ways that facilitate the flexibilisation of capitalism, and the internalisation of workplace norms (Foley, 1995). They can also create informal learning environments that enhance the awareness of learners to recognise the potential that can come from learning, and the decisions to learn from these experiences. Informal learning can be 'transformative' in a way that unmasks how 'perspectives on the world, others and ourselves can be challenged and transformed in our ongoing efforts to make sense of the world' (Hodge, 2011, p. 248). These forms of learning can create 'transcendent' possibilities as learners seek to disturb the way society 'thinks, feels and acts' with learning that is 'very real and … empowering' (Newman, 1995a, pp. 246–248).

4 The Elements of the Apparatus: Characteristics and the Nature of Their Connection

Foucault's concept of apparatus signifies a complex ensemble of norms, knowledges, power relations, and practices implicated and bound together with regard to a particular social problem, an 'urgent need'. In this section, we will investigate the critical connections within this ensemble that give meaning to the strategic function of the foundation skills apparatus. Our discussions are organised using some of Foucault's (1980a, pp. 194–196) understanding of the 'elements' constituting the 'ensemble' (discourses, institutions, architectural forms, regulatory decisions, laws, administrative measures, scientific statements, philosophical, moral and philanthropic propositions). One objective in investigating the connection between the elements is to reveal the historical, and then contemporary, discursive neoliberal construction of human capital, skills and the commodification of human abilities.

4.1 *Competency-Based Foundation Skills Training*

Over a significant period of time, the policy response to low foundation skills of the working-age population of Australia has primarily centred on training and education initiatives. The policy actions – the *National Policy on Languages* in 1987, the *Australian Language and Literacy Policy* in 1991 and the *National Foundation Skills Strategy for Adults* in 2012 (*National Strategy*) have principally coordinated the funding of registered training organisations (RTOs) to deliver foundation skills training. Despite a lack of policy before 1987, a series of programs were funded by Commonwealth, State and Territory governments to address the problem of low foundation skills. In Victoria, adult literacy programs were offered by the Council of Adult Education,[6] trade unions, or on a community volunteer basis, with tutors providing students with individual tuition. Migrant education, starting in the 1940s, consisted of classroom and home tutor programs through the *Adult Migrant English Program* [*AMEP*] (Martin, 1998). Class tuition and teacher expertise gradually advanced during the 1980s with programs delivered by adult education organisations and Technical and Further Education (TAFE) colleges (Gribble, 1994)

Training programs at this time reflected children's literacy pedagogies (DEET, 1991) despite the theoretical and practical approaches of Malcolm Knowles (1973) and others on adult education. However, fears that program development would shift from a process of 'imagination, flexibility and a willingness to take risks' to a process tied down by 'sets of guidelines or lists to follow' (Newman, 1995b, p. 54) began to be realised in the mid-1980s. As we detailed earlier, this shift was a transformation driven by a reorganisation of the labour market through concerted efforts of unions, industry and governments. Responding to business complaints that workers lacked the skills to succeed in new labour markets, governments embarked on reforms to identify, measure and increase the education and vocational skills of the workforce. This included restructuring industrial relations awards and agreements and developing career plans and pathways for workers. As part of this complex process, trades, occupations and professions were analysed and described in sets of skills, widely known as competencies (Newman, 1995b). By 1994, competency-based curriculums were established as part of the *National Training Reform Agenda*. Competency-based curriculums were credentialled by public and private training and educational sectors, which formed the basis of contemporary 'training programs' in adult education (Australian National Training Authority, 1994). A by-product of competency-based training was the alignment of foundation skills with VET, or as Rhodes (2016, p. 31) describes, the positioning of 'LLN within the wider VET space'.

The *AMEP* is one example of how competency-based training became embedded in foundation skills. Before competency-based training, standardised syllabuses were not prescribed in this program. From 1984, the only official guidelines or framework comprised assessing the learner's proficiency, prior to enrolment, in speaking, listening, reading and writing through an oral interview using the *Australian Second Language Proficiency Ratings* (Ingram & Wylie, 1979). This general proficiency rating scale was used, along with other information, to place clients in appropriate learning arrangements. Drawing on the *National Training Reform Agenda*, a competency-based curriculum framework called the *Course in Spoken and Written English* was introduced in 1994 for RTOs as the basis for curriculum planning and assessment (Brindley,

2000). At this time, the AMEP shifted to teacher-administered assessment and outcomes-oriented criteria (Brindley, 1998). The first iteration of the *Course in Spoken and Written English* consisted of certificates corresponding to four English language proficiency levels and providing a statement of the learning outcomes in the form of language competencies in oral interaction, reading and writing. Task-based assessments of competencies were administered by teachers at periodic points throughout the program and at the end of a course. Based on these assessments, learners could achieve a statement of attainment or be awarded a certificate if they fulfilled the requisite competencies. Several other competency-based curricula, such as general education, work education, and other variations of English language education, were developed, all of which began to form part of Commonwealth, State and Territory funded foundation skills training programs (Brindley, 2000).

Competency-based training contributed to the emergence of human capital perspectives in foundation skills. As Black and Yasukawa (2013) note, rationales in policy and funding were heavily skewed towards funding of workplace job seeker programs. Individuals were deemed to be lacking a set of 'skills' to compete in labour markets, and formal education and training was principally the approach to address this issue. A learner's progress in attaining foundation skills in Commonwealth programs, as well as satisfactory participation under mutual obligation and continued funding, was determined by their 'progression' against a set of 'competencies' known as the *National Reporting System*. The *Literacy and Numeracy Training (LANT) Program*, its later iterations, the *Language Literacy and Numeracy Program (LLNP)* and *Skills for Education and Employment (SEE) Program*, and more recently, the AMEP, adopted this mechanism to report learner's progress. As learners achieve these 'competencies', they can be eligible for another round of subsidised funding. This achievement is also attached to payments to RTOs (ACIL Allen Consulting, 2015b, 2015c).

State and Territory governments, specifically the Victorian Government, also contribute to the human capital/competency approach to addressing low foundation skills. Drawing on the competency-based methodology, the Victorian Government introduced its own foundation skills training competency-based curriculum, named the *Certificate of General Education for Adults*, in 1992 (Department of Education and Training, 2016). In a similar structure to the *AMEP-Certificate in Spoken and Written English*, as learners progress through sets of competencies (modules), they are awarded a certificate. They can then enrol in another set of competencies at a higher qualification level. The learner's progression through the modules and their qualification level can be used as an indicator of their foundation skills level in order to transition to other options such as higher secondary certificates, including the adult

Victorian Certificate of Education, courses that require a *Certificate II of General Education for Adults* (deemed a Year 10 equivalent for entry into the Army Reserves), or other VET options.

4.2 *Foundation Skills Training Programs*

Two of the most significant institutions to deliver foundation skills training programs are Technical and Further Education (TAFE) institutions and community education providers. TAFE institutions are the most prominent providers of VET, and apprenticeships and traineeships and foundation skills programs. Community education providers – usually non-profit community RTOs and neighbourhood houses – focus on non-accredited or entry-level industry qualifications, usually of non-trade varieties such as service and health industries (Whyte & Crombie, 1995). As the *National Training Reform Agenda*, and later in 2008, the *Victorian Training Guarantee*, introduced marketisation policies, the foundation skills and VET sector increasingly 'opened up' to private RTOs, including enterprise-based providers, industry organisations, and commercial businesses (Australian National Training Authority, 1994; Department of Industry Innovation Regional Development [DIIRD], 2008). Figure 1 illustrates how the foundation skills programs and the pathways of the Victorian training system, combined with Commonwealth-funded programs, are organised. This figure and the following discussion outline four major programs in the foundation skills apparatus and their connections, intended or otherwise. These programs, which formed part of the apparatus as it emerged responding to a historical 'urgent need' in the mid to late 1990s, have remained relatively stable in their structure and operation since then.

Adult Migrant English Program (*AMEP*): Earlier, we introduced the *AMEP*, Australia's largest language learning program for migrants. The Commonwealth Government developed the first adult migrant education policy in the mid-1940s to implement an immigration program that sought migrants from Britain and other European countries. The *AMEP* was introduced in the context of this migration program and offered new arrivals the opportunity to learn English (Martin, 1998). The *AMEP* is still operating with a similar objective to this present day. It is a voluntary program for eligible permanent migrants and humanitarian entrants who lack proficiency in English (ACIL Allen Consulting, 2015b).[7] Since 1997, the program has been delivered by TAFE, the migrant specialist public provider *Adult Migrant English Service* (*AMES*), and/or private providers, who are awarded contracts from the Commonwealth by competitive tender. The program's delivery is divided into service delivery regions to ensure appropriate national geographic coverage (ACIL Allen Consulting, 2015b; Martin, 1998).

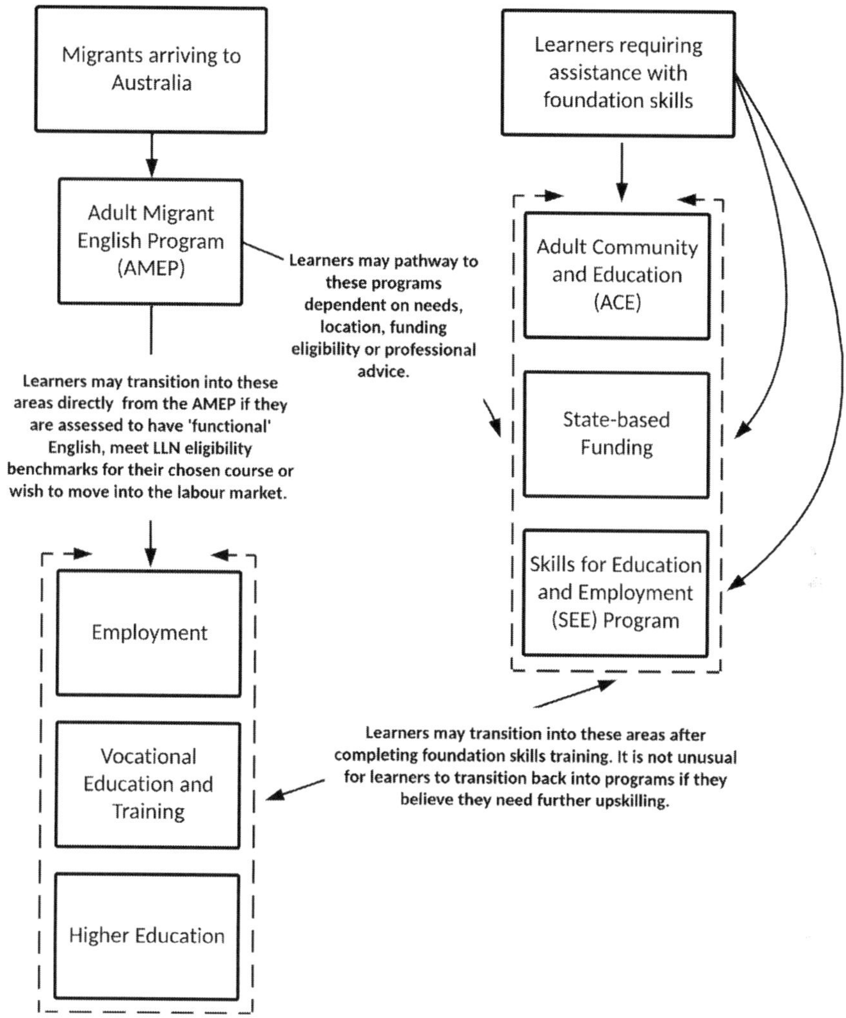

FIGURE 1 Foundation skills training programs, pathways and alignments (Adapted from: ACIL Allen Consulting (2015a, pp. 27–33), ACIL Allen Consulting (2015b, pp. 6–16), ACIL Allen Consulting (2015c, pp. 6–18), Australian Government (2021c, para. 5), State Government of Victoria (2013a, pp. 13–25) and State Government of Victoria (2016, pp. 3–12))

Before 2020, *AMEP* provided 510 hours of free English language tuition within the migrant's first five years of settlement. The primary objective of the *AMEP* is for learners to acquire the confidence and 'functional' English language skills they need to operate effectively in Australia (DEET, 1991). The program also introduces newly arrived clients to Australian social norms and practices, services, and the rule of law. The *AMEP* is delivered in various modes, including classroom training, correspondence or distance learning courses, home tutoring, small groups in community settings, and, more recently, using computers, video conferencing, and the Internet (ACIL Allen Consulting, 2015b). The *AMEP* also provides an education assessment, counselling, placement and referral service, professional and curriculum support, a national management information system, and free childcare (DEET, 1991).

From 2010, the *AMEP* underwent several reforms in its business model, one of which included the introduction, in 2018, of semi-competitive markets in regions where demand for programs was high (Australian Government, 2017). In 2017, the *AMEP*, previously positioned as a Commonwealth settlement responsibility under the provisions of the *Immigration (Education) Act 1971* (DEET, 1991), shifted to the responsibility of the Department of Education and Training (Scanlon Institute, 2019). The shift led to the inclusion of employment-related elements into English language learning in response to a significant number of participants being identified and registered as job seekers after nine months of residing in Australia (ACIL Allen Consulting, 2015b). In 2020, the Australian Government introduced reforms to address the non-completion of allocated training hours and lower English proficiency (Scanlon Institute, 2019; Stayner, 2020), which, according to the then Citizenship Minister Alan Tudge, was leading to lower integration rates and 'emerging ethnic enclaves' (cited in Acharya, 2018, para. 3).[8] These reforms removed the previous 510-hour limit on free English tuition to help migrants access additional free tuition until they reach a higher level of proficiency (Australian Government, 2020c). The five-year time limit from when a migrant is issued their eligible visa to commence classes was also removed (Australian Government, 2024a).

Skills for Education and Employment (SEE Program): This program was established in 1997–1998 as the *LANT Program,* and despite undergoing several restructures and name changes since its inception, it has remained the Commonwealth's primary mutual obligation program for helping eligible job seekers improve their foundation skills (UNESCO Institute for Lifelong Learning, 2013). In 2002, the *LANT Program* was renamed the *Language Literacy and Numeracy Program (LLNP)* and expanded to address concerns of unmet English language demands post the 510-hour limit of the *AMEP* and rising unemployment of cohorts other than young people. The changes included removing age restrictions to allow any individual registered as a job seeker with Centrelink to be eligible, differentiating between the needs of 'language' and 'literacy' learners by offering two distinct tuition streams, and seeking to establish a training pathway from the *AMEP* to the *LLNP* (Australian Council for Adult Literacy, 2001; Australian Government, 2013b).

The *LLNP* sought to improve job seekers' foundation skills, expecting that such improvements would enable them to participate more effectively in further training or the labour market and lead to more significant long-term gains for society (Australian Government, 2013b). Like the *AMEP*, *LLNP* contracts were awarded by competitive tender for service delivery regions across Australia. RTOs, including TAFE, community and private institutions, were contracted to deliver assessment and training services through face-to-face training, or by distance mode (Australian Government, 2013a). The program provided up to 800 hours (later reduced to 650 hours) of free training undertaken on a part-time or full-time basis over no more than two years. Job seekers exiting the *LLNP* could pathway into other foundation skills courses, a vocational course, or paid employment – the priority for Commonwealth and its employment services agencies.

Similar to the *AMEP*, the *LLNP* has undergone several reforms. In 2010, the Commonwealth conducted market research to determine obstacles to engagement for Australian-born job seekers. The study demonstrated a close identification between the name of the *LLNP* – particularly the terms 'literacy' and 'numeracy' – and perceived social stigma, which was understood to impact the participation numbers of 'literacy' learners. The Commonwealth, referencing strong support from key program stakeholders, recommended a name change to the *Skills for Education and Employment* (*SEE*) *Program* in 2013 (Australian Government, 2013b). In 2013, the program moved away from a one-provider-per-region model to a multi-provider competition model in high-demand regions (Australian Government, 2013b). The Commonwealth also researched ways to formalise and strengthen the alignment between the *AMEP* with the *SEE Program*. However, in this process, it strongly recommended that any alignment should not disturb client choice (ACIL Allen Consulting, 2015a).

Accredited State-Funded Foundation Skills Training Programs (*Victorian*): Another key 'element' within the foundation skills apparatus are programs funded by state governments. These courses differ from the *AMEP* and *SEE Program* in several ways. In Victoria, for example, RTOs are contracted, not through competitive tender, but through an application process to the State Government, provided they hold registration with their Commonwealth or State training regulator. Training is also funded in a fully marketised environment. In contrast, Commonwealth programs have restrictions on competitive markets and are bound by a notional cap on how much funding can be accessed. The eligibility criteria for learners also differs from Commonwealth programs. The *AMEP* is open to migrants who hold an appropriate visa, such as humanitarian and partner visas, and are not Australian citizens. The *SEE Program* is also available to appropriate visa holders, and to Australian citizens registered as job seekers with Centrelink. However, Victorian funding is open to Australian citizens and permanent residents, 15 years and above, irrespective of whether they are unemployed, working or retired (ACIL Allen Consulting, 2015b, 2015c; DIIRD, 2008; State Government of Victoria, 2019).

Outside of funding eligibility, there are few points of difference between Victorian-funded programs and their *AMEP* and *SEE Program* counterparts in pedagogical delivery. Programs will usually be delivered by similar providers, teach a similar curriculum, have comparable student contact hours, and students can move through the various levels within the curriculum to attain certificates. Often state funded learners will be in the same classroom as *AMEP* and *SEE Program* students. Students may combine a foundation skills certificate to value-add and support their state funded VET studies. Or, learners may use state funding to meet prerequisite foundation skills standards for further education.

Adult Community Education Programs (Non-accredited Programs): Foundation skills training can also be offered through Victorian state-funded programs known as non-accredited courses. These courses provide short-term, basic or introductory training for people as a pathway to work or accredited training (SCOTESE, 2012). Also known as the *Learn Local* or *Adult Community Education* (*ACE*) sector, these courses have been funded through the Victorian state-regulated Adult Community and Further Education Board since 1992. The State Government of Victoria (2013a), through their *Learn Local Focusing on the Future Strategy,* states that many of the ACE organisations are neighbourhood and community houses, with about half of the 300 registered organisations being located in regional areas. Non-accredited courses do not provide a person with a nationally recognised qualification on completion and are not based on a competency-based curriculum. The target group for students undertaking non-accredited studies can be populations that would otherwise find accredited training and large RTOs intimidating – likely due to negative educational experiences in the past – and prefer an informal and inclusive learning environment. These populations can include young people disengaged from education, people with a disability, Indigenous Australians, people from a culturally linguistically diverse background, unemployed people and vulnerable workers. Adults wanting to improve their foundation skills and digital literacy often use ACE organisations to re-enter education. Courses are frequently complemented by other services, such as childcare, family support and job placement services, that support the wellbeing of learners and encourage them to continue with their education and training.

4.3 *Academic, Economic, Industry and Social Support Agencies of the Foundation Skills Apparatus*

Of significant importance to the foundation skills apparatus is a group of institutions from academia, economic, welfare, advocacy and industry sectors – who, initially, might appear as 'peripheral' to the apparatus. However, these 'peripheral' stakeholders in the apparatus often work to meet the needs of the most marginalised populations and individuals with low foundation skills. All contribute to the operations of the apparatus in a variety of ways, ranging from the welfare support of learners, research into classroom and workplace-based pedagogies for RTOs and industry, lobbying of governments and research. There is potential in neoliberal policy for collaborations between cross-sector organisations that encourage innovative solutions, reduce implementation resistance, and improve information and resource sharing (Koon, 2020). Yet even if goals are intrinsically linked, conflicts and tensions can arise between stakeholders.

Welfare and advocacy organisations: Foundation skills learners are widely regarded as 'at-risk' populations. Studies such as those of Crowther et al. (2010) claim that foundation skills learners are disproportionately likely to come from areas of social deprivation and low-income families, lead unstable lives, experience ill health, and live with disabilities. In response, Commonwealth, State and Territory funding contracts strongly recommend collaboration between RTOs and welfare organisations when awarding contracted services (ACIL Allen Consulting, 2015b, 2015c). Welfare organisations can assist in refugee settlement, housing and homelessness support, youth services, family support, domestic and sexual violence, and legal services. As these matters are prioritised, welfare appointments and home-life (re)arrangements and interventions can disrupt foundation skills training. In these circumstances, the formal engagement of foundation skills learners is often marked by pauses in learning as they take breaks to manage life circumstances (Crowther et al., 2010). These breaks can be in opposition to the learners' mutual obligation requirements, where they face punitive sanctions for not attending classes and potential withdrawal from programs for not meeting attendance standards.

In a similar manner, migrant and refugee advocacy groups support learners in their transactions with the community, politicians and governments. Advocacy can be in the form of:

- individual advocacy – which focusses on helping individuals get access to existing services;

- collective advocacy – lobbying to change government policy and the creation of services that do not yet exist; and,
- public advocacy – running campaigns to influence the public's attitudes, behaviours and practices (Refugee Council of Australia, 2019).

Both welfare and advocacy organisations can receive government funding to deliver services. They can also raise money to fund activities and advocacy programs through corporate or philanthropic funding. A key emphasis of migrant advocacy is facilitating the integration of migrants and humanitarian entrants into society. However, the concept of 'integration' is frustrated by widely different meanings (Ager & Strang, 2008) and continues to be 'controversial and hotly debated' (Castles et al., 2001, p. 12). While lobby groups will advocate for their clients on platforms of 'rights and citizenship' (Ager & Strang, 2008, p. 185), they must navigate the policies, programs, instruments and public discourses that aim to condition, incentivise and shape migrants, through socialisation measures, into 'citizens' (Borevi et al., 2017).

Employment Services Agencies: Earlier, we introduced the emergence of Commonwealth-contracted employment services. This service has been named *Employment Services, Job Network, Jobactive* and, more recently, in 2022, *Workforce Australia.* Consisting of private, non-profit, charities and religious agencies, employment services agencies have strong relationships in the foundation skills apparatus. Many learners undertake programs as part of their mutual obligation to receive income support. Employment services agencies are contracted to work closely with employers to understand their recruitment needs based on their strong understanding of local labour markets. Through an agreement between the provider and the job seeker called a 'job plan', agencies tailor services to the assessed needs of job seekers to assist in obtaining and maintaining employment (Australian Government, 2015a, 2024b). The job plan is a binding agreement between the agency and the job seeker. The plan details the job seeker's mutual obligation requirements, including the prescribed number of jobs to apply for and documenting approved training activities such as foundation skills programs (Australian Government, 2015a).

Employers & Industry Groups: Employer groups, business councils, and other labour market and economic think tanks have profoundly influenced national governments of all political persuasions to pay more attention to foundation skills (Jackson & Slade, 2008). Two groups in particular have played a key role in shaping a human capital discourse of foundation skills. First, Skills Service Organisations, formerly Industry Skills Councils, have been set up with funding from the Australian Government to support industry reference committees to review and develop training products for the VET system. Part of their role has been to clearly identify the opportunities to underpin foundation skills as part of VET (Australian Industry and Skills Committee, 2021). A second group, known as industry associations, represents employers promoting the benefits of foundation skills development to employers and employees. Governments collaborate with industry associations to identify opportunities and support training and research initiatives to integrate foundation skills into workforce development and regular workplace training activities (Australian Government, 2021b).

Evaluation, Review and Academic Research Actors: The policy space in Australia has generated many follow-up research studies from key stakeholder groups and government-sponsored organisations. Peak foundation skills groups, the Australian Council for Adult Literacy and the Victorian Adult Literacy Basic Education Council, national and Victorian organisations, respectively, provide advocacy and advice on government policy and support significant research in foundation skills. Government-sponsored reports have also been prominent. Two notable reviews from ACIL Allen Consulting (2015b, 2015c) on the *AMEP* and the *SEE Program* produced recommendations to the Commonwealth on the program's efficacy, operations, and outcomes. These reviews were also an impetus for recommending the introduction of competitive market principles into these programs.

Academic research in Australia on foundation skills since the 1980s has largely been influenced by the work of Joseph Lo Bianco and Rosie Wickert. They have captured accounts of those deeply engaged in language and literacy policymaking and its effects. Other prominent researchers in foundation skills include Stephen Black and Keiko Yasukawa, who have co-authored and edited publications that have debated the 'human rights versus human capital' aspect of adult foundation skills in Australia (Black, 2002; Black et al., 2010; Black & Yasukawa, 2013; Black et al., 2013; Yasukawa & Black, 2016). Another prominent research body is the National Council of Vocational Education Research. *The* National Council of Vocational Education Research's role is to inform policy and practice in the VET and foundation skills sector on behalf of the Commonwealth, State and Territory governments. Their work has been prominent in progressing elements of the 2012–2022 *National Foundation Skills Strategy for Adults* (*National Strategy*), particularly in building the capacity of education and training workforces.

Advisory bodies: Three major advisory bodies are prominent in the foundation skills apparatus. Earlier, we noted the role of the Industry Commission in their review and advisory roles on micro-economic policy and regulation in a range of economic and social issues. The Productivity Commission's (formerly the Industry Commission) work on workforce productivity in 2008 was a fundamental justification for developing the *National Strategy* (SCOTESE, 2012). The second advisory body is the Organisation for Economic Co-operation and Development (OECD). The OECD advises member countries on developing, activating, and using foundation skills. It highlights the kinds of education, employment, tax, and other social policies that encourage and allow people to make the most of their potential (OECD, 2013). The OECD's influence on educational policy emerges mainly from its role in developing a series of international surveys measuring adult literacy and numeracy skills.

The third organisation, the United Nations Educational Scientific and Cultural Organization (UNESCO), has been at the forefront of global literacy efforts since 1946 in advancing the vision of a literate world for all. They partnered with the Australian Government through the *International Year of Literacy* in 1991 and continued to promote literacy through their *2030 Agenda for Sustainable Development* (UNESCO, 1990, 2015). As part of this agenda, *Sustainable Development Goal Four: Quality Education* (*SDG 4*) involves a commitment to quality and equity in education. Four targets of SDG 4 are particularly related to foundation skills:

- 4.3: By 2030, ensure equal access for all women and men to affordable and quality technical, vocational and tertiary education, including university;
- 4.4: By 2030, substantially increase the number of youth and adults who have relevant skills, including technical and vocational skills, for employment, decent jobs and entrepreneurship;
- 4.5: By 2030, eliminate gender disparities in education and ensure equal access to all levels of education and vocational training for the vulnerable, including persons with disabilities, Indigenous peoples and children in vulnerable situations; and,
- 4.6: By 2030, ensure that all youth and a substantial proportion of adults, both men and women, achieve literacy and numeracy (UNESCO, 2015).

Many OECD member countries have been relatively successful in their progress toward achieving a number of the SDG 4 targets with respect to school infrastructure, gender gaps in access to early levels of education, access to basic education, and completion rates of young people in primary and secondary education (Webb et al., 2017). However, according to Webb et al. (2017), significant challenges remain for many OECD countries concerning gender parity in adult education and learning outcomes, and a lack of focus on lifelong learning and access to tertiary education. In its voluntary national review of the SDGs in 2018, the Australian Government identified that improving outcomes for

Australia's Aboriginal and Torres Strait Islander peoples, and 'assisting workers through transitions related to technological and industrial change' would be priority focus areas (United Nations, 2018, para. 10). Australia has yet to formally report its progress on several SDG 4 targets,[9] however, Smith and Brolan (2020, para. 7) claim that the government has been 'incredibly slow on SDGs uptake relative to other countries'. They argue that for the Australian government, the SDGs are largely treated as a foreign policy agenda rather than a domestic one, and, as a result, governments have failed to develop an SDG implementation plan. In this context, Latham (2020) has also identified minimal political interest, and a lack of public interest in holding the government accountable, as possible reasons for a lack of interest, even urgency in relation to the SDG agenda in Australia.

5 The Foundation Skills Apparatus: Debates and Truth Claims

For Foucault (1980a, p. 194), an apparatus is the particular 'system of relations that can be established' between such things as discourses, institutions, and systems of thought. In the foundation skills apparatus, this system can be given meaning by the professional experts and agencies installed, or contracted, by governments. Governments rely on contributions from stakeholders to understand, regulate and deliver contracted services, and as this occurs, certain truth claims are promoted. These claims can create potential alliances dependent on mutual interests and benefits (Miller & Rose, 1993). Yet, they can also unexpectedly rupture when interests and benefits are no longer advantageous, or when ideologies conflict. Different claims, debates and discourses are promoted or silenced depending on the social, economic and political motivations of a particular social movement, public policy or market dynamic. Tensions between discourses are complexified even further through opposing and diverse scientific or academic statements embedded within philosophical and moral propositions. To this point, we have introduced several claims that are strongly, often heatedly, debated, and which are politically and economically significant enough to result in the functions of the apparatus being in a constant state of flux. These claims and debates include:

- The emergence and dominance of human capital discourses, and the subjugation of social capital discourses in foundation skills;
- Various subjectifications of the foundation skills learner – particularly as a 'job seeker', 'individual', 'customer' or 'Australian'; and,
- Influence of the reconfiguration of the welfare state – including the moral regulation of individuals.

In this final section we outline a number of key features of these debates in order to more fully explore these in later chapters.

5.1 *The Emergence of the Human Capital and the Subjugation of Social Capital Outcomes*

One recurring debate on how foundation skills are understood is the contest between discourses of human and social capital. The social capital form focusses on how literacy acquisition occurs in social contexts. The emphasis here is not so much on the text but on the relationship between comprehension, sight words, graphophonic cues and the context in which these are used (Falk & Millar, 2001). The human capital form views foundation skills as perceptual and cognitive skills, emphasising sight word recognition and phonics (decoding and encoding skill and fluency based on linguistic sound patterns). The assumption with foundation skills taught as basic skills is that they can be applied in those functional tasks that rely on them (Falk & Millar, 2001).

Human and social capital understandings of literacy can be further differentiated by referencing Brian Street's (1984) 'autonomous' and 'ideological' models. Characteristics of the 'autonomous' model – in this case, basic skills – largely reflect a human capital agenda. Street (cited in MacLachlan & Cloonan, 2003) describes the four assumptions of the autonomous model of literacy:

- literacy can be removed from its social context and treated as a skill devoid of social meaning;
- literacy development or skill level can be measured in terms of levels of capability;
- there are strong associations between literacy levels and social progress; and,
- there are strong associations between higher literacy skills and higher cognitive abilities, for example, problem-solving and self-reflection.

This model, he argues, assumes the homogeneity of literacy and the perception of it as being somehow a 'separate' parcel of transferable skills that exist in isolation from the social contexts in which those skills are to be used. The autonomous model imagines that individuals are the expression of their intellectual abilities and any deficit can be understood as primarily the individual's responsibility. Literacy can be reinforced as a disability, deficiency or remedial issue and is commonly aligned with special education. The underlying purpose of literacy development is that without these 'basics', the opportunity to acquire qualifications and employment is restricted (Street, 1984).

The ideological model assumes that literacy practices are embedded in various social activities (Street, 2003). The model is 'ideological' in that it offers a more culturally sensitive view of literacy practices as they vary from one context to another (Street, 2003, p. 78). By viewing literacy as an ideological and social practice, not simply a technical and neutral skill, these discourses foreground that literacy will be embedded in socially constructed principles. From this perspective, there is a strong focus on the social context in which literacy practices occur and how this affects the character of the literacy being developed and the ideas about literacy held by individuals. In contrast to the autonomous model that represents a skills-based focus for individual learners, Street (1984) argues the ideological model allows access to more holistic outcomes related to empowerment and capacity-building for individuals and communities. This accessibility includes multiple learner-centred literacies involving a diverse range of skills and understandings, including a shift away from print-based literacies to technology and computer literacies, and a focus on 'soft skills' (Street, 2003).

The many voices that advocate for the ideological model of literacy in policy do unsettle discourses of human capital in the neoliberal apparatus. Still, as Jackson and Slade (2008, p. 27) argue, the principal analyses of adult literacy now originate from employer groups, business councils, and other labour market and economic think tanks, and have significant influence on national governments. Attention is concentrated on economic growth and increased productivity as 'formal learning is privileged over informal learning' (Hamilton, 2012, p. 171). Education is positioned within national productivity agendas, dominated by industry interests, often at the expense of the needs of individuals who are treated as an investment rather than as social and cultural beings (Rizvi & Lingard, 2010). In the domains of skills focussed knowledge – and the discourses that support this knowledge – these interests become accepted as standard and are difficult to challenge (Gorur, 2014). Black et al. (2013, pp. 605–611), for example, argue that the governments, industry, workforce skills agencies and the media, speak with an unchallenged 'common sense' using the 'one voice on foundation skills'. Black and Yasukawa (2014) express concern that there has been no empirical investigation into the relationship between human capital and foundation skills, despite its widespread acceptance and influence in government policy and funding.

At the same time, research from Coulombe et al. (2004), Barton (2006) and Hartley and Horne (2006) maintain that both models can be complementary. Despite social capital not featuring in government thinking in earlier policy discourse, much has happened in the intervening years to change this (Balatti et al., 2006). There is a view that economic and workforce outcomes through education and training opportunities and investment can positively support and impact social capital outcomes for individuals and various target groups participating in foundation skills training. Tett and Maclachlan (2007) add that a focus on enhancing an individual's social capital can promote access to employment opportunities, enhance people's workplace efficiency, and bring wider benefits for the individual in the community. Other authors, such as Walker (2009), are more sceptical, suggesting that the inclusion of social capital in policy is more of a form of tokenism. They claim that policy and discourse from government and advisory bodies (such as the OECD) are usually framed in socially inclusive ways, but 'scratching beneath the surface of declarations of balance and equal concern for both the economy as well as society reveals a continued bias in favour of education for employment, productivity and wealth' (Walker, 2009, p. 348).

5.2 *The Moral Regulation of Individuals and Human Rights Approaches*

Regimes of 'truth' operate by representing the inherent qualities of the individual as something to be realised through a range of interventions that emerge primarily from the moral propositions embedded in governing practices (Harris, 2001; Hunt, 1999; King, 2009; Rubin, 2015; Saunders, 2013). Moral propositions or moral regulations focus on the social actions that attempt to influence an individual's conduct. Moral regulation provides instances of the relationship between the 'governance of others' and the 'governance of the self' (Hunt, 1999, p. 2). An important feature of this argument is that moral regulation can be generated from various social positions. Moralisation involves what Foucault (1982, p. 210) has called 'dividing practices'. An example is a division between what have been identified as 'deserving' and 'undeserving' population groups. Such a distinction can have two immediate consequences (Hunt, 1999). First, it moralises the categories by delineating between good and bad. Second, it operates as a legitimisation for the differential treatment of the divided categories. The deserving poor, in this sense, are granted relief, welfare and funding for training. All of which can be denied to the 'undeserving' poor who fail to meet their 'obligations'.

Despite this positioning of morality and the welfare state, governments have faced ongoing criticism that the primary moral obligation of government should be related to the importance of lessening human need and suffering. As Saunders (2013, p. 1) explains:

> the overriding priority… is to care for the vulnerable. If that is expensive and necessitates higher taxes on everybody else, so be it; if a few people at the margins claim benefits when they should be working, then that's a price worth paying for a decent, inclusive welfare system that looks after all its citizens.

This argument rests on a rights-based approach to accessing welfare support to alleviate such things as hunger, homelessness and poor health and well-being. It also contests notions that welfare is 'a state of mind as much as it is an economic plight' (Murray, 1986, p. 25) and advocates for a focus on structural causes of welfare dependency and the creation of sustainable and accessible opportunities in housing, health and employment as opposed to individual solutions (Buckmaster, 2009).

A rights-based framework submits that for the exercise of all human rights, then the human right of acquisition of literacy and accessibility to education is 'foundational' (UNESCO, 2006). Rights-based advocate Katarina Tomasevski (2003, p. 33) argues that: 'education should prepare learners for parenthood and political participation, it should enhance social cohesion and, more than anything, it should teach the young that all human beings – themselves included – have rights'. The framework rejects the association of education and literacy with moral obligations. Under a moral obligation, education must have some intrinsic value, provide human capital gains, or be 'seen simply as a good thing to be pursued if and when there are some funds available' (Robeyns, 2006, p. 75). A rights-based framework should understand education and literacy as the basis for everything that enters into shaping contemporary life and prioritise actions that fundamentally expand people's capabilities (Robeyns, 2006). For UNESCO (2006, p. 154), the wide-reaching purpose and value of literacy include the:

> whole range of people's functions, whether as citizens, as producers, as private householders in their families, villages or home neighbourhoods, or as individuals seeking answers to the questions they ask themselves about the physical, social, moral and intellectual world in which they live.

Our later discussions will demonstrate how these rights are inherently individualistic in the neoliberal foundation skills apparatus. The apparatus promotes the essential role of the individual as the transformative agent in society. In this sense, as neoliberal subjects, individuals are compelled to make choices throughout their lives and have greater freedom to construct their individual identity, including developing and protecting their 'human rights' (Allais & Wedekind, 2020; Robeyns, 2006).

5.3 *Dividing Practices and the Various Subjectifications of the Foundation Skills Learner*

The lines of subjectification of the foundation skills apparatus can be imagined in a diverse set of contexts. These contexts – economic, political, educational, welfare, academic, advocacy – produce discourses of foundation skills.

As these discourses are (re)interpreted and (re)imagined in the apparatus, a particular form of personhood, the 'foundation skills learner', is produced. The apparatus focusses on creating an active and lifelong learner, willing to engage with what the foundation skills market offers. Neoliberal discourses of individualisation and responsibilisation shape subjects to see themselves as responsible for developing foundation skills for a desirable future. The apparatus exerts a powerful shaping force through processes of subjectification, which offer recognition and inclusion for those who are able and willing to conform, and threats of exclusion and marginalisation of subjects who fail, or are unable to comply. In this context, these subjectivities include:

- Migrant as 'Australians'; and,
- Human capital subjectivities: Individuals as customers and consumers.

Migrants as 'Australians': the subjectification of migrants as 'Australians' has been a principal objective and debate as the foundation skills apparatus has emerged and consolidated. The earlier policy agendas of the *National Policy on Languages* in 1987 took a 'pluralism' approach to language (Moore, 2002, p. 123). The policy valued language learners as critical to Australia, with bi- and multi-lingual populations imagined as 'adding language to an existing linguistic repertoire' by learning English (lo Bianco, 1987b, p. 85). The achievement of 'stable bilingualism', rather than the perception that English should replace an existing language, was framed by the policy as potentially rewarding for Australia, both economically and culturally (lo Bianco, 1987b).

Notwithstanding the *National Policy on Languages*' claim that the pluralism of English and 'world languages' should be regarded as an asset to the economy, the *Australian Language and Literacy Policy* in 1991 took a principal focus on promoting 'Australian English' (Dawkins, 1991, p. 1). The prime objective of the *Australian Language and Literacy Policy* was that 'all Australians should develop and maintain effective literacy in English' to enable them to participate in Australian society (DEET, 1991, p. XIII). The policy argued that apart from the general need to improve literacy in various contexts, the people who do not have the functional foundation skills expected for everyday life in Australia constituted the group with the greatest need. This shift in thinking then imagined migrant populations and native English speakers as a single homogenised group, 'Australian' job seekers (Moore, 2002).

In response to rising unemployment, funds for foundation skills programs combined with job readiness training increased dramatically, and migrants were recognised as having the same learning needs as literacy learners. Once separated in classrooms, language and literacy cohorts were brought together with the aim that programs with a broader scope could accommodate multiple population groups (Moore, 2002). While Coates (1996) maintains that this approach ensured policy and programs were non-discriminatory and that no population would be overlooked, Moore (2002) argues that administrative and bureaucratic reasons were more apparent. One notable interview in her study revealed:

> The department would say 'If you've got English language and literacy difficulties, which is not the same as being non-English speaking background, we will address that need'. But they didn't want to differentiate against people's backgrounds or their learning needs. They were running such a massive system in labour market programs, they couldn't get down to that level of refinement. (Moore, 2002, p. 125)

As the foundation skills apparatus emerged, several migrant focussed initiatives were introduced or reconfigured. These include the continuation of the *AMEP* and dedicated tuition streams for migrants in the *LLNP*. However, these initiatives were not based on any perceived pedagogical advantages to migrant learners. Instead, they were based on longstanding concerns from governments, including Australian and other OECD governments, that migrants were not building 'new social links', were resisting 'social cohesion', and were not integrating into communities (Sarian, 2018, p. 129). Framed as a source of 'unity', the Howard Coalition's position was underpinned by the notion that multiculturalism could only be tenable if underpinned by a common (British-derived) Australian ethos (Sarian, 2018, p. 126).

These forms of subjectification of migrants have continued in more recent times. The program objectives of the *AMEP* state that the program is designed to guide learners to participate in Australian life, and to provide the English language skills to become a 'job seeker' and an effective participant in the economy (Australian Government, 2017, 2019a, 2021c). Migrants, seen as resisting the acquisition of sufficient English language skills, are subjectified as rejecting the Australian way of life by remaining in their 'cultural bubbles' (Acharya, 2018; Belot, 2018; Collins, 2018). A study of public attitudes to unauthorised arrivals in Australia by McHugh-Dillon (2015) revealed other concerns. These include that asylum seekers pose a threat to the nation's national security, and that asylum seekers are a drain on Australia's economy and welfare system. Alla-Mensah et al. (2019, p. 173) write that the integration of migrants into labour markets is a key element of the political contestations of migration in many countries. The promises of migrant contributions to society are disturbed by thoughts of 'xenophobia' and migrants 'taking our jobs'.

Human capital subjectivities and individuals as customers and consumers: The subjectivities of the foundation skills learner as a job seeker are often associated with negative connotations of the term 'unemployment'. In these discourses, individuals that are 'capable' but not employed, are lazy, untrustworthy and lack motivation and work ethic (Boland, 2016; Krug et al., 2019). For learners who understand and are responsive to the moral obligation of receiving welfare, their modes of subjectification are more supportive. In this sense, they are likely to be imagined as lacking the human capital skills – are 'not capable' – to participate in the labour market. Their human capital and opportunities for sustainable employment can be improved by dedicating time and resources to education and training, with immediate benefit (Black & Yasukawa, 2013; Street, 1984).

This subjectivity is supported by the neoliberal discourses structuring the *Hilmer Report* and the *National Training Reform Agenda*. The neoliberal characteristics of the apparatus understand 'skills' as a commodity in the labour market (SCOTESE, 2012). As foundation skills are imagined as a commodity, individuals deemed to be lacking these skills are responsibilised by various agencies (or themselves) in the apparatus, to acquire them. The core feature of these strategies and mechanisms is to place the individual, as the customer/consumer subject, at the centre of the process. The 'success' of the system is contingent on the development of responsibilised individuals who are capable of making 'correct' choices to build their human capital.

Dividing Practice: Foucault's (1982) concept of 'dividing practices' suggests that these practices become components of how those who are targets of regulation become subjects. In other words, how people are constructed, both through the actions of others, and through their actions upon themselves. Subjects may attempt to refuse the subjectification imposed on them, creating the possibility of resistance and the formation of an alternate subjectivity. Subjects may accept their position within the constructed category and accept or exist with the status of having 'low' foundation skills. These subjects may face lives of insecurity, with limited foundation skills to participate effectively in increasingly technologically structured labour markets. They may also face an uncertain occupational identity, a lack of a sense of a career trajectory, and almost constant stress (Standing, 2011a).

These subjectification processes always include the potential for contestation and struggle, and can involve some form of self-understanding or reflexivity. This reflexivity may be mediated through the participation of others, such as foundation skills practitioners, welfare organisations, and advocates, as external experts, who construct, reinforce, or interpret dividing practices. Within the diverse relationships of organisations, agencies and groups in the foundation skills apparatus, it is envisaged that the individual who emerges from foundation skills education and training will be a 'learner' who takes it upon themselves to be an active citizen. At this point, the learner is regarded as an individual who has developed those capabilities that characterise the neoliberal subject as autonomous, choice-making, risk-aware, prudent, and enterprising (Kelly, 2013). The foundation skills apparatus is a powerful means by which this contested form of subjectification is made real in and through the entanglements between a very particular rendering of an urgent historical need, the strategic function of putting in place the practices, processes and actors that can meet this need, and the relationships between the diverse and often competing elements of the apparatus.

Notes

1 Refer to OECD (2000) for a description of the *International Adult Literacy Survey* levels.

2 Brooker (1999) details the early difficulties in the *LANT Program*. In the first year only 15 percent of the projected 12,000 places had been taken up and many of the 69 organisations that had been contracted to supply this service had received no referrals into the program. Brooker's (1999, p. 32) dialogue with education and welfare professionals indicated that for many young adults who have experienced failure within mainstream schooling, the offer of a 'return visit' to a similar environment had little appeal.

3 Australia's 'strategic-political' initiative mirrored comparable initiatives from the United States and the United Kingdom at a similar time. The then United States President Bill Clinton, in his January 1999 *State of the Nation* address, spoke of the need to increase federal support of adult literacy provision for people in the workforce. Additionally, a 1999 report commissioned by the British government on the literacy and numeracy needs of adults in England identified the high numbers of adults who were not functionally literate as one of the reasons for relatively low productivity in their economy (Castleton, 2001).

4 These measures were principally in response to an Australian Council of Education Research report in 1996 that a third of Year 9 students (14-year-olds) didn't have basic skills. The then Federal Schools Minister of Dr. David Kemp claimed that the figures indicated that education policy and practices over the twenty years had failed, and in some cases, there had been a decline in standards (Kemp, 1996). Brock (1997) strongly refuted the claims and the assessment method used to justify these claims.

5 See Foucault (1980a, p. 194).

6 The Council of Adult Education, later named the Centre of Adult Education was established under Victorian Government legislation in 1947 with a broad charter to provide adult education (Gribble, 1994).

7 This program is voluntary in the sense that there is no obligation for migrants to undertake English language training once they arrive in Australia. Migrants, registered as job seekers may be required to attend training as part of their mutual obligation requirements.

8 After the re-election of the Liberal-National Coalition in May 2019 the government moved the *AMEP* out of the Department of Education and Training and back into the Department of Home Affairs (the successor to the Immigration Department). The Scanlon Institute (2019) suggests that declining enrolment numbers and non-completion of allocated training hours was a possible reason, with the Department of Home Affairs best placed to implement actions for improvement.

9 See Australian Government (2022d) for the reporting status of SDG 4.

CHAPTER 4

Creating a Skills Market

The Marketisation and Commodification of Foundation Skills

1 Introduction

> If someone can figure out a way to make a profit by selling something that was not previously for sale, pretty soon it will be for sale. (Brennan & Jaworski, 2016, p. 7)

Brennan and Jaworski's (2016) observation is a powerful way of pointing to the scepticism, even cynicism, that many stakeholders feel towards government and the private sector when free-market principles begin to reshape social policy. Vigourous debates persist about the role and limits of markets, and what sorts of things and activities should be allowed to be commodified. Recent contributions to the global literature on adult and further education have expressed reservations concerning the transformation of adult education into a space energised and governed by market practices. In an editorial on the 'Marketization and Commodification of Adult Education', in a special issue of the *European Journal for Research on the Education and Learning of Adults*, Andreas Fejes and Henning Salling Olesen (2016) indicate that in the context of the emergence of markets for educational goods and services, and the commodification of 'adult learning', concerns have arisen that learners may experience disadvantage and access and equity obstacles. There are also recurring fears that learners are at risk of exploitation in neoliberal markets. While they acknowledge the different ways in which these processes of marketisation and commodification have emerged and developed in different economies and markets, they suggest that key logics of neoliberal forms of governance and principles of new public management have been influential in these processes. The papers in that special issue explore these challenges and concerns in a variety of contexts, including: the so-called 'Europeanisation of adult education policies in Slovenia, and how such processes foster marketization of adult education and commodifies valuable knowledge and desirable forms of neoliberal subjectivity' (Mikulec & Krašovec, 2016); a 'historical account of the history of steering and the role of market mechanisms in adult education in the Netherlands' (Hake, 2016); an analysis of 'meaning-making among school leaders in adult education in Sweden', that seeks to explore the ways

 | DOI:10.1163/9789004724464_005

in 'which marketization is operating' (Bjursell, 2016); and an account of 'the marketization and commodification of adult education within universities in the US' (Zacharakis & Holloway, 2016) which highlights significant differences between the US and European processes of marketisation and commodification (Fejes & Salling Olesen, 2016, pp. 148–149).

In acknowledging the scale and scope of the range of possible similarities and differences in the ways in which these processes of marketisation and commodification in adult and foundation skills education emerge and operate in different economies and markets, our aims in this chapter include identifying and analysing a number of key dimensions of the ways in which the foundation skills apparatus in Australia has come to be characterised by these processes. In the first instance, we will provide some background of the elements of the foundation skills apparatus that promote it as a marketplace. As financial buy-sell market exchanges become embedded in education, learners are defined by the 'funding' they can bring to Registered Training Organisations (RTOs) and their 'acquisition' of the valued economic commodities of skills and knowledge that can benefit the labour market. In providing an account of the context of the foundation skills market, we then describe the 'free market' commodification and marketisation reforms of the four key programs in the apparatus and how they promote neoliberal processes of individual choice, and quality and efficiency by consumer demand. We also detail how regimes of new public management (NPM), relying on risk management, contracts, legal regulation and audit, are used to protect competitive markets to ensure public trust and consumer confidence.

In the section that follows, we discuss a key 'event' of the commodification and marketisation reforms in the foundation skills apparatus, namely the reform of the Victorian training sector, the *Victorian Training Guarantee*, between 2008 and 2013. We illustrate how this event can be understood through Stephen Ball's (2004) concept of 'hidden privatisation' and how it changed a number of key strategic aims, elements and relationships in the apparatus. As various agencies tried to understand what happened through the misuse of government funds, and budget blowouts that characterised this event, several possibilities and consequences followed – intended or otherwise. Our discussions include the correction of the initial reforms that deployed NPM regimes, and the emergence of a new Commonwealth regulator promoting risk and reputation management. We also analyse the intense anti-privatisation media discourse revealing the dynamics between the key 'players' in the reform, and the cautious approach to the introduction of competitive processes into Commonwealth foundation skills programs as a result of the Victorian reform. In our Discussion, we make a wider contribution to more global discussions of these processes by considering how the concept of reflexive governance can be understood as a way of understanding the recurring reconfigurations in the apparatus, as neoliberal 'arts of government' emerge as 'continually failing' activities in which audit, review and reforms are intrinsic to its function.

2 Foundation Skills as a Commodity: Students, Funding, Knowledge and Skills

2.1 *Commodification of Skills*

Processes of marketisation connect back to the emergence of neoliberalism in the 1970s and 1980s, which sought to implement basic economic market principles in all areas of society. In education, neoliberal marketisation presumes a commodification of education and training provision so that education and training can be directly organised as a market exchange, and the coordination and funding can be related to the principles of supply and demand in the market economy (Fejes & Salling Olesen, 2016). Even the realms of primary and secondary education – despite legislation that ensures that all Australian schools (independent, Catholic or government) are not-for-profit entities and hold a non-commercial status – are subject to elements of commodification (Australian Bureau of Statistics, 2001). Accompanying this legislation is the social, cultural and economic expectation that the government is the principal education provider. For higher education, the situation and expectations are similar (Rome & Smith, 2012). University assets are publicly owned, and profits are reinvested into the institution itself. Outside of VET private providers, publicly run TAFE and community not-for-profit RTOs follow the same expectations and regulations.

Many education policies now treat institutions in all education sectors (primary, secondary and tertiary) as a business. There is an expectation that they will increasingly fend for, and fund themselves. While Commonwealth legislation regulates that no financial advantage can be gained in public education (Rome & Smith, 2012), neoliberal processes of financial accumulation are still central to education policy. The accumulation, in this sense, is about student numbers and the various forms of capital – economic, social and cultural – that can enable growth over time. Institutions compete against each other for students and the funding that follows them. Funding is essential for financial viability. The more students, the more opportunities can open up to recruit 'quality' students, seek grants and funding for educational projects, research and infrastructure developments, and the likelihood of retaining and recruiting quality staff (Rome & Smith, 2012).

In this sense, mechanisms of funding or finance, well established in the economic world, are normalised and extended to education. Finance becomes a significant element in the 'grid of intelligibility' (Foucault, 1979, p. 93) through which everything is framed and understood. Education decisions made in this grid make use of concepts from economics. Institutions implement finance mechanisms such as cost-benefit analyses to determine if an investment in programs or infrastructure will achieve intended objectives at the lowest costs. Profit margins are set to establish if the combinations of student funding and student fees outweigh the costs of programs and overheads (ACIL Allen Consulting, 2015b, 2015c; Community Colleges Australia, 2019; Essential Services Commission, 2011a, 2011b; State Government of Victoria, 2012). In this sense, Harvey (2005, p. 3), when considering the spread of financial mechanisms in interaction with digital technology, argues that 'to bring all human action into the domain of the market… requires technologies of information creation and capacities to accumulate, store, transfer, analyse, and use massive databases to guide decisions in the global marketplace'. The synergies produced at the intersection of finance technologies and digital technologies are a defining characteristic of the neoliberalisation of education systems, processes and practices. Databases, for example, generate performativity metrics in the form of learner participation and attainment, training and assessment, quality data timelines, and records management. Performativity refers, here, to a 'technology, a culture and a mode of regulation' (Ball, 2003, p. 216) that monitors institutions and student's performance in return for contracts and funding. In this sense, these metrics act as a governmental technology that energises and enables performativity.

The emergence of markets for migrants and job seekers – and foundation skills learners – reflects the contemporary commodification practices of neoliberalism. The market is based on consumer culture and how it is embedded in daily lives through an array of subtle processes and the ongoing need to search for new markets, new products and new sources of profit (Gottdiener, 2000). The commodification of education reconfigures learning as a 'use-value' in its contribution to the development of the student as a person, as a citizen, or at least as a depository and carrier of culturally valued knowledge. However, the 'use value' is often displaced by a preoccupation of activities that will increase the 'exchange value' in terms of the resources that flow, directly or indirectly, from this commodification (Willmott, 1995).

It is possible, as Köpsén (2022) suggests, to interpret a learner as an identity that is framed by the logics of supply and demand in a market. Where the overarching objective of education policy is to efficiently supply output, this reasoning requires a material or resource to be processed to produce this output.

In this form, learners may be imagined as input material that, through training, are transformed into products with exchange value. Education providers are imagined not only as the suppliers, but also the manufacturers of the output. The commodity to be supplied are 'skills' that can aid participants in the labour market. In contemporary usage, skills are a commodity that are at least as important as physical and financial capital and natural resources as a source of economic growth. Populations of skilled workers are a national economic asset and the basis of national competitive advantage (Peters & Humes, 2003). The benefits of foundation skills are expected to flow like money in markets energised by the logic of supply and demand. Learners with 'skills' are required to seamlessly flow from the education system (supply) to employers' enterprises (demand) without disruption or interference. To facilitate this flow, individuals are encouraged to continuously upgrade and broaden their skills through formal education, lifelong learning, and learning in the workplace and less formal surroundings (Peters & Humes, 2003).

When understanding the 'exchange' value of foundation skills, we start to consider how the commodification of education has converted this knowledge into a commodity, into an item of commercial use. By drawing on the studies of Miller (2010), there are two ways skill commodities can be exchanged. The first commodity – widely applied to higher education but also the skills space – is a 'credential' or certification of learning (Miller, 2010, p. 200). This certification, when purchased, promises to have value in the wider community, a way of gaining entry into a particular employment market, and that can be exchanged for a job with higher wages (Miller, 2010; Noor, 2017; Willmott, 1995). In this sense, a credential in foundation skills is important in several ways. For migrant learners, attaining a qualification can demonstrate a certain level of English proficiency for employment or a vocational study pathway. For early school leavers, completion of a competency-based literacy curriculum such as the *Certificate of General Education for Adults* can be used as a proxy to meet requirements to have year ten secondary school levels for various courses or traineeships. Foundation skills qualifications are also teamed with VET qualifications if individuals are identified as having low foundation skills prior to enrolling in their course. The completion of both qualifications is useful as a route to profitable employment in that learners have a credential in both technical and foundation skills (Australian Industry Group, 2016; Cunning, 2007).

The second commodity, the 'set of skills', has increasingly formed the basis of contemporary education policy (Miller, 2010, p. 202). Rather than a proxy for skills expressed through credentials, this commodity is argued to be real in an economic sense. It represents the learning of techniques that improve a learner's capacity to work or function in the economy and develop transferrable skills that can be applied in different industries. For example, the 'set of skills' commodity is well illustrated in the *National Foundation Skills Strategy for Adults* (*National Strategy*):

> Research also shows employability skills are critically important to people gaining employment and remaining employed. The link between numeracy, literacy and problem-solving skills and the central use of technology in contemporary communication means that foundation skills are increasingly important for effective participation in modern workplaces and contemporary life. (SCOTESE, 2012, p. 2)

The 'set of skills' is a marketable feature in most foundation skills programs. For example, the *Adult Migrant English Program* (*AMEP*) claims that 'learning English will help you to participate more fully in Australian life. You will learn new skills to help you work' (Department of Home Affairs, 2021, para. 2). Similarly, the *Skills for Education and Employment* (*SEE*) *Program* 'is a great way to gain the confidence and English language, literacy and numeracy skills needed to get the job you want or go on to further study' (Department of Education, Skills and Employment 2021a, para. 3). The link between VET and foundation skills is also an essential feature of the 'set of skills' commodity. Workplaces demand higher levels of foundation skills performance from their employees. This can include completing complex forms, making multiple calculations, learning technological applications, and taking greater responsibilities for production errors, which has placed a greater need for VET to meet the needs of learners with low foundation skills (Benseman, 2014; Harris & Short, 2014).

Skills and knowledge are imagined as 'the heart of the education and training system' with governments faced with the challenge of organising education and training systems to help meet the needs of the labour market (Shah, 2017, para. 1). The foundation skills apparatus consists of several programs that can be understood as constituting a 'training market'. This market draws on neoliberal processes of marketisation and commodification as key elements to its function. Yet, these neoliberal processes are bound by limits, regulations and controls, which Hake (2016) describes as an essential feature of a quasi-market. A quasi-market secures the benefits arising from the supposed efficiency of free markets while retaining the benefits of individual rights guaranteed by public responsibility and government oversight. It is these features that we investigate in the following two subsections.

2.2 *The Marketisation of the Foundation Skills Apparatus*

In Chapter Two, we traced a series of events and practices that formed a neoliberal template used to guide interventions in social and education policy. This template drew on the rationalities of neoliberal thinkers such as Hayek (1976), who claimed that where effective competition can be created, it is a better way of guiding individual efforts than any other. As a consequence of this move, competition can be understood as inherently good, the most efficient way to distribute government resources, and one of the principles on which society is organised. This thinking was the basis of Commonwealth discourse such as the *Hilmer National Competition Policy* (1993), the *Competitive Principles Agreement* adopted by the (1995), and the *National Training Reform Agenda* (1994), all of which emphasised that their market-driven approaches would produce a system responsive to customers and provide an efficient and high-quality service.

Contemporary educational policies in Australia are increasingly constituted by the opening up of education markets and allowing new providers to operate alongside traditional public institutions (Catlaks & Dekoning, 2009). With ongoing concerns about budgets and accountability within education in the mid-1990s, Australian governments accelerated tendencies to model education practices, processes and institutions on free market values, prioritising quality, efficiency, fiscal restraint, and customer satisfaction (Schwartzman, 2013). Schwartzman (2013) argues that amid strong opposition, these practices appealed to economists, taxpayers, public administrators and, in some contexts, educationists. As a financial strategy, free markets would curb the growing demands on state resources in education. As a political strategy, it would appeal to consumers by improving the responsiveness of public services and allowing the choice of provider. In this way, choice is facilitated by moves to diversify programs alongside introducing combinations of per-student funding and the devolution of management responsibilities and budgets to providers. As an educational strategy, competition would encourage new pedagogic alternatives to strengthen institutions for the future (Hamilton & Zufiaurre, 2014). One outcome sought by policymakers was the production of competition between providers. Competition, in principle, is expected to raise standards across the system by closing down poor providers or boosting the performance of these poor providers due to the logics of competitive choice (Ball & Youdell, 2008).

Ball and Youdell (2008) argue that this embrace of principles of competition, often framed as 'education reform', marks a significant trend towards privatisation. They define privatisation in two forms:

- privatisation *of* Public Education, otherwise known as 'exogenous' privatisation. Such privatisation involves opening up public education services to private sector participation on a for-profit basis and using the private sector to design, manage or deliver aspects of public education; and,
- privatisation *in* Public Education, otherwise known as 'endogenous' privatisation. Such forms of privatisation involve importing ideas, techniques, and practices from the private sector to make the public sector more like businesses and more business-like. Endogenous privatisation emerges as a consequence of reform (Ball & Youdell, 2008, pp. 9–10).

The exogenous and endogenous forms of privatisation are all functional processes in the foundation skills apparatus, each having a role in how policy and programs are imagined, organised and governed. At this point, we will focus on the exogenous form of privatisation. This includes practices and processes such as the 'mix' of public, private and non-profit RTOs in programs selected by competitive tendering. It also includes entitlement, or eligibility-based funding, which involves individuals meeting specific criteria and being deemed eligible for access to publicly funded programs that compel providers to compete for students (The Allen Consulting Group, 2011). Table 4 provides a summary of this investigation, and a brief account of each program.

Adult Migrant English Program (*AMEP*)*:* From 1997, the *AMEP* underwent several reforms promoting processes of marketisation. Reflecting recommendations from the *Hilmer Report*, the Commonwealth introduced competitive tendering principles to optimise learning outcomes, attract the highest quality service providers, allow client choice, and provide the Commonwealth value for money and greater flexibility to respond to changing conditions. The program was released to tender every three years (Martin, 1998). Until 2010, the program was delivered nationally through one consortium group, led by the publicly operated migrant education provider Adult Migrant English Service (AMES). As a precursor to a greater emphasis from the Commonwealth on the involvement of the private sector in adult education, the metropolitan New South Wales region contract for *AMEP* was awarded to a private RTO, Navitas, in 2011. Later tender application rounds in 2015 and 2018 included more private, TAFE and community-led consortiums awarded contracts, with AMES losing significant market share.

The role of competitive markets, alongside a greater emphasis of the program on employment outcomes, was introduced in 2017. Semi-competitive markets replaced the one-provider-per-service delivery area in regions where

TABLE 4 Forms of privatisation/marketisation in foundation skills programs

Program	Forms of marketisation/privatisation
Adult Migrant English Program (*AMEP*)	Competitive contract tendering per region – open to public, community and private RTOs. RTOs are restricted to using funding only in their contracted region. Semi-competitive markets *within* the program in regions of high demand. Limited competition with other Commonwealth, State and Territory programs
Skills for Education and Employment (*SEE*) *Program*	Competitive contract tendering per region – open to public, community and private RTOs. RTOs are restricted to using funding only in their contracted region. Enrolment and funding caps on RTOs. Semi-competitive markets *within* the program in regions of high demand. Competition with other Commonwealth, State and Territory programs.
State-based Funding (Victoria)	No competitive tendering. Annual application for funding contract with State government. Open competitive markets with no enrolment or funding caps. No regional restrictions. Competition with other Commonwealth, State and Territory programs
Adult Community Education (*ACE*) Funding	No competitive tendering. Annual application for funding contract. Enrolment and funding caps on providers. Regionally restricted. May experience competition from other neighbourhood houses/community providers in their region with ACE funding. Competition with other Commonwealth, State and Territory programs

SOURCE: ACIL ALLEN CONSULTING (2015B, PP. 6–16), ACIL ALLEN CONSULTING (2015C, PP. 6–18), STATE GOVERNMENT OF VICTORIA (2013A, PP. 13–25) AND STATE GOVERNMENT OF VICTORIA (2016, PP. 3–12)

demand for programs was high (Australian Government, 2017). This reform was based on a review from ACIL Allen Consulting (2015b, p. xv) warning that 'existing models were at risk of falling behind other government policies and programs in terms of improved efficiency, innovation and client outcomes'. For the first time in selected regions in NSW, *AMEP* providers were awarded contracts within the same delivery region and they would be required to compete for the market share of migrant learners. The removal of the 510-hour limit on free English tuition to uncapped hours to meet demands for higher levels of English proficiency increased the number of migrants seeking training in this program. While the *AMEP* experienced a competitive environment *within* its program environment, the uncapping of hours also disturbed the market share of the *SEE Program* and state-funded programs, which we will outline next.

Skills for Education and Employment (SEE Program): From its inception out of the *Language and Numeracy Training (LANT) Program*, and subsequent reform through the *Language Literacy and Numeracy Program (LLNP)*, contracts have been awarded to RTOs for the *SEE Program* by competitive tender, specific for each service delivery area in Australia. In 2015, the program moved away from a one-provider-per-region model to a multi-provider competition model in regions where providers, like the *AMEP*, would be required to actively market programs to job seekers and their referring agencies. The Commonwealth introduced this model, it claimed, to manage the doubling of program funding from three years prior, to create an environment of improved quality training, and to introduce a market that was more responsive to demand within geographic areas (Australian Government, 2013b).

A review from the Commonwealth in 2015 sought to strengthen the alignment of the *AMEP* with the *SEE Program*. Though never defined as a formal pathway, an additional 650 hours of funding available for migrants registered as job seekers could be available for individuals exiting from the *AMEP* (ACIL Allen Consulting, 2015a). Data provided to this review indicated students were not utilising this pathway between programs. Learners bypassed the *SEE Program* and remained with their *AMEP* training provider by accessing largely subsided funded training through State governments (ACIL Allen Consulting, 2015a). In other words, as many *AMEP* providers held both Commonwealth and State contracts, they could effectively retain students in their organisations. Despite the implementation of the review's recommendations, such as addressing the language proficiency gaps between the programs (the level of proficiency for the *SEE Program* classes were often set too high for exiting *AMEP* clients), and promoting the advantages of both programs to referral agencies, the outcomes of the alignment post-review were unclear. The Commonwealth was unable to report on how many learners shifted between programs, stating only that it was a 'fair proportion', and that many women were still unable to access the *SEE Program* as, unlike the *AMEP*, it did not provide childcare (Scanlon Institute, 2019, p. 5). The program also experienced $37 million of funding cuts in the three years to 2019–2020, which the Scanlon Institute (2019) argued excluded many refugees from accessing classes.

The *SEE Program*'s alignment with the *AMEP*, and overall viability, has continued to be disturbed by the 'opening up' of the *AMEP* to all migrants by removing the 510-hour training cap. In a similar way to the informal measures between the *AMEP* and State funding, migrant learners could effectively complete their English tuition within the *AMEP* and not utilise the *SEE Program*'s offerings. With *AMEP* including a focus on employability skills, its delivery could also supersede the *SEE Program*'s job-seeking benefits. As two-thirds of the *SEE Program*'s participants comprise migrants and refugees – the remaining are native-born English speakers and Indigenous Australians – these changes impact a significant slice of their cohort (Scanlon Institute, 2019).

State Government Funding (Victorian): As well as the reform to the national VET sectors in the late 1980s with the introduction of competency-based training, another significant reform involved the introduction of 'user choice' as an element of the marketisation of the sector. User choice was introduced into the apprenticeships and traineeships sector, largely drawing on recommendations by the *National Training Reform Agenda,* which allowed employers to choose any RTO to deliver the formal training component of the apprenticeship or traineeship (Australian National Training Authority, 1994). In progressing the concept of 'user choice', in 2008, the Victorian Labor Government released a 5-year reform called *Securing Jobs for Your Future* that introduced marketisation and competition practices into all programs and components of the sector. The reform, abbreviated to the *Victorian Training Guarantee*, was based on the objectives of the government to 'drive Victoria's growth as an innovative, productive and internationally competitive economy… as the national leader in skills development and most importantly secure the jobs that will deliver a strong future for all Victorians' (DIIRD, 2008, p. 1).

Before the *Victorian Training Guarantee*, the State Government set aside funding for registered training providers (RTOs) based on local training needs, student demographics, infrastructure and operating costs, and historical operating performances (DIIRD, 2008). This approach provided a guaranteed market share of funding for public providers, such as the TAFE colleges and community providers, and reduced funding to other providers, such as private providers (Ball, 2005). The *Victorian Training Guarantee* removed the fixed allocation of hours and regional restrictions and invited private and non-profit providers – after meeting requirements through Commonwealth, State or Territory training regulatory bodies – to enter the market in direct competition with TAFE and community providers. The principal basis of the reform was for RTOs to market programs to students who had the freedom to choose their RTO and access a government-subsidised course provided they met eligibility criteria (Karmel, 2011). DIIRD (2008, p. 23) claimed that:

> For the first time, providers will be able to deliver government subsidised training in response to demand rather than by fixed allocation. More providers will be able to customise training products to the needs of individuals and businesses and offer specialisations that reflect their own expertise.

In this context, funding flows with each student, with payments given to RTOs for each unit from completed qualifications. To fully utilise the available per-student funding, RTOs were encouraged to ensure students remained studying in their course and fully complete their qualification.

Foundation skills were identified as an important component of the reform. Under a key objective of 'better outcomes' for individuals, employers, and the wider Victorian community, the reform indicated that 'school leavers and adults without solid foundation skills in literacy, numeracy and language skills will be able to acquire them. This will greatly improve their employment and further education opportunities' (DIIRD, 2008, p. 23). Unlike the requirements of VET qualifications, in which students must enrol at a qualification *higher* than the one they hold to be eligible for subsidised funding, the enrolment into foundation skills programs was unrestricted. Individuals enrolling in qualification levels such as Diploma or Advanced Diploma qualifications could potentially access foundation skills funding. As well as being a state-funded alternative to Commonwealth foundation skills programs, the open eligibility for any learner was a point of difference from the *AMEP* and *SEE Program*s. *AMEP* and *SEE Program* held proficiency levels for enrolment, with students deemed to have 'functional English' unable to access funding for classes (ACIL Allen Consulting, 2015b, 2015c). Up until changes in 2013, state government funding included no limitations on enrolling in a foundation skills course (State Government of Victoria, 2013b).

Adult Community Education Programs (Non-accredited Programs): This funding continues to be accessed by providers with a fixed allocation each year. This allocation is determined by local training needs, student demographics and historical operating performances (State Government of Victoria, 2013a). While there are situations of competition between neighbourhood houses (a region or council area may have several providers that service local communities), processes of marketisation are not built into the funding structures. However, a neighbourhood house that is an RTO may also access state government funding alongside their non-accredited funding, which places them in a competitive market. They may also market their non-accredited programs against competency-based qualifications by highlighting that their programs do not involve assessments, are less formal than larger TAFE provider offerings, and have connections to local services such as childcare and welfare (Gribble, 1994; State Government of Victoria, 2013a).

While the competitive logic between Commonwealth and State programs in the apparatus might exemplify the 'untidy' nature of the competitive markets (Ball, 2004, p. 13), Pincus (2010, para. 4) identifies this sort of arrangement as 'vertical competition'. He claims that vertical competition is unique to federal systems such as Australia, and comprises competition between the Commonwealth and the governments of the states and territories. Vertical competition recognises that a changing mix of uniformity and diversity is possible between levels of government. It can leverage off consumer markets, as consumers provoke businesses to differentiate their products and tailor products to what consumers want and are willing to access. At the same time, academics, politicians and political commentators criticise duplication, 'buck passing' and the 'blame game' when more than one government is responsible for a role or function (Hollander, 2010; Pincus, 2010, para. 5).

In Australia, there are several examples of a problematic relationship between the Commonwealth, State and Territories in the histories of adult education and foundation skills policy. Lindgard et al. (1995) suggest that national leadership has found it difficult to obtain full collaboration and support of State and Territories. National collaboration has variable meanings for both levels of government. Despite the dependence on 'transfer funding' (funds which are diverted from the Commonwealth to the States and Territories for compulsory education sectors), Moore (2002, p. 118) observes that State and Territories 'jealously assert their constitutional authority over all non-university education'. In the development of the *Australian Language Literacy Policy* in 1991, simply holding the State and Territories to the actual process that allowed policies and projects to be described as national and cooperative was deemed 'collaborative' (Moore, 2002). The *Australian Language Literacy Policy* and the *National Training Reform Agenda* in 1994 produced policy descriptors that provided an 'aura' of 'widespread acceptance' (Moore, 2002, p. 120). Yet, the collaborative processes between the Commonwealth and States and Territories were conflictual and vulnerable to destabilisation (Lindgard et al., 1995). 'Collaboration' can be 'used by the Commonwealth in an attempt to incorporate the States into its own agenda', and 'by the States to resist this process and assert their primacy in determining school policy' (Lindgard et al., 1995, p. 48).

Often the possibilities and consequences that arise from competitive arrangements, like vertical competition, are influenced or corrected by new public management (NPM) regimes that defend market dynamics and regard any failures as 'waste and inefficiency in resource use', and/or the result of 'inadequate mechanisms of accountability' that have not ensured the quality, efficiency and effectiveness of public policies (Promberger & Rauskala, 2003, p. 1). Indeed, NPM regimes have become crucial to protecting the commodification and marketisation functions in the foundation skills apparatus.

2.3 *New Public Management and the Australian Skills Quality Authority (ASQA)*

Contrary to the early political economists who argued that competition is a natural phenomenon that justifies a 'hands-off' approach from government, competition in the neoliberal apparatus is imagined as 'fragile' (Foucault, 2008). As a consequence of this fragility, competition requires nurturing and monitoring. For Davies (2014a), the normalisation of competition frames social relations in terms of winners and losers. Participants may not seek to act in an altruistic or moral fashion, so practices and processes are needed to protect consumers from exploitation while maintaining conditions favourable to competition.

During the last four decades, the public sector in many countries has been reshaped by reforms under discourses of new public management (NPM). Discourses of NPM have disrupted the 'Weberian' model of public administration in which a centralised bureaucracy of apolitical agencies, hierarchically organised and governed by formal procedures, managed the demands for government services (Hekman, 1983; Hood, 1990). As a new paradigm of public administration, NPM emerged to address the claimed 'failures' and 'inadequacies' of public sector performance by reorganising public sector bureaucracy to bring their management approaches closer to business methods (Dunleavy & Hood, 1994). NPM signalled a shift from the guidance of policies to concentrate on the administration and regulation of these policies. The studies from Promberger and Rauskala (2003), Ranson (2003) and Stewart and Stoker (1995) illustrate the distinctive dimensions of NPM. A summary of their studies is detailed in Table 5.

TABLE 5 Key features of public-sector management practices

Practice	Features
The valuing of the customer	Rationalisation of services focussing on customer demand, charging arrangements and marketing of services.
Competitive tendering	Compulsory competitive tendering arrangements generated 'contracting out' or 'outsourcing' of services.
Contract culture	Adopting the contract culture to ensure the efficient delivery of services with the growth of contractual arrangements.
Strengthening legal regulation	Contracts regulate adherence to clear accountabilities, ensuring they are answerable for the service levels delivered, the set resource targets and the outcomes achieved.
Service level agreements	Service level agreements are written into contracts to ensure that services will be delivered in a business-like way through indicators, standards, capability statements and benchmarks.
Strengthening the audit-state partnership	Audit services contracted out to implement accountability regimes.

SOURCE: PROMBERGER AND RAUSKALA (2003, PP. 5–19), RANSON (2003, PP. 463–476) AND STEWART AND STOKER (1995, P. 3)

In broad terms, NPM is the product of specific social, organisational and managerial processes that are recognised and described in terms of 'risk' (Power et al., 2009). Such processes signal a potential/possible harm, danger, vulnerability or opportunity that is transformed into a risk when it is articulated as a social fact, in turn, to be managed and made into the responsibility of an organisation (Hilgartner, 1992).

NPM processes have been important in reshaping governance and regulation regimes in the foundation skills apparatus. Since 2011, VET compliance has been regulated by a national body, the Australian Skills and Quality Authority (ASQA), under the *National Vocational Education and Training Regulator Act 2011*. Before establishing ASQA, registration and audit activities for VET providers were undertaken by eight state and territory registering bodies. ASQA was set up by the Council of Australian Governments' recommendation to maximise efficiency, facilitate greater consistency of regulation, and ensure better responses to emerging quality issues in the sector (Braithwaite, 2018). ASQA has assumed the regulatory responsibility of most training and assessment in Australia from state-based regulators by evaluating the accreditation of RTOs (Productivity Commission, 2017). Foundation skills programs are funded through the particular Commonwealth, State or Territory department responsible for them. To be eligible for contract status with the specific government department, the RTO must have accreditation under ASQA. While there is an interconnectivity between ASQA and government departments in this sense, the compliance regimes of each government body and department are autonomous. For example, an RTO will be accountable against standards from ASQA for accreditation and the separate – albeit similar – standards from their specific government department. This distinction is important to note as it underscores that RTOs are often accountable to more than one regulator in the apparatus.

Under the *National Vocational Education and Training Regulator Act 2011*, NPM processes underpin ASQA's function. ASQA's responsibility includes overseeing RTOs in the market, assessing new RTOs, monitoring operations in terms of training and assessment quality and relevance to industry, ensuring an RTO's ethical marketing to students, provision of appropriate facilities, and compliance with staffing qualifications requirements (Braithwaite, 2018). ASQA deploys risk-based regulation by collecting and analysing data and intelligence on various risk factors that determine where RTOs may fail to deliver the quality of training and education that the community expects. The risk factors fall into three general categories:

- performance-related risk factors – including complaints and non-compliance against contract guidelines;
- governance – stability of management, length of registration and revenue; and,
- the profile of the RTO – including training in multiple regions (Australian Government, 2015b).

ASQA takes a dual-focused risk management approach (Braithwaite, 2018). The first focus for ASQA is the provider risk associated with RTOs who exhibit characteristics that arouse suspicion in their operations. This focus includes the range of courses offered, staffing levels, changing enrolment numbers, low completions, a history of non-compliance, and complaints. These characteristics are triggers that could lead ASQA to look more closely at the operations of a particular provider. The second focus is systemic risk, which relates to problems occurring among groups of providers, particularly when market competition is keenly felt. For example, this can include cheaper, shorter, online courses that tend to create markets where low quality providers can undercut high-quality providers.

The emergence of ASQA as the Commonwealth VET regulator in 2011 coincided with the third year of the *Victorian Training Guarantee* reform, which, at that time, was experiencing a multitude of negative media reports and student complaints about the quality of funded training. Despite one year remaining in the reform, the Victorian Government commissioned the Essential Services Commission (2011a, 2011b) to conduct a review that revealed an extensive lack of regulatory oversight in the program's operations. The consequences of these findings resulted in a series of interventions implemented by ASQA that not only resonated within the Victorian system, but also with other Commonwealth, State and Territory programs, as they all attempted to make sense of how the fully contestable Victorian market collapsed as it did.

3 Hidden Privatisation: The Victorian Training Guarantee

Ball and Youdell (2008) label various forms of marketisation in the education sector as 'hidden privatisation'. These forms are often camouflaged by market reform vocabulary of 'choice', 'accountability', 'performance management', 'devolution', 'contestability' or 'effectiveness'. Privatisation can be hidden, either as a consequence of educational reform, or as a means of pursuing such reform. Ball and Youdell (2008) add that even where privatisation involves the direct use of private companies to deliver education services, this process is often not publicly well understood. In addition, opponents of privatisation and competition may claim that this confusion is just a game of semantics. As van Leeuwen (cited in Ball & Youdell, 2008, p. 3) implores:

> We need to get the trend towards privatization out into the light of day. We need greater transparency, we need to get a better understanding of what is happening, so that we can engage in an open public debate about the future of education in our societies.

While Ball and Youdell's interpretation may assume that this form of hidden privatisation is an intentional or planned education reform on behalf of governments, the example of the *Victorian Training Guarantee* as 'hidden privatisation' was not as calculated in the way they suggest. Our analysis of the *Victorian Training Guarantee* investigates the chaotic response to a marketisation policy that changed a number of key strategic aims and relationships in the apparatus, as various governments and agencies attempted to rationalise such a radical reform. Following Foucault (1980c, p. 146), we reveal 'the accidents, the minute deviations… the complete reversals… the errors, the false appraisals, and the faulty calculations' which continued to protect and double-down on, not evaluate, the marketisation policies in the VET sector despite the widespread reports of funding misuse.

3.1 *Rorting, Budget Blowouts and the Essential Services Commission Review*

The Victorian funding system was thrust into the spotlight as a consequence of the explosive growth of funding for VET courses between 2008 and 2012. This growth followed the uncapping of government-funded enrolments leading to concerns of budget blowouts. The number of private providers increased from 200 to 430 in three years (State Government of Victoria, 2012). Many entities recognised the business opportunities to establish themselves as RTOs and access markets of potential students who would be eligible for subsidised training. This included a market of migrants and job seekers under mutual obligation requirements. TAFE and other public and not-for-profit providers that had historically received a fixed allocation of funds from the Victorian Government, began to experience a fully competitive market for the first time. RTOs began to aggressively market and incentivise students with low or no-cost and low-time programs. With the advantage of low overheads compared to larger RTOs such as TAFE institutions, smaller RTOs enrolled high volumes of students to achieve high completion rates.

Accusations that the integrity of training and assessment was at risk due to funding misuse and rorting arose throughout the reform. One observation characterised the *Victorian Training Guarantee* as 'open slather' resulting in:

> a budget blow-out, a misallocation of funding to low priority training and millions of dollars of profit from the public purse to private providers, as well as debasing qualifications. Not to mention a public system which is now destabilised with big gaps likely in provision and stranded public assets. (Wheelahan, 2012, para. 18)

In response, the Victorian Government commissioned a review in 2011. Consultations by the Essential Services Commission (2011b) revealed the frustration and anxieties of public and community providers in this unfamiliar competitive environment. There was an underlying belief from many that the VET system was at risk from private providers. This included accusations that low-cost, low-time programs from private providers were not providing quality outcomes, and that many RTOs were deploying inappropriate marketing strategies and engaging in the fraudulent enrolment of students (Essential Services Commission, 2011a, 2011b). Examples included: qualifications – that were obtained in days – being issued to students who had no demonstrable skills; providers claiming taxpayer funds for non-existent training; enrolled students being paid to undertake training; learners enrolled in multiple programs simultaneously to boost payments for training; and students offered gifts such as iPads to enrol (Department of Education and Training, 2015; Tomazin, 2015; Wheelahan, 2012).

The reviews also received repeated stakeholder criticisms about administration and compliance. Many RTOs were concerned that regulatory burden, red tape and student administration were excessive. One observation from an RTO argued that 'we're auditing at the wrong end. We're not auditing at the outcome' (State Government of Victoria, 2012, p. 5). Other criticisms identified that administrative costs associated with the new student funding model were having a negative impact. It was suggested that compliance requirements directly influenced RTO's ability to deliver a quality course and meet their student cohort's needs flexibly and efficiently. While there were calls that compliance requirements should be rationalised to reduce the administrative burden on providers, there was a consistent acknowledgement that additional scrutiny and transparency would assist in regulating training quality (Essential Services Commission, 2011b).

Many submissions strongly pushed an anti-competition and anti-privatisation discourse in the Essential Services Commission review. Some expressed observations that increased competition between providers was not delivering benefits associated with quality and efficiency. However, others identified that regulation failures, rather than competitive practices, were responsible for the failing system. Some RTOs gave positive perspectives that the current funding model had delivered benefits to learners and communities as a whole. The Essential Services Commission (2011b, p. 31) highlighted that: 'several submissions indicated that competition has delivered a number of significant advantages to students, including increased opportunities for training and greater choice in terms of the quality, content and flexibility of the training offered'.

The Commission recommended the continuation of competitive markets while maintaining an appropriate level of government involvement where there was an inadequate provision of competition in course delivery, consumers and thin market providers (Essential Services Commission, 2011a). The Essential Service Commission review findings were largely incorporated into the next iteration of the Victorian funding model (State Government of Victoria, 2013b).

3.2 *The Baillieu Coalition Reform and the Anti-Privatisation Media Discourse*

The 2011 election of the conservative Baillieu Liberal-National Coalition Government in Victoria saw a quick and substantial response to the failings of the *Victorian Training Guarantee*. The Baillieu Coalition criticised their predecessors for providing 'endless subsidies' for low job outcome industries, leading Premier Ted Baillieu (cited in Arup, 2012, para. 3) to claim: 'what we have seen in vocational training in Victoria was a massive blow out without an effective response in terms of generating training for jobs'. Arguing that the budget blow out was also being exacerbated by the challenges of declining revenue and national and global uncertainty (Arup, 2012), the Baillieu Coalition introduced major changes to funding models, which largely impacted TAFE institutions. Framed as an investment in skills shortage training areas and making TAFE sustainable (Savage & Bell, 2012), the Baillieu Coalition placed TAFE funding on the same basis as funding to community and private providers and reduced funding subsidies for courses not deemed to be addressing a skills shortage. The then Victorian Higher Education Minister Peter Hall (cited in ABC Melbourne, 2012, para. 11) described the setting of training subsidies as a 'recognition of what job needs, employment outcomes in communities across Victoria are'. Premier Baillieu (cited in Savage & Bell, 2012, para. 9) claimed that 'over the next few years there will be a billion dollars more than Labor provided in vocational education'.

As other states and territory governments planned their own processes of skills reform, the evaluation of the Victorian process was observed closely. Commentary largely emerged from the media giving considerable voice to key education lobby groups accusing both the Baillieu Coalition and Commonwealth Governments of a privatisation plan of TAFE. The 'literally hundreds of media reports' (Wheelahan, 2012, para. 3) established the media as a crucial platform in arguing against a 'hidden privatisation' reform agenda. Wheelahan (2012, para. 1) remarked that:

> For years, those concerned with vocational education and training have worried about how to lift the public profile of TAFEs. But what has taken many years for some – without much success – the Baillieu government in Victoria has done in a matter of weeks.

Many reports were damning of the changes with accusations of a '$300 million hit to TAFEs' (Arup, 2012, para. 1). The Australian Education Union's Federal TAFE Secretary Pat Forward (2013, p. 6) strongly accused all levels of government of an anti-TAFE, pro-privatisation agenda:

> Recently, a VET 'insider' said: I don't think what happened in Victoria was an accident. To see it as an over-zealous, efficiency obsessed government looking for a savings in tight economic times is wrong. They knew what they were doing. They were turning TAFE Colleges into RTOs – just another provider on a level playing field. They were saying 'TAFE is a 40-year-old Labor experiment which hasn't worked and we're going to kill it'. He is, of course right. Anyone who thinks what happened in Victoria was an accident – first by a Labor and then by a Liberal government is wrong. Governments have been intent on privatising TAFE for twenty years.

And:

> TAFE was always about working class education, and it was always about opportunity for those who were marginalized or dispossessed. TAFE was about lifelong learning, not lifelong toil, or lifelong debt... slowly, over the last twenty years, in a calculated way, and not without the active resistance of teachers in the sector, governments have moved to dismantle public vocational education – TAFE. (Forward, 2013, pp. 5–6)

This media interest could be attributed to a number of factors. At one level we can identify a form of 'media hegemony' (Mueller, 1973) which highlights the tendency of media to shape the conduct of political debate. This not only involves informing public opinion but also strategically shaping the political strategies pursued by key policy stakeholders (Deacon & Golding, 1994). At another level, we can see the media choosing to report issues favourable to the status quo (Golding, 1981). Or a traditional media claim that they are autonomous from the state and marketing forces and serve to defend the public good (Chaney, 1981). Setting aside the reasons for determining the media interest in this reform, the consequences of the media narratives were also felt by TAFE's two largest competitors, the private and community training sectors.

The counter-narrative to what has been argued as a TAFE-centric view of VET can be likened to Foucault's (2004, p. 7) concept of 'subjugated knowledges', those blocks of knowledges 'present in the functional and systematic ensembles, but which were masked'. Locating a counter-narrative to the media-driven anti-privatisation discourse in the apparatus requires an investigation outside of common media channels. Claims similar to the Australian Education Union (2019, para. 8) that 'privatising vocational education has failed. Public TAFEs need to be the centre of our vocational education system... only public TAFEs can be trusted to deliver educated and skilled graduates that employers need for the future' were publicly criticised by private training and community education stakeholder groups. These groups argued that the media discourse was TAFE-centric and did not reflect the actual state of affairs in the VET system.

The then Australian Council for Private Education and Training (2013, p. 7), a peak body that represented private and independent providers in the higher education and VET sectors, claimed: 'some twenty years ago it was fair to say that TAFE was VET and VET was TAFE. Indeed, a surprising number of academics and commentators seem to hold the same view even after two decades of growth and change in VET'. The Australian Council for Private Education and Training (2013, p. 7) described that media discourse around the role of TAFE as 'emotive' and 'has done little to serve the system it seeks to protect' by obscuring facts and ignoring 'the real successes and challenges of VET in this period of reform'. The peak body pointed to the TAFE media discourse that strongly promoted the failings of private-sector providers and downplayed TAFE's involvement in similar controversies. These include several 'legal, though dubious practices by public TAFEs' (Hall cited in Wheelahan, 2012), where these practices were justified in the media as a means for 'cash-strapped TAFEs in their desperation to maintain services and provide support to students' (Herbert cited in Preiss, 2013). There are two notable examples here. One was reports of some TAFE institutes putting staff and students through foundation skills programs so they could maximise government subsidies. This included some TAFEs enrolling teachers with postgraduate degrees and others enrolling every student, including those doing diplomas and advanced diplomas, in foundation skills courses (Preiss, 2013). The second was public inquiries held by the Victorian Independent Broad-based Anti-Corruption Commission (2017) into allegations of serious corruption involving South West Institute of TAFE and Bendigo Kangan Institute of a lack of oversight into $2.2 million of VET funding that was paid to a subcontractor in which the training did not take place. Arguing that TAFE endlessly expects to be funded to 'reconfigure themselves in a reactionary manner to meet the changing education and training environment', Australian Council for Private Education and Training (2013, p. 7) proposed that a 'nimble and flexible training market of private and public providers, meeting the needs of learner and industry', would benefit the nation.

The criticism of a largely TAFE-centric training discourse was also made by Community Colleges Australia (2019), the peak body representing and providing services to community-owned, not-for-profit education and RTOs. They claimed that:

> Despite the extensive political and media attention that is given to state and territory TAFE systems, in 2017 community education providers

> delivered training to more than one-half as many students as TAFE providers did... community education providers consistently reaches Australia's most vulnerable and disadvantaged learners, in almost all cases much more capably than other types of providers: TAFE and the private for-profit providers. (Community Colleges Australia, 2019, pp. 3–4)

Community Colleges Australia (2019, p. 19) went on to claim that: 'the community sector loves TAFE. However, it's almost always an unrequited love' due to TAFE's perception of a lack of integration between the two sectors. They were also sceptical of the negative, and possibly unintended, impacts of TAFE-centric policies such as 'free TAFE courses', which quarantined funding for TAFEs for training in skills shortage areas. This group claimed that 'if additional TAFE funding damages community providers, the whole training sector loses' (Community Colleges Australia, 2019, p. 19).

In closing, commentary from Lambert (2018) agreed that the Commonwealth, States and Territories faced difficulties in delivering national leadership on a shared vision for VET. She argued that policy is 'too TAFE-centric to capture the totality of the issues facing VET', and was inadequate 'to address wider issues such as VET quality, roles and funding responsibilities across governments and the capability of the sector to deliver the skills needed in the workforce' (Lambert, 2018, para. 5–6). Lambert (2018) concluded that current discussions between Commonwealth, State and Territory Governments remained problematic. She insisted that a collective effort to establish a collaborative workforce development strategy focused on the skills needed for the economy is long overdue. Braithwaite (2018), in her review of ASQA and the *National Vocational Education and Training Regulator Act 2011 Act*, added to the debate of the conflict between public, community and private sectors by observing that for many, the status of being a public or private provider was the main indicator of quality training provision. She argued that in some areas, the private sector was surpassing the quality of public provision, and that the VET sector should be open to the proposition of how profit seeking is managed – and how this impacts the undermining of quality – and not resist the presence of private providers in the sector.

3.3 *Responding to Open Market Policies: ASQA and Reputation Management*

Miller and Rose (2010, p. 275) maintain that when analysing the problematics of government, a key objective is no longer one of accounting for government in terms of the 'power of the State', but of ascertaining how and to what extent the state is articulated into government activities: 'what relations are established between political and other authorities; what funds, forces, persons, knowledge or legitimacy are utilised; and by means of what devices and techniques are these different tactics made operable'. As the Victorian VET sector became identified as a market characterised by poor quality and corruption, both Commonwealth, State and Territory governments began to question, not the efficacy of marketisation policies, but rather, the 'devices and techniques' deployed to protect and make markets 'operable'. The Victorian Government tightened its risk management approach in 2013 with stronger entry requirements for RTOs, and the creation of mechanisms to monitor levels of competition and trends in quality and price (State Government of Victoria, 2013b). The Commonwealth Labor Government of Prime Minister Julia Gillard produced a much stronger response, deploying the Australian Skills and Quality Authority (ASQA) to regulate RTOs under the *National Vocational Education and Training Regulatory Act 2011*. Here the 'tactics and devices' of training compliance, historically delivered as 'guidance', began to be profoundly felt in the forms of risks and threats of punitive action against breaches of legislation. As RTOs made sense of the severe criminal and monetary repercussions of legislation breaches, 'risk management' in the apparatus began to be imagined as forms of reputation and crisis management.

ASQA played a critical role in the next iteration of Victorian funding, known as the *Next Steps for Refocusing Vocational Training in Victoria – Supporting a Modern Workforce* (State Government of Victoria, 2013b). While not a stakeholder involved in the implementation and regulation of the funding contract – this was a Victorian Government responsibility – ASQA could regulate the Victorian training market and training registration of RTOs under the *National Vocational Education and Training Regulatory Act 2011*. ASQA oversaw RTOs that held registration in more than one state or territory – this usually included larger providers or RTOs based in other states – but operating in Victoria. Many RTOs were expelled or driven from the Victorian market (Braithwaite, 2018; State Government of Victoria, 2015, 2016). Braithwaite (2018, p. 9) describes ASQA's management of marketisation driven policies (not just the Victorian reform) as: 'few regulators in Australian history have cancelled registrations for such a large number of businesses in a relatively short period of time; yet few have faced such major challenges of profound importance to Australia's future'.

ASQA's regulatory power was based on the risk of significant breaches being subject to penalties under a legislative test. A legislative test involves the calculation of the monetary penalties for offences under legislation. A penalty unit is a set dollar amount that determines the amount to be paid as a fine. The value of the penalty unit is multiplied by the number of penalty units that are set for the offence (Australian Competition & Consumer Commission, 2021b).

ASQA could issue administrative, civil and criminal sanctions against providers delivering inadequate training (Braithwaite, 2018). Its risk management principles were based on the satisfaction that contracted RTO's implementation of management systems must establish public trust (Australian Government, 2012). In terms of a marketised system, where the promotion of individual choice is paramount, risk management includes protecting the consumer and establishing consumer confidence in the training sector.

According to Power et al. (2009, p. 307), consumer confidence and trust, together with reputation, are complex relational concepts that are qualities of social perceptions and 'perceptions of perceptions'. In this sense, perceptions may or may not be accurate. However, they are social facts that generate actions and reactions. A good reputation is seen as a significant intangible asset. There is an assumed relationship between having a good reputation and more robust performance for the business or, often, lower costs, or reducing other risks (Csiszar & Heidrich, 2006). Reputation, positioned as reputational risk, has been a by-product of expanding the reach and significance of risk management (Power et al., 2009). It requires reactive approaches to limit reputational damage to the community (Eccles et al., 2007). For higher education systems, reputational risk has been established in an organised manner with national and global evaluations and ranking systems (Power et al., 2009). Despite unsuccessful attempts to introduce similar techniques, such as star-ratings systems reflecting customer satisfaction, the VET sector has yet to replicate such a system.

With the unfamiliarity of legislative authority, including the significant media discourse regarding 'shonky' training, ASQA's risk management auditing began to be identified as something to be feared. For RTOs experiencing a non-compliant audit with ASQA, risk management emerged as reputation and crisis management. An investigation by the Federal Member for the seat of Bowman Andrew Laming (2019) highlighted how reputational risk, or more aptly, the fear of reputational damage, was used to regulate the VET sector. His investigation revealed reports of RTOs experiencing 'aggressive and adversarial' audit activity from ASQA, designed to 'damage and wipe out' some training colleges. Other complaints focused on ASQA using the Administrative Appeals Tribunal as a means of managing appeals of their regulatory decisions even over 'trivial matters'. The Administrative Appeals Tribunal was construed as being a vehicle for ASQA to extinguish appeals through barriers of legal costs and reputational damage and delay by 'deliberately engaging in legal tactics designed to damage the respondent rather than just arriving at some form of clarity'.[1] The 'cultivation of student complaints' to build a case against RTOs was also a concern. There were also accusations that ASQA was targeting private providers, with TAFE providers allowed leeway to 'shuffle things between units, close a module down and shift students across to something else' (Laming, 2019).

Other aspects of ASQA's regulatory regime also translated into further significant reputational damage to providers. Every month, ASQA publishes lists of RTOs and their corresponding regulatory decisions on their website and via email newsletters. This process was implemented by ASQA with the objective that:

> transparency as a principle of good governance is a mechanism for accountability. It is important that RTOs can view each other's accomplishments and learn from each other's failures for purposes of building a culture that values quality, shares good ideas and also tempers hubris. (Braithwaite, 2018, p. 62)

Yet many stakeholders and commentators condemned this process as a tactic of 'name and shame' (Sandhu, 2021; Tomazin, 2015; Travers et al., 2018, p. 48). Combined with infringements calculated through penalty rates and suspensions of registration, RTOs questioned accumulating considerable debt to engage external auditors to rectify problems, or legal services to appeal the decision through the Administrative Appeals Tribunal, or to discontinue their registration.

These considerations placed pressure on the Executive Officers and Board of Directors of RTOs to understand the law and risks associated with failing to act in accordance with their responsibilities. As well as being tasked with making key decisions for an RTO, directors were also required to declare that they were a 'fit and proper person' and that they have the 'characteristics and principles necessary to ensure the delivery of high-quality services and outcomes' (Braithwaite, 2018, p. 14). This included disclosures if they had been convicted of a criminal offence, had been declared bankrupt, or disqualified from managing corporations (Braithwaite, 2018). Disclosing information of this nature, and the heightened responsibility of managing an RTO under legislative authority, may have led many directors, particularly non-profit directors, to question the worth of sitting on a board. As many directors voluntarily sit on boards to contribute to causes they are passionate about, in these circumstances, their lack of familiarity and required knowledge of their obligations under the legislation could 'punish' their otherwise 'good deeds' (Kester & Miller, 2020, para. 2).

Returning to Miller and Rose's (2010) 'problematics of government', the extent of the tactics, devices and reach of the Commonwealth's regulatory arm into training activity has been substantial. This example of 'reputational' risk management encompasses a complex space of diverse issues that RTOs need to identify and negotiate. These issues are not uncommon in higher education sectors with formal mechanisms that evaluate, rank and generate reputational risk. Power et al. (2009) argue that the expansion in the reach and significance of risk and reputation management in the higher education sector has formalised specific processes, and promoted a generalised concern with responding to ranking systems and other reputation metrics such as student complaints.

Yet, for VET and foundation skills, reputation management has been more pervasive, leaving RTO s to comprehend the consequences of 'reputation' with limited formal structures and/or little assistance. For example, in the *Braithwaite Review*, there were strong criticisms of ASQA strictly maintaining a position as a regulator but not providing advice or recommendations on meeting compliance obligations (Braithwaite, 2018). The review recognised that the inability of RTO s to work with the regulator to acknowledge shortcomings and find solutions created a 'climate of fear, defensiveness and adversarialism' (Braithwaite, 2018, p. 78). These findings are not unusual in environments of reputation management, according to Power et al. (2009) and Drori (2006). Reputational risk 'inscribes a generalized sense of organisational vulnerability' (Power et al., 2009, p. 316), and without a central steering mechanism, organisations will struggle to define, elaborate, manage and coordinate their identities (Drori, 2006). In this context, the suggestion that RTO s 'respond well when authority treats them with respect and offers avenues for help' was considered a simple, yet powerful way that ASQA's regulatory processes could be reformed (Field, 2019; Laming, 2019; Sandhu, 2019; Travers et al., 2018).

3.4 *Impacts of the Victorian Reform on Commonwealth Programs and Migrant Education*

Wheelahan (2012, para. 17), in her commentary on the *Victorian Training Guarantee*, described the reform as a 'great template in how not to reform vocational training'. The initial reform, and subsequent 'corrections', were monitored closely by all Commonwealth, State and Territory stakeholders in the VET system. Perhaps, this was one reason for the Commonwealth to take a somewhat cautious and pragmatic approach to introduce marketisation processes into the *AMEP* and *SEE Programs* in 2015. Competition within Commonwealth foundation skills programs had existed through competitive tendering arrangements from 1998 and had caused some disturbance to the status quo of the public provision of the *AMEP*, with a private provider awarded a contract in the popular and lucrative metropolitan Sydney region in 2010. Yet in both programs, no other commodification and marketisation processes had been introduced following recommendations from the *Hilmer Report* or the practices from the *National Training Reform Agenda*.

As well as a wariness resulting from the Victorian reform, a number of researchers and consultants had examined the role and limits of markets and whether programs for migrant and other vulnerable populations should be allowed to be commodified. The Commonwealth's own commissioned research from The Allen Consulting Group (2011) identified that fully contestable, demand-driven markets could impede equitable access for vulnerable groups. Their research highlighted some concerns that could be present in a training market, including:

- learners with the most intensive and costly learning needs, and those in geographic areas where provision was not economic, would face reduced access as providers concentrated at the profitable end of the market;
- reduced prices from increased competition would compromise intensive learner support and limit provider's capacity to use resources to meet learner needs flexibly;
- learners with major learning needs and with significant and multiple disadvantages would not be in a position to make informed choices; and,
- the risk of loss of continuity of provision and expertise and local capacity if a provider loses a tender for a program (The Allen Consulting Group, 2011, p. VI).

Other scholars have also attached an 'amoral ethos' to what can be regarded as 'for profit education' (Brennan & Jaworski, 2015, p. 358), particularly in relation to concerns that vulnerable populations, like foundation skills learners, can be exploited (von Platz, 2017). For example, Schwartzman (2013, p. 1), in an analysis of processes of marketisation in the US, claims that modelling education along competitive, free market lines and treating education as a commercial transaction, 'frays the moral fabric of education and short changes students who are configured as consumers to please rather than characters to build'. In addition, the promises of commodification and marketisation are meaningful, but are 'ultimately incapable of delivering what they propose: transferable skills, at most, but not education' (Brancaleone & O'Brien, 2011, p. 501). This brings an 'educational dislocation', which signals the loss of the intrinsic worth of things and forecloses on the potential of education (Brancaleone & O'Brien, 2011, p. 515). The possibility of education can be disturbed by focusing on competition, not cooperation; on reduction, not creativity; and satisfying a customer, not on supportively challenging each other (Saunders & Blanco Ramirez, 2017a, 2017b). Yang (2006) adds that commodification reduces bonds of human relationships in the production of value and instead, structures these relationships within formal covenants and contracts.

Nevertheless, concerns about quality, efficiency, and meeting consumer demands of foundation skills programs in local communities drove the introduction of commodification and marketisation processes in the *AMEP* and *SEE Program*. Recommendations from the ACIL Allen Consulting (2015a, 2015b, 2015c) reviews emphasised that the one-provider-per-region model was at risk of falling behind other government policies and programs in relation to offering a greater provider choice to learners. Consultations indicated RTOs could not meet the demand in their contract region, leading to clients facing considerable delays in commencing training and, often, negatively impacting employment, English language, and settlement outcomes. Referral agencies to the *AMEP*, such as employment providers and Centrelink, reported that the limit of one-provider-per-region restricted their ability to provide meaningful feedback to enact change regarding the quality of teaching and course content. Without alternative local options, many learners travelled long distances to study with another RTO. Earlier research from Australian Council for Adult Literacy (2001) had identified the tendency of RTOs to 'recycle' migrant learners back into short term focus programs. The ACIL Allen Consulting (2015b, 2015c) reviews advocated that a diversity of providers and contextualised programs would promote renewed, sustained, and continuous skills development with a lifelong learning focus to empower and lead to the betterment of outcomes for learners.

The next round of competitive tendering in 2017 resulted in a significant change to the adult migrant education space. By acknowledging that the introduction of increased client choice should not in any way compromise the standards of service provision, the Commonwealth implemented a multi-provider model trial in an area of high training demand for the *AMEP*, and a continuation of this model in the *SEE Program*. For example, the large migrant areas of Southwest Sydney introduced two providers – private and TAFE – with learners given the opportunity to choose their provider for the first time in the *AMEP*. The frustrations – from private and community providers in particular – of the difficulty of entering the *AMEP* market, largely dominated by AMES and TAFE (ACIL Allen Consulting, 2015a, 2015b, 2015c; Social Compass, 2019), were seemingly addressed with the large, well known, migrant provider AMES, continuing to lose significant market share, this time in metropolitan Victoria, to TAFE-community consortiums.

The consequences of the 'opening up' of migrant education to marketisation processes were felt beyond the financial wins and losses for individual providers. Australia has a long and rich history of immigration from the European migration post-World War II, to humanitarian immigration from Asia, Africa and the Middle East in the 1990 and 2000s. Immigration is an emotive issue in Australia, with contentious, often heated debates related to illegal boat arrivals, offshore detention, localised movements promoting nationalism, underpayment of visa workers, expectations of English language proficiency, and cultural bubbles in the suburbs. These concerns have formed and sustained a durable, (informal) multicultural network of advocacy and charity groups, RTOs, settlement and welfare agencies, with long histories of supporting new arrivals to Australia. The network seeks to create a public profile that can effectively lobby governments to bring multiple benefits to migrants and refugees. This profile includes:

- opportunities to showcase work with vulnerable populations;
- leveraging to build funding partnerships and specific projects within the community;
- opportunities to engage in academic research; and,
- training and work collaborations with industry (Refugee Council of Australia, 2016, 2019).

Within these networks, there can be a sense of worry (for the well-being of clients) and status (of the work and advocacy undertaken) for agencies that support local migrant communities. The loss of training contracts for long-standing RTOs, the negotiating of partnerships with new RTOs, or navigating new relationships within an already crowded charitable and non-profit market was a confronting experience for many organisations. Understandably, organisations were reluctant to 'let go' of their relationships with vulnerable migrant populations in these circumstances. For instance, Balatti et al. (2009), in their study of social capital and partnerships, speak of the apprehension and mistrust when new service providers are contracted to deliver programs to local communities. They speculate that this unease could be the result of a lack of community input, or awareness, in the choice of a new provider. The Australia Council of TESOL Associations (2014, p. 21) labelled the *AMEP* competitive process as 'unthinkable' and called for foundation skills programs to reflect compulsory education and not be subject to competitive tendering unless sustained poor performance was identified. While this position could be regarded in one corner as a self-interested entitlement to government funding, from another perspective, Ross (1977, p. 1257) had claimed that it is a 'burden' that many advocacy and non-profit groups carry, as they often imagine themselves 'as the only or best hope' for vulnerable groups.

A review of the *AMEP*, commissioned by the Department of Education and Training, undertaken by Social Compass (2019), investigated the marketisation processes in the program. The review found a lack of stakeholder support to extend the multi-provider competitive model. Social Compass (2019), using a small comparative focus of student participation, progress and experiences data between a region with a multi-provider model and two regions with one provider, found no convincing evidence that competition was driving greater outcomes. The review noted submissions from community organisations that claimed the potential benefits of 'increased choice for students, including more convenient class locations, more convivial, community-based classes, and more diverse delivery options' (Social Compass, 2019, p. 91). The submissions also highlighted the benefits to the 'players', or referral agencies to the program, knowing 'that clients have a choice and can change if they are not happy' (Social Compass, 2019, p. 91). These claims were effectively silenced in the review. Social Compass (2019, p. 91) deemed this feedback 'hypothesising', and within their small comparative focus study, indicated that 'there is little evidence that this is occurring'.

Submissions to both the ACIL Allen Consulting (2015a, 2015b, 2015c) and Social Compass (2019) reviews called for an environment of collaboration between providers and between providers and the Commonwealth. On several occasions, the Australia Council of TESOL Associations (2014, 2019) advocated for a model of deliberate government intervention in regions in which one provider could be responsible for foundation skills funding and another responsible for the vocational pathways post-foundation skills training. This model resembled a study from The Allen Consulting Group (2011), which advocated for a method known as place-based funding that seeks to assist in better outcomes for vulnerable populations. With place-based funding, programs are designed and negotiated to meet the needs of communities in specific localities and may or may not involve a competitive tendering process. Learners would be allocated to one provider in that locality. This model promotes cooperation and collaboration between providers, as learners would then pathway to other providers post-training, and would, ideally, deliver more effective outcomes for learners than contestable arrangements.

Yet, no reviews articulated a clear picture of what collaboration would look like in a marketised setting where providers compete in the same region *and* for the same funding source. In this way, providers are delivering training in the same region but catering to different cohorts of learners that will, by design or intervention, organise themselves to access their preferred funding. While stating that providers 'would much prefer to collaborate', the Australia Council of TESOL Associations (2019. p. 78) argued that the pressures of financial viability would inevitably thwart any forms of collaboration in a competitive environment. The lack of conversation, detail, or clarity of cooperation could be attributed to what Ball and Youdell (2008) identify as the normalisation of competition across social, institutional and cultural fields. In environments of 'winners and losers', advocating against competition could jeopardise hard-earned market share or the potential to obtain an increased percentage of available funding. As commodification and marketisation become further normalised in education, Ball and Youdell (2008) argue that these processes are less likely to be questioned or disturbed.

Brennan and Jaworski (2016, p. 7) suggest that those who resist commodification and marketisation are more concerned with 'how it's being sold' than 'what is being sold'. They contend that if selling particular goods and services a certain way might be wrong, there is always a different time, place, and manner for selling those goods and services that would remove those objections. Our genealogical analysis somewhat reflects the 'different time, place, and manner' examples. The three competing public-community-private sectors all enunciate their own 'truth claims' to how the market should be operated, regulated and unsurprisingly, how it best supports their existence. This is perhaps related to what Ball (2004, p. 13) claims is the 'multi-faceted, untidy, often unpredictable and both creative and destructive' nature of education markets. As governments attempt to organise and respond to the negative consequences of open markets, such as corruption, poor quality training and exploitation of learners, they rely on the truth claims of the public-community-private sectors to formulate an appropriate response.

4 Discussion: Policy Change and Reflexive Governance

Mitchell Dean (1999, p. 18) highlights an important feature of the 'arts of neoliberal government' – its reflexivity – that has significant resonance beyond our detailed analysis of Australia's foundation skills apparatus. Reflexivity here describes how:

> On the one hand, we govern others and ourselves according to what we take to be true about who we are, what aspects of our existence should be worked upon, how, with what means, and to what ends. On the other hand, the ways in which we govern and conduct ourselves give rise to different ways of producing truth.

The different ways of producing truth, according to Foucault (cited in Gaventa & Pettit, 2011), emerge from and shape scientific discourse and institutions. Here, 'truth' is reinforced – and redefined – constantly through the education system, the media, and the flux of political and economic discourses and rationalities. In times of market failure, the reinforcement, redefinition and production of different 'truths' are profound.

Under certain conditions, the production and distribution of a commodity, such as foundation skills, through a competitive market in which stakeholders pursue their own self-interest, can result in an allocation of that commodity that is socially inefficient or inequitable (le Grand, 1991). In neoliberal arts of government, when the market fails to produce positive outcomes, the government will decide whether and how to intervene. Governments run the risk of interfering in the economy to fix and create more problems, a situation known as 'government failure' (Dolfsma, 2013).

Reflexive governance is a form of governance that seeks to protect markets from government failure. This mode of governance has emerged to be reflexive and respond to complex risks (Leonard, 2021; Leonard & Lidskog, 2021). Dean (1998, p. 27) describes reflexive governance as:

> the governmentalization of government… the shifting of the liberal problematic of security from the security of social and economic process to the security of governmental mechanisms. The hypothesis of 'reflexive government', however, does not imply the government has ceased to try to change society. Quite the contrary.

In the foundation skills apparatus, governmental mechanisms include the processes of audit, review and reform. Schwella (2014) claims that when effectively deployed, these processes can bring ethical governance based on democracy. Governments can benefit from many influences and inputs from informed public participation that contribute to the quality and legitimacy of government analysis and action. Some commentary, such as Major (2018), argues that democracy as a basis of government action can be stifled by the processes it promotes. Major (2018, para. 2) observes that as democracy operates on consent, 'it is slower to make decisions… Democracy must cajole. Must persuade. Must seek consensus'. He questions the effect on the citizens it seeks to assist. Indecisiveness and the inability to deliver promises and act in a crisis are some of the problems associated with reflexive governance.

Australia's VET sector has a long history of reflexive governance. The National Centre of Vocational Education Research (cited in Zoellner, 2011) calculated a total of 70 national reports since 1969, and 60 landmark state and territory reports from 1976 to 2011 on vocational education. More recently, Commonwealth, State and Territory governments have invested considerable resources into collecting stakeholder data through regular program reviews of foundation skills programs. Over the last decade, the *AMEP*, the *SEE Program*, and the Victorian training system have, as we have outlined, been subject to multiple reviews. Adding to these reviews, three studies have been conducted into the regulation of VET through the *National Vocational Education and Training Regulator Act 2011 Act* and the role of ASQA, and numerous discussion papers and briefings into the *National Strategy*.

Zoellner (2011, p. 1) challenges the conventional narrative that 'the contemporary history of VET in Australia is based upon a linear progression of externally imposed and sometimes conflicting changes and breakpoints that have kept the sector in constant turmoil'. He argues that despite the multitude of reports and reviews over 40 years, there has been consistency and continuity of themes such as higher skills, responsiveness to individual needs, flexibility, national consistency and increased access and articulation across sectors. Zoellner's argument can apply to the *Victorian Training Guarantee* as well. Despite a significant failure of the Victorian training market, there was no serious unsettling of the neoliberal rationality underpinning the reform. The reviews of the *AMEP*, *SEE Program* and the *Victorian Training Guarantee* all continued to promote and protect processes of commodification and marketisation, centered on skills agendas and individual choice. Any questioning of the processes was attributed, not to the efficacy of marketisation, but to the deficiencies in regulation to protect these processes.

Despite its best intentions, Leonard (2021) and Leonard and Lidskog (2021) claim that reflexive governance finds difficulty in managing the plethora of potential contestations and negotiating the legitimacy of claims. It also risks ignoring or fragmenting divergent views. There can also be an unclear distinction between what reflexive governance is, and what it enables and hinders. Leonard (2021) and Leonard and Lidskog (2021) add that if neoliberalism influences reflexive governance approaches, then governance may potentially safeguard or protect neoliberalism. In a similar vein, Zoellner (2011) discusses the reflexive governance of the Australian VET system, suggesting that the limits of neoliberalism restrict the framing of problems in specific ways amenable to the relatively limited range of government responses. Through this lens, governments can only conceive issues in particular ways, prepare and implement programs under tightly controlled conditions, and monitor the outcomes that validate neoliberal rationalities. We will return to discussions on reflexive governance, which is a significant theme of our work in our final chapter where we explore the reflexivity of the apparatus in relation to how the 'elements' might respond to events such as the COVID-19 pandemic and its aftermath, future OECD survey results, and the conclusion and evaluation of the *National Strategy*.

Note

1 The Administrative Appeals Tribunal is the body that considers appeals against ASQA's regulatory decisions from RTOs. The appeals are not dealt with by ASQA themselves. To have an appeal heard by the Administrative Appeals Tribunal requires legal representation and a substantial wait time. Providers that have their registration suspended or severely modified by ASQA, can apply to have a 'stay' put in place, to continue training until their appeal is heard, however these applications are also subject to substantial wait times. See Laming (2019) and Braithwaite (2018).

CHAPTER 5

The Choice-making Learner as a Customer

The Individualisation and Responsibilisation of Foundation Skills

1 Introduction

The *National Policy on Languages* in 1987 generated collective responsibility for foundation skills programs by creating incentives for Commonwealth, State and Territories governments, education providers, lobbyists, and industry leaders to think and act in collective terms. By establishing efforts to coordinate foundation skills priorities and resources, all stakeholders could envisage the benefits to the nation and its citizens, such as external economic and political needs, labour market productivity, workforce participation, community awareness, preparation for technological changes, and the reduction of social inequities through skills use and learning. But as Australia's neoliberal foundation skills apparatus emerged with a greater emphasis on competitive market principles, a range of social, cultural, and political practices and policies contributed to the dominance of discourses of individualised responsibility and self-governance. Here, individuals, as foundation skills learners, were positioned as self-directing and autonomous, irrespective of context, and tasked with carrying the burden of developing their 'human capital' so that they could hope for more secure participation in the increasingly precarious labour markets of a globalising, neoliberal capitalism.

In this chapter, we continue to examine how the power relations in the apparatus allow for different ways of thinking about the foundation skills learner, and what possibilities and consequences emerge from imagining subjects in these ways. In the first section, we analyse components of the *National Foundation Skills Strategy for Adults* (*National Strategy*). The *National Strategy* is a key example of how processes of individualisation and responsibilisation have manifested into foundation skills. We will detail how the strategies are grounded, in quite fundamental ways, in practices designed to work on the psychological choice mechanisms of individuals through processes of moral self-evaluations. The aim here is to responsibilise foundation skills learners to recognise the benefits of, and take up opportunities to, increase their foundation skills.

In the second section, we explore three problematisations that have emerged as governments promote, and contracted service providers interpret,

 DOI:10.1163/9789004724464_006

the processes of individualisation and responsibilisation at a program level. As the flow-on effects of these processes, both intended and otherwise, impact the foundation skills learner, we analyse the possibilities, opportunities and challenges that confront learners when they are tasked with the responsibility to make choices and manage their own risks. These new responsibilities highlight the incongruity of learners with low-level foundation skills having to comprehend complex information to facilitate choice; the governmental technologies that hinder, not promote, individual choice in the apparatus; and the marginalisation of populations in discourses that promote 'outcomes' not the 'process' of foundation skills development.

Finally, we consider how processes of individualisation and responsibilisation can 'pervade contemporary social, political and moral life' (Halse et al., 2017, p. 1) of foundation skills learners. As we will suggest, these processes of individualisation and responsibilisation have emerged as key characteristics of neoliberal 'arts of government' in many of the neoliberal democracies of the high-income economies around the world, characteristics that signal:

> modern forms of self-government that require individuals to make choices about lifestyles, their bodies, their education, and their health at critical points in the life cycle, such as giving birth, starting school, going to university, taking a first job, getting married, and retiring. 'Choice' assumes a much wider role under neoliberalism: it is not simply 'consumer sovereignty' but, rather, a moralisation and responsibilisation, a regulated transfer of choice-making responsibility from the state to the individual in the social market. (Peters, 2017, p. 142)

In these processes, the complexities that many foundation skills learners face are reduced to an employment-focussed agenda that acknowledges, then subjugates, factors of disadvantage that impact how individuals might access learning opportunities. We argue that this form of subjugation is embedded into neoliberal policy and displaces responsibilities for broader systemic social problems to the family, community and government-contracted agencies.

2 The Emergence of Individualisation and Responsibilisation in Foundation Skills

The release of the OECD *Adult Literacy and Life Skills Survey* in 2006 detailed relatively similar results to the previous data series by revealing that 44 percent of Australia's working-age population, around 6 million people, did not possess the foundation skills to meet the complex demands of work and life in contemporary economies (Australian Bureau of Statistics, 2006). At the time of their release, these results were cited extensively in policy and position papers from foundation skills peak bodies and prominent industry bodies. Here, stronger 'human capital' perspectives of foundation skills emerged from employer groups, business councils and other labour market and economic think tanks (Jackson & Slade, 2008). There were several prominent publications, including the Industry Skills Council's (2011) position paper titled: *No More Excuses*, and the Australian Industry Group's (2010) *National Workforce Literacy Project: Report on Employer Views on Workplace Literacy and Numeracy Skills*, which claimed that foundation skills shortfalls had emerged as a major issue for employers as they evaluated their skills base against opportunities presented by the improving economy. The Productivity Commission estimated that, together with improvements in early childhood education and higher education attainment, increases in literacy and numeracy could increase total labour productivity by 1.2 percent (cited in Gillard, 2010). Also, industry groups stressed positive returns on investment for employers who implemented workplace foundation skills training for their workforce (Australian Industry Group, 2010; Industry Skills Councils, 2011).

The *National Strategy* was the first policy response to foundation skills for over two decades and advanced the 'human capital' discussions of the importance to Australia's economy and productivity of enhancing foundation skills. In the Foreword to the *Australian Core Skills Framework*, Julia Gillard (cited in Industry Skills Councils, 2011, p. 3), who was the then Minister for Education, Employment and Workplace Relations, argued that:

> We are living in a time of skill shortages arising from demographic and technological change and the proportion of jobs requiring vocational education and training qualifications is expected to significantly increase in the future, yet the capacity of many individuals to re-skill and up-skill is constrained by poor language, literacy and numeracy.

Neoliberal processes of commodifying and marketising the training sector were well established within program operations before the *National Strategy's* release in 2012. However, the strategy was novel in that it aligned and enhanced these processes with emerging practices of individualisation and responsibilisation strongly influenced by policy directions from the re-regulation of key dimensions of the 'liberal' welfare state, such as health and vocational education.

2.1 *The National Strategy: A Policy Characterised by Individualisation and Responsibilisation*

The release of the *National Strategy* signified a shift away from government as being responsible for the implementation of foundation skills policy, to making the individual foundation skills learner, and the community and organisations that influence them, more accountable for the choices they should make (SCOTESE, 2012). The strategy was premised on adult learners' needs being placed at the centre of all policy actions. The strategy's components were designed around four key priority areas to enable adult learners to access and benefit from foundation skills development opportunities. These objectives included increased information and community awareness, increased ability of learners to navigate and engage within a responsive market to meet their training needs, workplace literacy, and capacity building of the sector.

The *National Strategy* identified 'engagement' as the critical aspect of its priority action areas: 'four key priority areas for action focus on the conditions necessary for adult learners to successfully engage with foundation skills provision' (SCOTESE, 2012, p. 3). The strategy is contingent on the engagement of, and meeting the needs of, the adult learner. The assumption is that regardless of background and circumstance, learners will be motivated and confident to access opportunities if their needs are met. It advocates for the importance of developing foundation skills for individuals to improve their employment and social participation outcomes by designing tools and products to inform, guide and create opportunities while promoting personal choice.

By placing the learner at the centre of practice, the *National Strategy* reflects the dominant principle informing teaching and learning in adult literacy and numeracy courses (Balatti et al., 2006). The *National Strategy* progresses this principle further by shifting away from the idea of relative passivity of an individual 'treatment', towards the concept of a more active and autonomous individual who is engaged in the management of their self-care. The 'responsibilisation' processes are the point of differentiation from traditional adult education pedagogies. One key principle of adult learning is for learners to be supported to become self-directed and empowered to control, motivate, supervise and adjust their own learning. Here, adults also have the flexibility to learn from experience, even if they make mistakes (Foley, 1995; Knowles, 1973). Yet neoliberal discourses of responsibilisation can be less sympathetic to an individual's mistakes and poor choices. Brown (2005, p. 42) argues that:

> [people's] moral autonomy is measured by their capacity for self-care – the ability to provide for their own needs and service their own ambitions... the individual bears full responsibility for the consequences of his

> or her action no matter how severe the constraints are on this action – for example, through lack of skills [and] education.

For individuals with low foundation skills, adult education is often understood as the 'last chance' education to make the 'right' choices about developing their skills (Adult Literacy Information Office, 1999; Rogers, 2006; Street, 1984).

The *National Strategy* promotes the importance of individuals being responsible for their foundation skills. Individual responsibility is energised by representations of what broadly constitutes an individual with low foundation skills. Incorporated within these representations are several scenarios illustrating the effects of low foundation skills and the consequences of unmet responsibilities – to the person, the economy, and for health and family – if these skills are not addressed.

The representations rely on data from the OECD *Adult Literacy and Life Skills Survey* from 2006 to frame the benefits of foundation skills training for 'all Australians'. The *National Strategy* is selective in its use of the OECD data. It cites Australian population data that claims 'nearly half of adults in Australia do not have the foundation skills to work within complex contemporary economies' while insisting that it does not claim that adults have no skills at all (SCOTESE, 2012, p. 5). The *National Strategy* highlights data that indicates that the tasks required in work or personal environments are sometimes beyond the skill level of many Australian adults, but does not frame this as a cognitive issue for an individual. Instead, it points to the lack of clear information and community awareness of the benefits of increased foundation skills. For example, the strategy argues that individuals with low foundation skills are:

- unaware of the extent to which they could benefit from foundation skills development and participation in learning more broadly;
- unable to recognise the need to continue building skills due to the stigma and traditional notions that are often associated with having trouble with reading, writing or maths;
- unaware of their potential to benefit from some form of additional foundation skills learning;
- not good at assessing their foundation skill levels or recognising their skills gaps;
- require more support or development than others, many require alternative learning styles and some face highly individualised barriers to training and will not fit a one-size-fits-all approach; and,
- can be aware of the need to strengthen their foundation skills but are deterred by the difficulty of fitting learning activities into their day-to-day life (SCOTESE, 2012, p. 14).

The *National Strategy* seeks to emphasise that a lack of foundation skills is not 'blamed' on the individual, at the same time as it directs the responsibility for developing and curating foundation skills to the individual.

In this instance, the socio-economic demographics from the surveys that are understood to impact an individual's foundation skills, are absent from the representations in the *National Strategy*. Stressing that 'all' individuals can benefit from improved foundation skills, the *National Strategy* only minimally refers specifically to populations such as the unemployed, people with a disability, Indigenous Australians, young people, or migrants with an increased likelihood of having low foundation skills. It describes its target group under the general categorisation of 'adult learners' with 'different backgrounds'. For example:

> Adult learners come to foundation skills education and training with different needs, expectations and backgrounds and at different stages of life. Different learners also take on foundation skills development in different contexts and for different purposes. (SCOTESE, 2012, p. 14)

We discussed possible reasons for this kind of 'generalisation' of the foundation skills learners in Chapter Three. Coates (1996) suggested that having separate frameworks for people from different backgrounds would have been a discriminatory practice. Moore (2002) argues that this practice has more administrative and bureaucratic reasons, with massive welfare systems restricting the Commonwealth from that level of refinement. The *National Strategy* seeks to form an alternative representation of the foundation skills individual. For example, the first objective, increased information and community awareness, sets out to raise 'awareness and a collective commitment to action, particularly promoting benefits, removing stigmas of foundation skills, fostering positive attitudes about engagement and providing clear and easily accessible information' (SCOTESE, 2012, p. 13). Once provided with appropriate information and support, the individual can be positioned as a responsible choice maker and recast as a 'consumer' and a 'customer'. For example:

> A significant commitment of time and effort is needed to substantially develop foundation skills and adults have competing claims on their time and financial resources. Foundation skills programs will need to be innovative, highly effective and learner-centred in order to attract and retain new customers. (SCOTESE, 2012, p. 14)

Implicit in this example of a shift to a 'customer' model is that learners are imagined as consumers of services that promise to enhance their human capital. RTOs are recast as 'service providers', and made increasingly responsible for understanding 'what adults most want to learn and for what purpose and then design programs that are likely to be attractive and useful' (SCOTESE, 2012, p. 14). The arrangement is based on two assumptions. First, consumers are rational, have freedom of choice, and receive all the available information to make decisions. Second, RTOs will adapt and respond to consumer preferences. However, due to market constraints and political dynamics, individual choices will be impacted by resources, time and capacities. Choice may not always be realised or desired, and RTOs will only respond to personal preferences if they lead to the development and purchase of profitable products.

2.2 *Self and Moral Responsibilisation: The Nudging of the Individual to the Benefits of Foundation Skills*

Peters (2017, p. 142), as we indicated earlier, argues that 'choice' assumes a much more significant role for the individual in the neoliberal apparatus, and is not simply a matter of 'consumer sovereignty, but rather, a moralisation and responsibilisation, a regulated transfer of choice-making responsibility from the state to the individual in the social market'. The foundation skills apparatus seeks to (re)assemble the understanding and relationships that individuals have with/of themselves by conducting moral evaluations of their ongoing actions to mitigate harm and risk and maximise the benefit to themselves. Central to the understandings and relationships is the vision of the individual as *homo economicus,* the fundamentally self-interested 'entrepreneur' who continually strives towards self-maximisation and self-capitalisation in competitive markets and social arrangements (Foucault, 2008). Peeters (2013) suggests that humans behave less like a rational 'homo economicus' and are just as likely to follow group pressure, impulses, desires, and emotions. Embedded in Peeter's characterisation is the widespread mobilisation of a governmental technique called 'nudging' in neoliberal democracies. 'Nudging' is a governmental technique that aims to influence and incentivise people's behaviour to conform to politically defined norms by working upon the psychological mechanisms underlying the choices they make. These techniques 'nudge' people into behaving according to the public interest and government terms. Nudging aims to connect policy ambitions to presumed individual interests by organising the opportunity structure in such a way that people are seemingly spontaneously directed towards desirable behaviour (Thaler & Sunstein, 2008).

A prominent application of nudging occurs in the field of public health. Cognisant that motives such as money, pleasure, comfort and habits determine many of the lifestyle choices people make as much as objective knowledge, governments seek to nudge citizens to make healthy choices by:

- choice architecture – making healthy products more readily available;
- regulation – age limits to purchase alcohol and cigarettes, raising taxes, banning television commercials, smoking bans in buildings;
- communication – using social marketing techniques to promote the ease and benefits of healthy lifestyles; and,
- facilitation – increasing the number of sporting grounds, cycling lanes and walking paths (Peeters, 2013).

Using similar techniques, the *National Strategy* deploys nudging to promote the benefits of increasing foundation skills through education and training. Nudging occurs in the *National Strategy* in three ways. First, it constructs an alternative representation of an individual with low foundation skills by emphasising the opportunities individuals have to develop their foundation skills. The strategy argues that individuals with stronger foundation skills will experience enhanced economic benefits, which will contribute to the broader quality of life outcomes and that 'people with higher LLN skills are more likely to be employed, participate in their community, experience better health and engage in further training' (SCOTESE, 2012, p. 2). Additionally, the strategy claims that foundation skills are 'important for maximising employment opportunities, learning new skills, adapting to changing circumstances and requirements, and progressing or changing careers' (SCOTESE, 2012, p. 4).

The *National Strategy* also nudges individuals to conduct a moral evaluation of their actions by highlighting the importance of foundation skills to their family's health and wellbeing. It claims that 'people with strong foundation skills are more likely to maintain and enhance their own health and wellbeing and that of their family', and 'studies have also shown that within a family environment children's literacy improves as a result of increased adult participation in foundation skills building' (SCOTESE, 2012, p. 6). The strategy also highlights the link between low foundation skills and 'poor access to health services, poor health, higher risk of hospitalisation, higher rates of depression and an inability to understand and comply with the use of prescription drugs' (SCOTESE, 2012, p. 7).

A second technique of nudging within the *National Strategy* is the promotion of the 'entrepreneurial self' (Kelly, 2013). Though acknowledging that individual needs may not be employment-related and may relate to personal, family or community imperatives, the *National Strategy* delivers a strong and repeated message of the relationship between foundation skills and increased workforce participation and productivity. The strategy assumes a linear relationship between foundation skills and employment, in that increased foundation skills will seamlessly boost employment opportunities. Other examples are also deployed to nudge individuals to develop foundation skills, such as the self-maximisation of their position in labour markets:

> As modern workplaces become increasingly complex and supporting technologies evolve, there are rising expectations around acceptable levels of foundation skills. The need for individuals to continually build and adapt their foundation skills for new contexts, technologies and purposes means that these skills extend beyond the entry-level skills required to obtain employment and enter the workforce. Foundation skills exist across a continuum of levels and affect an individual's ability to progress through a career, change career paths, participate in education and training and engage with their community. (SCOTESE, 2012, p. 2)

Further:

> Strengthening the skills of those who are currently employed also has the potential to free up jobs at entry-level for those Australians who are unemployed and would like to work, or who would like to work more hours. At the same time, many unemployed individuals would increase their ability to participate in work or pursue further education and training if they developed stronger foundation skills. (SCOTESE, 2012, p. 6)

At this point, the *National Strategy* references data that individuals with higher foundation skills are likely to work in higher-skilled industries, with higher income streams, and are less likely to face downsizing or restructuring than workers in low-skilled occupations with lower proficiency (Australian Bureau of Statistics, 1996, 2006, 2013).

The third technique of nudging is what Peters (2017, p. 140) refers to as the removal of 'all collective value'. This occurs in ways that responsibilise 'individuals to take care of themselves through enhanced choice-making [where] the state forces responsibility and responsibilisation on the individual, families, and professionals'. The *National Strategy* appeals to the community and stakeholders to take a 'shared sense of responsibility' for foundation skills (SCOTESE, 2012, p. 14). The strategy terms this a 'call to action' and seeks to responsibilise an extensive list of actors, including families, LLN practitioners, RTOs, employers, unions, trusted intermediaries and active agents, to increase community awareness and break down the stigma of foundation skills that are a barrier to individuals improving their skills (SCOTESE, 2012, p. 25). It suggests that the community, including employment services and housing organisations, are the most capable stakeholders in connecting to 'hard-to-reach learners' (SCOTESE, 2012, p. 14), and those with 'highly individualised barriers to learning' (SCOTESE, 2012, p. 25) who may need extra assistance in understanding the benefits of foundation skills learning.

The *National Strategy* takes no account of social policy research that warns that the shifting of responsibility to communities and other non-state actors who lack public accountability, and the technical know-how, resources, authority or power to carry out responsibilities of the state is problematic (Garland, 1996; Ilcan & Basok, 2004). Indeed, the *National Strategy* suggests this process of responsibilisation is a crucial action to success:

> Everyone has a role to play in supporting potential learners, including putting potential learners in touch with adult foundation skills learning opportunities. A shared sense of responsibility will go a long way to assisting those who are seeking opportunities to develop their foundation skills. (SCOTESE, 2012, p. 14)

The *National Strategy* is a framework that has had a wide-reaching impact on the foundation skills apparatus during its development and release. The Standing Council on Tertiary Education Skills & Employment (SCOTESE) received many submissions from RTOs, industry organisations and peak foundation skills professional bodies recognising the need for policy intervention after two decades since the *Australian Language and Literacy Policy.* The findings of the strategy were varied. Positive feedback from industry (Australian Industry Group, 2011) was mixed with critiques from some academics and warnings that the targets and actions of the *National Strategy* would be in jeopardy without continued funding (Conway, 2016; Wignall, 2015; Yasukawa & Black, 2016).

A review by PhillipsKPA (2015) evaluated the *National Foundation Skills Strategy Project,* an initiative that supported priority action areas in the first three years of the *National Strategy.* The review concluded that the project successfully achieved its overall aim of supporting the strategy's priority areas. Despite this early evaluation of the ten-year strategy, it can be argued that the *National Strategy*, produced by the Gillard Labor government, was less prominent within Commonwealth discourse since the election of the Liberal-National Coalition Government in 2013. For example, the commitment to funding for the training of migrants and job seekers has continued (Andrews, 2017b). However, this is likely a result of historical investment into programs, irrespective of the objectives of the *National Strategy*. No other projects from the *National Strategy* were funded and implemented since 2015, until the Commonwealth commissioned an inquiry into foundation skills titled *Don't take it as read,* in 2022, followed by developing a draft of the *National Foundation Skills Framework* for 2022–2032.

3 The Impact of Individualisation and Responsibilisation at the Program Level

In this section, we progress our discussions on the emergence of processes of individualisation and responsibilisation in the apparatus by problematising the relations of power that allowed the idea, and the practice of the responsible and choice-making foundation skills learner to emerge. To do this, we describe and discuss three events that disturb the assumptions the neoliberal processes are based on and investigate the possibilities and consequences that occurred as these events took place.

3.1 *The Disruption of Choice: Complex Information and (Un)responsive Markets*

The *National Strategy* and the programs that operate within the foundation skills apparatus strongly suggest that RTOs should be responsive to the customer's needs and provide high-quality learning opportunities. The concept of 'choice' for the foundation skills learner has a somewhat conflicted history in the neoliberal transformation of education policy. Critics of processes of individualisation in adult education point to experiences of self-blame among learners if the outcomes of such choices are experienced as unfavourable. They also argue that the structural factors that impact lives are not the learner's direct responsibility, even though they are made to feel otherwise. Others argue that the individual has a right to choose. Individualism is strongly tied to the notion of self-directed learning. Self-directed learning is the idea that learning is facilitated rather than taught, and adults are free to develop relationships and direct their own learning while being challenged and extended, rather than being indulged by their teachers (Foley, 1995; Lee & Wickert, 1995). For the adult learner, this rationality can be extended to empowering choice in an open market as they take charge of their learning experience.

Logics of learner choice quickly emerged as an accepted process in foundation skills and VET, with most Commonwealth, State and Territory programs creating an entirely, or partly, open market. The *National Strategy* is a powerful example of the ways in which logics of 'choice' emerge as dominant forces in framing foundation skills markets. It promotes the need to develop 'awareness' as a critical element for individuals to engage with information that is easily accessible, up-to-date and relevant to personal circumstances and needs. Within a commodified and marketised training system, the *National Strategy* promotes an environment where individuals will access information and resources to inform their 'choice' of an RTO and training package. The RTO will respond in turn to their customer's needs with a suitable training product. Embedded in this information is the detailing of 'learning opportunities that are appropriate, engaging, relevant... and, most importantly, available when and where they are needed' (SCOTESE, 2012, p. 14). Yet, these critical aspects of these forms of choice, or the information that informs the ability to choose, have taken on additional dimensions when joined with new public management (NPM) processes in the apparatus.

In Chapter Four, we analysed the legislative changes to the national VET system. These changes were introduced due to the widespread fraud and rorting of state-based funding entitlements. One significant and repeated breach of training and assessment standards was the deliberate targeting and misleading of disadvantaged students through fraudulent or unfair marketing practices. As a result of legislative changes, new regulatory accountabilities included an increased focus on the provision of information to individuals seeking to undertake training (Braithwaite, 2018). To achieve this, the Australian Skills Quality Authority (ASQA) monitors RTOs to ensure that they have provided sufficient information to prospective learners to understand and to be in the position to make informed decisions about the training 'product' they are considering 'purchasing'. In summary, the provision of information to learners, set out in the *Users' Guide to the Standards for RTOs* 2015, includes:

- the training and assessment and related educational and support services the RTO will provide to the learner;
- the RTO's obligations to the learner, including that the RTO is responsible for the quality of the training and assessment in compliance with standards;
- the learner's rights, including details of the RTO's complaints and appeals process;
- the learner's obligations, including any requirements the RTO requires the learner to meet to enter and successfully complete their chosen training product; and,
- information on the implications for the learner of government training entitlements and subsidy arrangements concerning the delivery of the services (Australian Government, 2015b).

To ensure the integrity of training and verify many of the requirements, RTOs are obligated, under the standards, to collect enrolment information (contact details, date of birth, residential address, emergency details), proof of identity, and citizenship or visa categories from learners to ensure they have study entitlements in Australia and can confirm the authenticity of the enrolment.[1] For migrants and refugees, their visa status and eligibility to study in Australia, depending on specific classifications and requirements, are additional complexities to comprehend. All learners need to create a *Unique Student Identifier*. This lifetime personal education number provides an online record of VET training and is required for RTOs to issue qualifications or statements of attainment (Australian Government, 2022e). In addition, learners are required to sign an acknowledgement that the necessary information has been explained before proceeding with enrolment and payment of fees. Learners also need to acknowledge their understanding of the privacy obligations and rights of the RTO and ASQA in accessing and using their personal information (Australian Government, 2015b). As regulated by ASQA, information provision is further complexified if the learner is enrolling in government-subsided training. Learners will need to understand the information that underpins their eligibility and obligations to access this government subsidy. The learner will then need to sign and acknowledge that they understand this information. To complete the enrolment process, the learner will need to accept and agree to any specific requirements and obligations relating to their conduct in terms of health and safety, attendance, assessment and classroom expectations. Outside of the regulatory components of the enrolment, students also need to discuss their campus locations, timetable, study modes, technology, resources and equipment requirements.

These requirements can appear as profoundly incongruous as learners with low foundation skills must attempt to comprehend, and then acknowledge, their understanding of extensive and complex information. In signalling their understanding of this information, they are also faced with choosing a suitable qualification level, funding option and RTO. These issues were not explored within the *National Strategy*. They took on greater significance due to the problems relating to the Victorian system and the regulatory reform emerging after its development and release. The *National Strategy* would argue that the framework reinforces the role of family, trusted intermediaries, stakeholders and communities in supporting individuals to build their foundation skills by assisting with program eligibility requirements and information provision (SCOTESE, 2012).

The issue of information and choice was briefly explored in one foundation skills review. ACIL Allen Consulting (2015b), in their study of the implementation of competition and choice in the *AMEP* contract, claim that learners can only realise the benefits of choice if they are sufficiently informed about which providers are likely to be the most suitable for them. The review adds that given that *AMEP* learners, by definition, suffer from a language barrier, the ability of eligible migrants to make choices cannot be assumed. ACIL Allen Consulting (2015b, p. xv) suggests that it is likely that for at least some learners, the choice will be 'at best inconsequential, and at worst daunting', but also acknowledge that it is not necessary for all clients to be highly discerning for the benefits of choice to be realised. For some migrants:

> it is conceivable that notwithstanding the language barrier, some (possibly many) *AMEP* participants will be able to identify the types of courses that meet their needs, seek advice from others in their community who have previously had experiences with prospective providers, consult other relevant *AMEP* service providers on their options, and choose or change *AMEP* service providers as appropriate. (ACIL Allen Consulting, 2015b, p. xvi)

Even if only a tiny proportion of learners could identify positive traits and switch providers accordingly, ACIL Allen Consulting (2015b) claims that this is sufficient to deliver broader benefits and drive improvements across the system.

The Australia Council of TESOL Associations (2019) has vigorously opposed arguments that learners can make an informed choice, even without sufficient English language proficiency and knowledge. They point to the complexity of the training system as a barrier, and that the choice is usually made 'for them' by referring agencies such as humanitarian settlement services and employment providers (Australia Council of TESOL Associations, 2019, p. 78). They add that in the absence of interpreters, which many organisations have limited access to for their clients, migrants have 'no clue' as to why they are referred to a specific provider (Australia Council of TESOL Associations, 2019, p. 78). While the *National Strategy* advocates the role of trusted intermediaries to assist learners, this assumes that in the first instance, the learner has access to such a resource, and second, the intermediary has a sufficient understanding of the information themselves. Another consideration, according to a study from Biddle et al. (2019, p. 173), is the public concern that the Australian Government and commercial entities have suitable safeguards in place to be trusted with their data. The report found that trust tended to be lowest for those with low levels of education – we can correlate this with low-level foundation skills – and those who live in relatively disadvantaged areas. This mistrust can arise from past experiences and perceptions from others, which likely problematises the role of the trusted intermediaries in the

National Strategy even further. The current environment of regulation, which involves a high level of information provision and comprehension of eligibility rules and guidelines, could lead individuals – even with support – to disengage from participation, believing it to be too difficult, or to accept requirements without complete comprehension, expecting (or hoping) for no consequences of these actions.

The partial opening of Commonwealth programs as a competitive market and their 'competing' relationship with state-funded programs promotes the assumption that a learner has an unimpeded ability to 'choose'. Choice is subject to the responsiveness of the market to the learner's needs. In highly populated areas, the availability of training options, funding, and RTOs can promote processes of 'choice'. Individuals may have access to various learning opportunities that fit their needs, and RTOs can cater to the needs of large cohorts of learners. However, in 'thin' markets – markets in less populated areas that provide fewer training options – the ability to 'choose' is significantly impeded. Learners can often only broaden their choice by travelling outside their locality (ACIL Allen Consulting, 2015c; Essential Services Commission, 2011b). In thin markets associated with remote and regional areas, the fragmentation of delivery in which RTOs compete for a small cohort of learners, the duplication of infrastructure, and the loss of economies of scale can outweigh the benefits of competition. In this case, all providers struggle to remain financially viable and meet the needs of their learners, resulting in limited training options overall (ACIL Allen Consulting, 2015c).

A consistent theme from RTOs in the ACIL Allen Consulting and Essential Services Commission reviews has been the financial pressures associated with training. These pressures are still prevalent in highly populated areas with greater economies of scale. Customers can 'purchase' a training 'product' or 'service', but this purchase is determined by a critical mass of customers for this 'product-service' to be provided. In short, a foundation skills class must have viable numbers to run, if not, the class would likely be cancelled. A training product can be provided in many different modes – full-time, part-time, day, evening, and online – and at the level appropriate for the learner's skills. While the *National Strategy* claims that 'learners need learning opportunities appropriate, engaging, relevant to their needs and, most importantly, available when and where they are needed' (SCOTESE, 2012, p. 14), it does not engage with the financial constraints of choice. The financial constraints on RTOs – learner numbers, paying qualified staff, operation of facilities – all determine the running of a program. Here, the likelihood of a flexible, responsive market to individual choice can be unrealistic. Failing to acknowledge that these factors are a barrier for potential learners in the current training market (and for RTOs) simplifies and exaggerates the responsiveness of a market that still grapples with the complexities of competition.

3.2 *Problematising Choice and Agency with At-Risk Populations*

The foundation skills learner is situated in this neoliberal apparatus as a choice-making consumer responsible for making the 'right' choices in developing their 'human capital'. While these neoliberal systems expect individuals to manage their own risks and demonstrate self-care, concepts of individualism and autonomy are interwoven with social policies regulating individuals (Bondi, 2005). Peeters (2013) identifies this as the preventative paradigm of government. The regulation of individuals by interventions is not meant to correct behaviour, but to ensure that negative consequences of choices made, or not made, do not occur in the first place. Neoliberalism has centralised state power in ways that result in a more authoritarian approach preoccupied with 'security' and 'prevention', which places the responsibility for both on the individual (Liebenberg et al., 2013). This approach is preventative in nature to ensure individuals are not a burden on society and seeks to manufacture new forms of individual responsibility.

Embedded in this approach is the implementation of technologies that evaluate, manage and track citizens, particularly those who are 'at risk' or whose behaviour is 'risky'. This approach may imagine that there is a distinct divide between 'active citizens' (capable of managing their own risk) and 'targeted populations' (the 'disadvantaged', the 'at risk', the high risk) who require intervention in the management of risks (Dean, 1998, p. 35). However, the delineation between the two is more of a fluid, than strict divide. It positions agencies in the apparatus as 'calculators' of 'high risk' individuals through an array of educative, estimative and preventative functions (Dean, 1998, p. 35). The calculation of risk is intertwined with two different types of governmental technologies: 'one is invoked from below. The other… from above' (Dean, 1998, p. 35).

In a similar way to the 'nudging' of individuals to the benefits of foundation skills, the technology invoked from 'below' is what Cruikshank (1996) calls 'technologies of citizenship'. These are the techniques of self-esteem, empowerment and negotiation to engage individuals as active and free citizens, the consumers of services, and agents capable of identifying and managing risks. Yet, when certain individuals, groups and communities are 'calculated' as being at risk and become 'targeted', such as populations with low foundation skills that are disengaged from the labour market, sets of technologies are invoked from 'above'. These technologies, what Dean (1998) calls 'technologies of agency', are used to make active citizens capable as individuals and communities, and enable individuals to manage their own risks and purchase services that fit their needs.

Rose (1996, p. 60) has referred to this kind of monitoring as a form of 'ethical reconstruction', which involves training, counselling, community action, and empowerment, or punishment for those deemed unwilling or incapable of taking responsibility. Technologies of agency are entrenched in both the operations of education and training programs, and in processes of job seeking and mutual obligation. These technologies aim to shape the conduct of the foundation skills learner. First, when considering training programs, there is a concern that learners may not have had positive educational experiences in the past. For some, formal schooling is a disabling experience that reinforces an internalised belief that they are not capable of being a learner. As a result, learners can be anxious, reluctant, and often deemed at risk of disengaging from programs (MacLachlan & Cloonan, 2003). Here, the technology of agency, or as Dean (1998, p. 35) describes, the 'learning contracts of the schoolroom', monitor learners in order for them to develop as 'responsible' students. For both Commonwealth, State and Territory programs, these responsibilities vary. Commonwealth programs involve individuals meeting language and literacy proficiency targets to continue their funding, maintaining agreed attendance requirements, and demonstrating a capacity to benefit. Every 200 hours, a learner will need to demonstrate they have progressed higher in a core skill (learning, reading, writing, numeracy or oral communication) as outlined in a document named the *Australian Core Skills Framework* (Wyse, 2008). A 'capacity to benefit' is a requirement that allows RTOs to deny enrolment to a student, who may satisfy eligibility requirements to access funding, but may have personal circumstances that reduce the likelihood they will benefit from training. In state-funded programs, meeting curriculum standards, attendance, assessment requirements and demonstrating regular participation within each curriculum module are required. If these responsibilities are not met, a learner's enrolment can be withdrawn.

For learners under mutual obligation and job-seeking requirements, their responsibilities are monitored by an agreement known as a *Job Plan* (Australian Government, 2024b). The *Job Plan* subjects individuals to technologies of citizenship such as counselling, foundation skills, labour market and job search training, but also a range of 'obligations' such as fortnightly job application targets, mandatory training hours, and attendance at meetings. The plan is, in effect, a 'contract', in which the job seeker's obligations are underwritten with sanctions, such as the cutting-off of income support, if components of the contract are not met (Australian Government, 2019b; Dean, 1995; 1998). For Dean (1998, p. 36), this kind of agreement is an 'obligatory point through which individuals are required to agree to a range of normalising, therapeutic and training measures designed to empower them, enhance their self-esteem, optimize their skills, entrepreneurship and so on'. Or, as Mendes (2009, p. 105) argues, these measures are deployed to 'motivate.... reintegrate... with mainstream social values... such as self-reliance and... work ethic'.

As technologies of agency and citizenship are manifested in the foundation skills apparatus, the representation of the individual as a responsible choice-maker is blurred. The construction of 'choice' is confined within a limited set of possibilities allowed within an individual's *Job Plan*. If, as part of this agreement, job seeking is prioritised over foundation skills training by an employment agency, then, in effect, an individual's choice to develop their foundation skills is removed. In this situation, individuals who wish to continue to build their foundation skills are prevented from doing so, and must do so in their 'own' time with their 'own' resources, or they can participate with the understanding that their enrolment may be short-term if a reasonable offer of employment is received.

This disturbs the *National Strategy's* claim that programs should be relevant and 'most importantly, available when and where they are needed' (SCOTESE, 2012, p. 14). Several examples illustrate the impact of employment services and mutual obligation on choice. First, a review of the *Jobactive* program from The Senate Education and Employment References Committee (2019) revealed that individuals were assessed as 'job ready', even when they have barriers to employment, such as low literacy levels. As a result, intensive job search training is prioritised over foundation skills learning even if the likelihood of permanent employment is low. Second, ACIL Allen Consulting (2015c) highlighted examples of *Jobactive* agencies encouraging clients to take up opportunities often in low-skill, low-paying, and insecure employment, resulting in individuals exiting training programs with minimal notice before meaningful gains in foundation skills can be made. This situation can be likened to what Jacobson (2020, p. 4) describes as 'educational churn', a disruptive and disorienting process by which large numbers of people move in and out of the education system – particularly adult basic education – to what seems like no productive end. At the same time, the Scanlon Institute (2019) reported the frustrations of some RTOs unable to get some migrants to attend classes because they are too focused on finding a job. A lack of attendance or engagement in programs could be a result of migrants feeling pressure to gain immediate employment to support family or community members. Migrants may end up finding work in low-skilled jobs and have little opportunity to improve their English through, or outside of, work. Learners were also compelled to miss classes to attend appointments with their employment agency or Centrelink

(Scanlon Institute, 2019). As strongly expressed by one agency in a Commonwealth review into the settlement of refugees:

> there needs to be some way of getting rid of the nonsense where people are penalised for not attending their Centrelink interview because of their English class… [and that] there is a lack of coordination between agencies. (Joint Standing Committee on Migration, 2017, p. 53)

Third, refugees undertake initial assessments with a minimum of four providers – settlement providers, AMEP, employment agency and Centrelink. This represents significant duplication of resources and, according to Shergold et al. (2019, p. 40), 'sends refugees round in circles'. All examples highlight how conflicted the concept and practice of learner choice becomes when mutual obligation and contractual program requirements shape learner choices.

Many of these examples of the prioritisation of employment over foundation skills result from how employment services agencies have understood, regulated and delivered their Commonwealth contractual obligations. As part of their contract, *Workforce Australia* agencies are bound to meet performance measures based on sustained employment outcomes, leading to public performance ratings and payments based on outcomes (Australian Government, 2024d). These performance metrics depend on the actions by agencies to help 'Australians find and keep a job, change jobs or create their own job', with jobseekers under mutual obligation requirements required to self-manage their obligations and job search through an online platform that tracks progress, reports tasks and activities and indicates the number of jobs applied for (Australian Government, 2024b). Within the employment services contract, *Workforce Australia* agencies are funded by employment outcomes after 13 and 26 weeks of sustained employment (Australian Government, 2024d), unlike earlier iterations, which provided outcome payments for education and training (Jobs Australia, 2015). Simply, the financial viability and contractual performance of *Workforce Australia* agencies are principally reliant on employment outcomes.

This narrower outcome focus is a significant influence on the ways in which the strategic aims and relationships of the foundation skills apparatus shape its functioning and outcomes, with employment agencies being the prime referral agency of programs. The pressures of generating income, attaining a high public performance rating, and meeting contractual obligations create demands on RTOs to modify the operations and structure of foundation skills programs. RTOs find themselves encouraged or obligated to meet the 'demands' of their most critical 'customer'. These demands include adjusting timetables to provide additional hours of tuition to learners to meet 'full-time' study obligations, completing administrative attendance diaries after each class, and re-enrolling participants who have exited programs due to short-term work assignments on short notice. By placing time restrictions on training, there is also a sense that for some employment agencies, there should be an endpoint, limit, or finality to foundation skills training. In this sense, six months or 12 months of training should be 'enough', and the skills should be learned by then (ACIL Allen Consulting, 2015c; Australian Government, 2019b; Scanlon Institute, 2019). This is another example of how foundation skills can be thought of as a set of skills that can be 'fixed' in a certain timeframe (Black & Yasukawa, 2013; Street, 1984).

At this point, we have identified and described technologies in the foundation skills apparatus in a somewhat 'oppressive' sense based on the view that some individuals will not express the desired forms of self-governance to actively engage with the labour market (MacIntyre, 1999). Governmental technologies can be seen to support the punitive treatment of some disadvantaged groups (Mendes, 2009) and limit their capabilities and capacities to act individually or collectively to further their own interests (Narayan & Petesch, 2007). However, adult education can play a productive role in building positive relationships with learners who may have had disabling experiences in compulsory education. Embedded in these relationships are program technologies such as attendance and participation expectations that can scaffold 'at-risk' populations that have the potential to disengage from learning. Technologies can provide structure to simplify what might be initially regarded as a complex and threatening environment and inform students exactly what to expect and what is expected of them. Curricula that are underpinned by competency-based training can facilitate a student-centred approach by giving learners the tools to understand the goals of their chosen qualification and gauge their own progress (Hodge & Harris, 2012). These technologies can provide support to those with little structure and stability in their home life (Crowther et al., 2010; Foley, 1995; Vaughn et al., 2000) and promote instruments of 'voice' and 'representation' by which the claims of consumers (or learners) can enter into negotiations over needs (Yeatman, 1994, p. 110).

Yet the balance between the support of learners and the meeting of contract obligations is an increasing concern for many RTOs. In the foundation skills apparatus, monitoring at-risk learners is crucial, both in a supportive and financial viability sense. Financialisation processes for both Commonwealth, State and Territory programs are structured on the capacity of RTOs to maintain learner attendance and participation. For Commonwealth programs, RTOs are paid a set amount per training hour that a learner attends and are not reimbursed for times of absence. The RTO is not paid a progression payment for learners who do not meet proficiency requirements (Australian Government, 2016, 2017b). In state-funded programs, for learners who cannot provide evidence showing participation and assessment for each module, the RTO cannot claim the monetary amount allocated for that module (State Government of Victoria, 2020b). Central to this form of management is tying the RTO's ability to manage learners with financial incentives. An RTO unable to engage and manage at-risk learners will not receive the total monetary payments for that learner, subsequently impacting their short and long-term financial viability in the training market.

These financialisation processes and practices, dependent on the monitoring of at-risk individuals, also depend on the cooperation of wrap-around services or welfare organisations to support learners facing hardship. The relationship between RTOs and welfare organisations – as well as employment agencies – is designed as a complimentary one, yet in the foundation skills apparatus, it can be one of opposition. A learner may experience difficulties in family, housing, transport, legal, health and financial matters and work with a welfare agency to manage and resolve their issues. Often, when dealing with these matters, a learner's participation can be distracted and attendance impacted. However, technologies, narrow in their interpretation and implementation, provide no allowance for the impacts of hardship. If the mandatory participation requirements are not met, learners are expected to withdraw or be withdrawn by RTOs regardless of their welfare issues and the advocacy of the welfare organisation. Learners are obligated to engage with Centrelink and their employment agency to be deemed exempt from attendance, and if no exemption is granted, they are expected to attend, despite these factors impacting attendance and participation. The pressure on RTOs to, on the one hand, support learners into wrap-around services, and at the same time, regulate them against obligations to meet contract requirements, is a source of contradiction and unease.

This contradiction and unease can add to what Goode (1960) defines as role strain for vulnerable populations. Role strain is the felt difficulty in fulfilling role obligations. The foundation skills learner may face an extensive, distracting, and sometimes conflicting array of role obligations as a job seeker, caregiver, patient, parent and wage earner. If the learner conforms fully or adequately in one direction, fulfillment could be difficult in another. Goode (1960) problematises role strain as the individual attempting to make their whole role system manageable. That is, how to allocate their energies and skills to reduce role strain to some bearable proportions. The threat of not meeting their mutual obligations at the risk of punitive consequences, while managing other roles is something the foundation skills learner is likely to find confronting. They may carry a heavy burden to meet the opportunities provided by education and employment, while potentially experiencing physical and mental health challenges, and a fragile sense of self.

3.3 *Problematising the Discourse of Outcomes in Foundation Skills*

In the foundation skills apparatus, outcomes can be defined in terms of employment, further study, or increased social interactions. As Slater and Tonkiss (2001, p. 162) argue, outcomes are embedded in all sectors of contemporary education: 'everything is viewed in terms of quantities; everything is simply a sum of value realised or hoped for'. There is an ever-increasing demand to focus on simple inputs and outputs to address learning and institutional effectiveness and report on individual outcomes. One provocation we introduce here is the problem in the apparatus between the 'intended' objectives of programs and the 'actual' measurement of outcomes. In other words, as the apparatus grapples with the kinds of outcomes that are important to foundation skills learners, it still favours more easily measured data. However, an increasing body of literature recommends shifting the focus away from the problematic discourse of 'outcomes' to value the learning process of participation, resilience, and informal learning. In this section, we explore these recommendations by problematising the extent of the relationship between foundation skills policy and the importance of the learning process, and the increased risk of marginalising the vulnerable even further if learners cannot attain the promises – or the outcomes – on offer.

The discourse of outcomes in foundation skills emerged from concepts of 'proficiency'. For instance, in the *Australian Language and Literacy Policy*: 'all Australian residents should develop and maintain a level of spoken and written English which is appropriate for a range of contexts, with the support of education and training programs addressing their diverse learning needs' (DEET, 1991, p. 33). Motivated to ascertain the population's specific foundation skills 'level', the Commonwealth developed the *National Reporting System* in 1994 (Coates et al., 1994). The *National Reporting System* was created as a mechanism for reporting the outcomes of adult English language, literacy and numeracy provision through five levels of competence. It was used as a collective means to develop consistent national and coordinated approaches to the conversations in this area, guide government spending, and provide a reference for curriculum developers and industry consultations (Coates et al., 1994). At this time, the Commonwealth began to use the *National Reporting System* to measure the 'level' or 'proficiency' of learners as an 'outcome'. For example, it was initially deployed in the *Language and Numeracy Training* (LANT) *Program* to measure a student's progression from one level of competence to another and indicate if their foundation skills were no longer a barrier to accessing employment (Kemp, 1998b).

The *National Reporting System* and its later iteration, the *Australian Core Skills Framework*, expanded further into Commonwealth foundation skills programs. This proficiency assessment was used to determine enrolment eligibility and continuation of funding for learners and tied to RTO payments and other key performance indicators. In a similar way to the International English Language Testing System entrance exams for migrants seeking to enrol in university courses (Australian Government, 2020c), from 2008, the Victorian VET system mandated that RTOs set their own proficiency level benchmarks using the *Australian Core Skills Framework* for native and non-English speakers to enrol in all VET courses. This process was implemented by the Victorian Government not only to protect learners from being coerced into registering and paying for certificates that they did not have the foundation skills for, but also as a way for learners to understand the skills benchmark they need to attain before accessing subsided training (State Government of Victoria, 2020b). The proficiency levels of foundation skills of migrants also featured prominently in political debates in 2018. Concerns for flagging proficiency levels in communities, and calls for reinforcing the importance of the English language through increasing proficiency benchmarks in acquiring citizenship, were debated in the federal parliament (Acharya, 2018; Australian Government, 2020b).

As data from OECD surveys (1996, 2006, 2013), Productivity Commission reports (Gillard, 2010), and the *National Strategy* argued that low foundation skills of the nation were impacting performance in global productivity and workplace participation, narratives from both Commonwealth and State governments overwhelming shifted to the human capital, and a lesser extent social capital, outcomes of foundation skills. The Commonwealth began to increasingly promote employment and skills outcomes, not foundation skills proficiency, as the critical objective of foundation skills provision. For example, the Australian Government, in their 2017 rounds of funding for the *AMEP* and *SEE Programs*, claimed:

> We look forward to working with providers to deliver improved learning outcomes for migrants and Australian job seekers with language, literacy and numeracy barriers... the Coalition Government's continued commitment to *AMEP* and the *SEE Program* supports the development of knowledge and skills that significantly improves the lives of participants, by providing pathways to greater social participation, employment, further study and training. (Andrews, 2017b, para. 3–4)

In both *AMEP* and *SEE Programs*, employment-related skills became mandatory components of program teaching objectives alongside the foundation skills of speaking, listening, reading and writing.

Despite this explicit shift, Commonwealth and State governments faced difficulties measuring and reporting on 'outcomes' and continued to rely on frameworks and benchmarking (The Allen Consulting Group, 2011) such as the *Australian Core Skills Framework*. These difficulties are not new to adult education globally. Allais and Wedekind (2020, p. 326) argue in their study of the *Sustainable Development Goal* (SDG) 4 and technical and vocational education (TVET) that this education sector is not amenable to target setting due to a 'heterogeneous' and idiosyncratic' nature that arises from its varying definitions within each country. The sector also lends itself to a focus on simpler measurable targets and indicators that have shifted away from 'complex, open-ended, and multifaceted processes, which had shaped many of the earlier approaches' (Allais & Wedekind, 2020, p. 323). Saunders and Blanco Ramirez (2017a, p. 400) share a similar view that complex processes in adult education have been reduced 'to simple quantifiable and comparable metrics'. For Ball (2004, p. 14), the construction of 'simple' metrics has only valued individuals solely on their performance and contribution rather than 'their intrinsic worth'. Karpov (2013, p. 76) echoes these sentiments and argues that current 'measurement materials' are not capable of determining the 'quality of the intellectual world, the genuineness of a civic position, the ability to engage in human understanding and interpretation'. In foundation skills specifically, despite social outcomes being 'highly valued by students and teachers alike', the sector has been hampered in formulating metrics that formally assess and report the benefits of these social outcomes (Balatti et al., 2006, p. 6).

Reviews of the *AMEP* and *SEE Programs* reflected these warnings by acknowledging broader further study outcomes, employment outcomes and social participation were difficult to measure and not consistently reported (ACIL Allen Consulting, 2015b, 2015c; Scanlon Institute, 2019). An example of these findings is reflected in the websites for the *AMEP*, *SEE Programs*, Victorian state-funded, and ACE programs. All provide generic statements that acknowledge a program's contribution, such as the *SEE Program*, which provides 'high-quality, flexible training' and 'help for jobseekers' (Australian Government, 2021a, para. 4), and the *AMEP* assists 'around 60,000 new migrants and humanitarian entrants to learn English each year' and is 'currently delivered nationally across 58 regions' (Australian Government, 2019a). However, no website contained any publicly accessible data that supported their contribution to their participant's employment and social outcomes. For example, there were no illustrations of a program's historical and current performance and the highlights of localised and nationwide successes – such as the number of job seekers that obtained employment or moved into a VET or university course – that demonstrate performance against the intended employment and social outcomes of programs.

The difficulties in reporting learners' employment and social outcomes led the then Assistant Federal Minister for Vocational Education and Skills, Karen Andrews, to address this issue specifically at the *AMEP* and SEE Providers forum in 2017. Minister Andrews (2017a, para. 49) claimed that the 'best way to illustrate the value of the services you provide is to talk not in terms of research results or statistics, but examples of real people'. She highlighted two student examples of the benefits of foundation skills 'to make a change for the better' (Andrews, 2017a, para. 50). These kinds of case studies, or what Eastmond (2007, p. 248) describes as storytelling, highlight the 'interplay between life, experience and story', and has emerged as common practice in adult education (Hall, 1999). Foundation skills programs such as the *AMEP*, *SEE Program* and ACE non-accredited programs have approached the promotions of outcomes through learner success stories in a similar way, highlighting individual examples of a learner's barriers and how the program has re-engaged them in education and pathways to further study or work (Australian Government, 2020a, 2021a; State Government of Victoria, 2020a).

A further problematisation is not only how the 'discourse of outcomes' should be interpreted and administered but also what outcomes should be prioritised over others. In Chapter 3, we introduced discussions of social capital's role alongside human capital outcomes as possible benefits of increased foundation skills (Balatti et al., 2006). These discussions are highly contested (Lonsdale & McCurry, 2004) within the apparatus, with accusations that human capital approaches subjugate social capital outcomes when planning policy and program agendas. The complicating factor in any discussion of foundation skills is that the arena has become 'highly politicised and contested' (Waterhouse & Virgona, 2004, p. 12). Many practitioners, motivated by social justice agendas, reject human capital rationalities by claiming that government's dominant human capital approach targets marginalised populations to reduce public expenditure (Perkins, 2009). This contestation led Mackay et al. (2006, p. 15) to declare an 'identity crisis' and an 'ideological dissonance' in the sector. Perkins (2009, p. 15) even suggests that while arguments are an accepted and important aspect of academic discourse, they can be 'intimidating', and make debates about literacy and numeracy seem inaccessible and incomprehensible to non-specialists.

What can be understood within this 'ideological' and identity 'crisis' is that the foundation skills apparatus has a broad remit concerning outcomes.

Individuals can benefit in many ways and in many forms, all of which can include human and social capital outcomes or personal achievements. This diversity was revealed during student focus groups conducted in reviews of the *AMEP* and *SEE Programs* (ACIL Allen Consulting, 2015b, 2015c; Scanlon Institute, 2019). In a departure from thoughts of an ideological crisis, many participants celebrated and embraced the broad scope of programs. The focus groups praised the program's human and social capital benefits in relation to employment goals, transition to further education or training, and settlement/integration into the Australian community. For migrants, the importance of learning about Australian cultural and social practices, understanding laws, regulations and fair trading, being independent, and fitting into the community were repeatedly expressed as an outcome of increased foundation skills (ACIL Allen Consulting, 2015b, 2015c; Scanlon Institute, 2019). Students viewed a greater 'proficiency on basic LLN skills such as speaking, listening, reading and writing' as a desired outcome (ACIL Allen Consulting, 2015b, p. 18). For migrants, this includes learning pronunciation, word usage, and rate of speech in Australia, essential for increased confidence, integration and settlement (ACIL Allen Consulting, 2015b).

The listening to learner voices is another illustration of those subjugated knowledges and voices that are disqualified as 'inadequate', 'insufficiently elaborated' or 'low down on the hierarchy' (Foucault, 1980c, p. 82). These knowledges can provide a richness of 'implicit knowledge' and voices of people 'who are the first to experience a technology of power' (Habermas, 1994, p. 92). The foundation skills learner can be understood as a valuable resource to provide experience and insights into the outcomes and worth of programs. As Freebody (1992, p. 73) observed:

> We are never describing literacy activities, no matter how commonsensical our assertions may be. We are always prescribing, saying what should be, and so presenting ourselves as arbiters of what counts as literacy to a community that has not generally learned to read our announcements critically.

The risk in prescribing what literacy 'should be' – for example, providing outcomes of greater employment, higher wages, improved health, better family relationships and developing connections with the community – sets expectations related to what a learner can or should achieve. The potential for a vulnerable person to imagine themselves as being 'not good enough' (Sennett, 1998, p. 118) if they do not achieve outcomes in the time, or in the context they expect, risks the learner becoming increasingly marginalised. As well as questioning their self-worth and choices they have made, learners could question the efficacy of foundation skills learning as 'so-called promises' have not been met, and in turn, may continue to be further disengaged from education.

An increasing body of literature has advocated a more limited construct of foundation skills in policymaking, in which these skills are imagined as a set of tools focussing on an individual's participation in society (Lonsdale & McCurry, 2004; Wickert & McGuirk, 2005). This construct emphasises foundation skills as a 'means' (the learning process of attaining skills) rather than an 'end' (concentrating on the outcome). Taylor et al. (1998, p. 438) argue that this kind of construct deters the forms of 'wishful thinking that not only fails to help in the achievement of goals but at least in some cases may actively interfere with it'. Or, it avoids the dualism of success/failure by imagining failure, not as the opposite of success itself, but as part of understanding the 'process' of the literacy event (Castleton, 2001). By focussing on the processes involved in reaching a goal and attempting to understand or manage a stressful event, a value is placed on the ability to plan, strategise and bring about goals. Taylor et al. (1998, p. 438) suggest that learning as a 'means' will bring 'joy or at least satisfaction in that process'.

Black's (2002, 2013) work on the 'social' construct of literacy is an effective way to describe this. A social construct does not predicate that foundation skills learning must bring outcomes of employment and study. It also does not frame a construct around social outcomes. Rather, a focus on the 'social' aspects of literacy assumes that development occurs through social interactions and is enhanced, but not dependent on, institutionalised training-based learning. This interpretation acknowledges that most everyday foundation skills practices are not formally learned, but are acquired through self-discovery or help from friends, or are modelled from others in the process of one's changing life circumstances, needs and motivations (Appleby & Barton, 2008; Black & Yasukawa, 2013). Here, a social practice approach takes account of students' lives and draws on their familiar everyday literacy and numeracy practices, rather than focusing on what they cannot do (Black & Yasukawa, 2013). Acknowledging persistence – rather than completion or attainment of education, work or proficiency goals, or other 'outcomes' – is a contributing factor to increasing a learner's foundation skills (Crowther et al., 2010; Hodge, 2014).

The possibilities of promoting the 'process of learning', 'social language and literacy', 'persistence' and other representations may alleviate the risk of marginalisation of learners and disturb the problematisation of 'outcomes'. However, it would take a significant transformation in policy approach for this to be the dominant rationality of the apparatus. It could also invite a new round of problematisations. A rationality where process, not outcomes, are prioritised could be understood as a return to times that many laud as the 'good old days', prior to competency-based training and curricula that focussed on the earlier interpretations of literacy (Hauenschild, 1990, p. 3). Others argue that the 'good old days' are 'nostalgic nonsense' (Hauenschild, 1990, p. 3) in which the approaches do not adequately address the complexity of skills that exist now (Adult Literacy Information Office, 1999; Brock, 1997). It also reveals debates on the strategic position of foundation skills in relation to VET. Some stakeholders regard the relationship as intertwined, whereas other foundation skills scholars believe that foundation skills training should be clearly distinguished from VET. Policies that promote foundation skills with an overriding employment focus can stretch staffing expertise and dilute the specialisation of foundation skills teaching. Hence, any specific work-related skills should be the domain of VET, or employment service agencies, as they have the expertise and links with industry. A transformation of this type would also call for rethinking how foundation skills can be reported and measured, the needs of learner's identified and acknowledged, and provider performance evaluated under changed NPM regimes. It would also responsibilise governments to confront concerns for how to manage the diversity that the human and social capital aspects of foundation skills foreground.

4 Discussion: The Subjugation (and Responsibilisation) of Socio-Economic Disadvantage in the Foundation Skills Apparatus

This chapter demonstrates how key policy actors employ market rationalities that naturalise self-care regimes, and responsibilise RTOs and learners in the foundation skills apparatus. The individuals who become subjects in the apparatus are imagined and constructed as consumers who will come to know and govern themselves through the motivation and desire to pursue the development of their foundation skills, and view employment success as the primary outcome of developing their foundation skills. The problem in the foundation skills apparatus is that the learners may not recognise themselves as subjects of 'human capital' discourses, may not conform to the rules governing their participation and performance, may not comply with the set criteria that monitor their progress and performativity, and may not attain the 'panacea' of foundation skills by accessing meaningful employment. Social benefits are imagined as a seamless by-product of employment success to those who make the 'right' choices, but individuals who do not make the 'right' choices are labelled as 'at-risk'.

As we suggested earlier, these processes have emerged as widespread in neoliberal democracies over the last four decades. Rik Peeters (2013, p. 583), for example, in an 'analysis of 'Dutch political discourse' at the start of the 21st century, suggests that 'traditional connotations of the notions "responsibility" and "solidarity" are transformed in order to mobilise citizens and approach them as both part of the problem and part of the solution to various social issues'. His analysis focuses on Dutch youth policy, and shows how 'this brings about a politicisation of citizen behaviour and implicates citizens as co-operators of political will formation'. Peeters (2013) suggests that policies of this nature can appear to be a constructive approach to managing the conditions of a social problem, however, they seldom account for the context in which such populations live and the historical content that can contribute to particular outcomes. Contexts can include the rate of unemployment in their community, wider structures of inequality built into the labour market or the educational system, lack of public housing, precarious employment, increased costs of living, medical expenses, and other forces such as family, legal issues, being a victim of crime, health problems, and drug and alcohol dependency. Historical conditions and factors such as discrimination against women and Indigenous communities, access to compulsory schooling by individuals, and the marginalisation of people with a disability are also factors. From this perspective, low foundation skills are a structural, as well as an individual phenomenon. People experience struggles in developing foundation skills because they find themselves in spaces in a social and economic system that delivers inadequate income, housing, health and disruptive education. Considering these structural influences as root causes of social problems is one way of developing public initiatives that invoke collaborative ways to address issues such as low foundation skills.

In this sense, we want to argue that in the neoliberal foundation skills apparatus, the complexities that many foundation skills learners face are reduced to an employment-focussed agenda that acknowledges, then discards, factors of disadvantage that impact how individuals might access learning opportunities. A Commonwealth sponsored report from the National VET Equity Advisory Council (2011) argues that the adult education system's success comes from monitoring populations who experience particular challenges. Yet, how socio-economic disadvantage differently shapes and forms individual responsibility can be absent from human capital-influenced discourse. These discussions, for example, remain absent from the *National Strategy*, despite a large body of policy discourse – as detailed in our exploration of the *No Single Measure* (1989), OECD surveys of 1996, 2006 and 2012–13 – that highlights the effect of socio-economic factors in the development of foundation skills.

Human capital discourses, as they shape and find expression in the contemporary foundation skills apparatus in Australia, fail to take account of those factors that signal the influence of broader social, geographical and economic forces of globalisation, labour market change, financial booms and slumps. Various 'resources' such as family, health and wellbeing, and housing that enable and limit capacities to engage in learning and make choices are also subjugated. The subject in human capital discourses is conceived, essentially, 'as a rational, autonomous individual in all its behaviours [and is] expected to "look after herself" modelled on assumptions of individuality, rationality, and self-interest' (Peters, 2017, pp. 140–141).

The subjugation of socio-economic disadvantage in the foundation skills apparatus is a distinct shift from earlier foundation skills policy – the *National Policy on Languages* of 1987 and the *Australian Language and Literacy Policy* of 1991 – which acknowledged and explored the connections between low foundation skills and socio-economic disadvantage. The *National Policy on Languages*, for example, claimed that four major social goals need to be promoted to justify the significant efforts to improve foundation skills. These include enrichment, economic, external and equality – with equality pertaining to social justice and overcoming disadvantage (lo Bianco, 1987b). The policy also argued that 'since language permeates all social life there are inevitable correlations between social inequalities and language' (lo Bianco, 1987b, p. 54). Here, the *National Policy on Language* sought to 'initiate action to alleviate and overcome problems, disabilities, inequality and discrimination which may be encountered because of language' (lo Bianco, 1987b, p. 5).

The *Australian Language and Literacy Policy* continued to acknowledge the relationship between foundation skills and disadvantage by establishing it as the key issue for the policy's rationale. The policy claimed that English skills development is 'fundamental to improving the quality of life and opportunities for disadvantaged members of our society' (DEET, 1991, p. XIV). The *Australian Language and Literacy Policy* also highlighted that 'people who are socio-economically disadvantaged have the greatest difficulty achieving social justice' (DEET, 1991, p. 14). Both policies acknowledged that with policy work in its infancy, more discussion, planning and action was required to address the needs and demands of the society, including related social policy such as social justice and multiculturalism. Moore's (2002) investigation into the implementation of the *Australian Language and Literacy Policy* highlighted the ad hoc nature of how assistance provided to the most disadvantaged was administered. Her discussions with Commonwealth staff involved in the policy revealed: 'The department doesn't actually target people. Apart from Aboriginal people. And single parents, but single parents can be male or female. But they're only special purpose things' and 'the only way in which the department tended to separate them [i.e. clients] out would be the very disadvantaged – at some stage they used to have this concept of the very disadvantaged and the less disadvantaged. That was a queuing mechanism' (Moore, 2002, p. 125).

The gap in policy from *Australian Language and Literacy Policy* in 1991 to the *National Strategy* in 2012 did not progress debates on disadvantage at the policy level. As processes of individualisation and responsibilisation were introduced into the foundation skills apparatus through the *National Strategy* and other social policies, factors of disadvantage were increasingly subjugated. In contrast, employment agendas were vigorously promoted. One prominent example of this is the repeated citing of OECD data in government discourse that indicates that nearly half of the population has difficulty with foundation skills. Yet data from the same source that indicates gender, educational attainment in compulsory schooling, parental education, labour market participation, and age as factors that impact foundation skills development (Australian Bureau of Statistics, 1996, 2006, 2013) were absent from the strategy. Instead, foundation skills discourse, notably the *National Strategy*, positions the individual as responsible for developing their own skills, and managing any extenuating circumstances that may impact their learning. The discourse does not refer to wider structures of inequality built into the labour market or the educational systems that may directly impact learners.

The *National Strategy* takes a risk-based approach to foundation skills and its connection to socio-economic disadvantage. It focusses on terms such as 'learner-centric', 'some learners require more support or development than others' and 'alternative learning styles' and suggests that a 'one-size-fits-all' approach is inappropriate (SCOTESE, 2012, p. 25). The strategy highlights the social relations that render individuals 'at-risk' and possibly threaten social and health orders. It uses the link between low foundation skills and 'poor access to health services, poor health, higher risk of hospitalisation, higher rates of depression and an inability to understand and comply with the use of prescription drugs' as a notable example (SCOTESE, 2012, p. 7). The *National Strategy* argues that foundation skills are the critical aspect, along with initiatives in the areas of health, housing and community services to understand and use information relating to issues such as drugs and alcohol, disease prevention and treatment, safety and accident prevention, first aid, emergencies and staying healthy (SCOTESE, 2012, p. 6). Central to this risk-based approach is that socio-economic disadvantage can be readily overcome with stronger foundation skills.

The *National Strategy* argues that one way an individual will act on their responsibilities to develop their foundation skills is to recognise and overcome (with help from close intermediaries) the 'stigma' that people experience when having trouble with their foundation skills (SCOTESE, 2012, p. 3). The *National Strategy* does not define its notion of 'stigma'. However, Crowther et al. (2010) suggest that the stigma of low foundation skills relates to the shame, embarrassment and poor educational experiences that people with low skills face. A Special Broadcast Service (SBS) documentary named *Lost for Words* is a recent example that demonstrated the stigma and shame people with low foundation skills can experience in education settings and society. This documentary followed the stories of eight people as they undertook an intensive adult literacy program that revealed learning difficulties, life circumstances, linguistic intricacies and shame that prevented them from learning foundation skills in the past (Endemol Shine Australia, 2021).

The stigma of low foundation skills can be attributed to the term 'illiteracy'. Illiteracy, defined as the inability of a person who cannot, with understanding, both read and write a short, simple statement on everyday life (UNESCO, 1978, p. 18), is now discouraged because of its often inaccurate use, and the stigma attached to such a description (DEET, 1991). A 'stigmatised' individual is represented in the *National Strategy* as lacking knowledge of the importance of foundation skills, and as a person who can be resistant to improving their skills (SCOTESE, 2012, p. 3).

However, another subjectivity is attached to the foundation skills learner, the notion that they lack knowledge, or the inability to comprehend, what is understood to be best for them. This mode of subjectification amplifies the various moral propositions that form part of the foundation skills apparatus. Many moral propositions attribute unfavourable outcomes to the individual by promoting the view that their situation would be better if they made better choices. In this sense, individuals are constructed as not being 'incapable' of improving their foundation skills. Instead, they are imagined as having personal failings and inadequacies such as a lack of understanding of the benefits of increased skills, a lack of a work ethic, or disorganisation, endeavour or ambition. The individual should have worked harder, stayed at school longer, or accepted the opportunities that have been presented previously. These representations work to create other subjectivities of laziness, immorality and irresponsibility and, as Black and Yasukawa (2013, p. 577) observe, 'blame the victim'.

What is assumed in the *National Strategy* is a relatively simple, straightforward and clearly apparent bridging and correlation between certain complex interactions in the apparatus. For example, if a learner overcomes the stigma of low foundation skills, they will effortlessly engage and reap the benefits of increased foundation skills. Yet, these complex interactions can confront an individual as they seek to restructure an identity as a learner. Discourses that promote terms such as lifelong learning, acquisitional, informal or task-conscious learning – the everyday learning that is unavoidable when living in and enacting with the world – construct everyone as a learner (Rogers, 2003; Tett & Maclachlan, 2007). Adults may recognise their competence with the acquisitional learning they regularly encounter in their daily lives, such as learning a new skill at work, learning a new application on their phone, or building an understanding of health and fitness. Rogers (2003) argues that an adult's perceptions and experience of education inhibit the transfer of this positive self-construct in formalised learning contexts. Many adults have negative experiences of compulsory education, which produces a struggle to marry their construction of themselves as capable learners with their sense of self as able learners in structured educational contexts. Adult learners may revert to constructing themselves as not able, as not competent, recalling past experiences of how the educational world has historically labelled them. They have negative or, at best, fragile identities as learners. Their engagement in learning requires them to take on a form of 'social capital' to scaffold their 'fragile identity'. Here, 'social capital is important for learning, and learning is important for social capital' Field (2005, p. 110). Foundation skills can advance social capital if the learner can override their negative self-image of a non-capable learner. If not, obstacles still exist for adults that inhibit not only the creation of an alternative self-image of a capable and competent learner, but also as a capable and competent individual.

As a final comment, the subject positions that exist in the foundation skills apparatus, be it a disadvantage, stigmatisation, or poor learner identity, follow a similar trajectory. These problematisations of the person frame these characteristics as individual issues that can be resolved by an individual attaining the right information and making the right choices from the 'second chance' education offered (Rogers, 2006, p. 129). And, where an individual does not make responsible choices, the responsibility falls to families and professionals to have the mediating and coercive means to facilitate engagement and encourage meaningful outcomes in learning (Peters, 2017). Policy is now designed and implemented from sets of principles that frame these issues as local issues concerning discrete members (individuals) in the community, that can be resolved by localised and private initiatives (Teghtsoonian, 2009). In the foundation skills apparatus, RTOs are responsibilised for managing the factors that can impact learner's ability to sustain their engagement in training programs. RTOs, tendering for contracted government services, are invited to analyse their service area – their local community – for socio-economic and labour market conditions that impact their learning cohort. Contracted RTOs are requested to develop their own measures, contextualised to their local area, to alleviate potential barriers that may burden an adult's learning (Australian Government, 2013b, 2017; State Government of Victoria, 2013a, 2016). As the foundation skills apparatus faces challenges from 'events' such as the COVID-19 pandemic and its aftermath, perceived skills shortages, upcoming OECD survey results, and employment services reform, responses to these events may remain increasingly localised and individualised. We explore these and other possible future events, and problematise how they may shape the apparatus, next.

Note

1 The authenticity of enrolment has become a focus of ASQA and state governments in response to situations of RTOs falsifying identification and/or enrolments to claim funding for training that has not occurred, for students that do not exist. See Independent Broad-based Anti-Corruption Commission (2017) for a notable example of this situation.

CHAPTER 6

A History of the Future of Foundation Skills

1 A History of the Present of Foundation Skills

The work we have undertaken here has attempted to identify and analyse the foundation skills policy and program apparatus that has developed in Australia during the last three decades. By drawing on Michel Foucault's conceptual frameworks of genealogy, governmentality and apparatus, we have discussed several 'episodes' and 'events' in the stories of neoliberal capitalism, globalisation and labour market skills as they have been implicated in the emergence of the 'problem' of foundation skills. Our main argument is that in Australia, as in many other high-income economies, the foundation skills learner carries an increasingly onerous burden to make sense of, and navigate, the complex entanglements of marketised training environments, the commodification of skills, and changing labour markets as an individual, choice-making, responsible consumer. These individuals are increasingly made responsible for making the right choices in developing their foundation skills – their 'human capital' – so that they can secure a less parlous participation in the increasingly precarious labour markets of a globalising, neoliberal capitalism.

What Foucault's genealogical tools have offered is a critique of present systems in the foundation skills apparatus in light of their history. Genealogy is an approach characterised as a 'critical and effective history' (Dean, 1994). Vucetic's (2010) 'three E' model for the 'doing' of genealogy suggests that genealogies can be organised by the identification of 'episodes', 'events' and 'effectiveness'. This approach has provided us with a means by which we have identified the force relations evident in significant episodes and events in the emergence of this foundation skills apparatus. This 'critical and effective history' has disturbed any sense that these events follow a chronological and continuous pattern by reconstructing their apparent certainty or necessity as contingent and historically produced.

In the first instance, we identified and analysed a number of the most important characteristics of the foundation skills policy and program apparatus since the emergence of the Commonwealth Government's policy, the *National Policy on Languages*, in 1987. It was important to do this work to identify the 'heterogenous ensemble' of elements – the policy and program discourses, institutions, and systems of thought – that make up the foundation skills apparatus. This work also provided a way to analyse the character

 | DOI:10.1163/9789004724464_007

of the relations and connections between the elements that can be named as 'neoliberal'. In Chapter Two, we investigated several historical policies and discourses from the Labour Hawke-Keating and the Howard Coalition Governments during the 1980s and 1990s. These emergent policies were influenced, as we demonstrated, by a shift to rationalities framed by the ideals of neoliberal markets, flexible capitalism, and human capital development that were made to align strongly with discourses of 'national economic recovery' during this period. In Chapter Three, we illustrated how these policies and discourses formed the strategic function of the apparatus as it emerged to meet the demands of the population that were identified as needing the 'upskilling' or 'retraining' of their foundation skills to meet the demands of changing labour markets. This training was re-structured by various governments within the logics of 'competitive, free markets', so that foundation skills were re-imagined as a commodity. Here, 'skills products' were developed by registered training organisations (RTOs), and then commodified in a manner that foundation skills customers could be identified as subjects who 'should' choose, based on their individual needs. In that chapter, we identified and analysed a number of the most significant characteristics of the Victorian Government's foundation skills policy and program apparatus. The Victorian example was an important 'event' as it was the first state-based policy to introduce a fully commodified and marketised training system. As this 'open' demand-driven system collapsed because of widespread corruption, inadequate regulation, and budget blowouts, the consequences echoed not only in the Victorian market but also in other Commonwealth, State and Territory training markets. We also analysed how rationalities that foregrounded skills as commodities, and 'open' market competition, were key features of the *Victorian Training Guarantee*. In this context, public, community and private RTOs were permitted to compete against each other, for the first time, for government subsidised student enrolments. We also described how, upon the collapse of the system, the Victorian system became characterised by new public management (NPM) risk management regimes, which were introduced to monitor regulatory requirements of quality, efficiency and 'consumer' confidence. Chapter Five further developed the analysis of how the Victorian system was modelled on neoliberal processes of individualisation, in which learners were imagined as choice-making consumers of services, capable of identifying training opportunities that promised to enhance their employment opportunities as well as collectively contribute to the development of the Victorian economy as 'innovative', 'productive' and 'internationally competitive'.

Another key purpose of our work has been to analyse the various ways in which the foundation skills apparatus imagines processes of globalisation and technological change, labour market change, labour market skills, and the sorts of person one must become to participate in paid labour markets. Here, we highlighted how key policy moments, documents and discourses have developed, and deployed, market rationalities in diverse attempts to produce novel regimes of individualised self-care and new forms of responsibility for learners in the apparatus. In Chapter Four, for example, we analysed the 'exchange' value of foundation skills for learners. Rather than as a proxy for skills expressed through credentials or learning as something valuable 'in itself', the exchange value represents foundation skills as real to the learner in an economic sense, and as 'things' that can be transferred into different industries and contexts. As we demonstrated in Chapter Five, the importance of foundation skills to a person's human capital was a significant focus of the *National Foundation Skills Strategy for Adults* (*National Strategy*). There we explored how this policy works on the psychological choice mechanisms of individuals through processes of moral self-evaluations, in efforts to responsibilise learners to take up opportunities to increase their foundation skills. This chapter also discussed how learners, when confronted with the challenge of being tasked with the responsibility to make choices and manage their own risks from social problems, are encouraged to imagine foundation skills as the 'panacea' to solve their social issues. Importantly, where learners are unable to regulate themselves in ways that are determined by the key actants and discourses in the apparatus, various practices and processes in the apparatus advocate that support from family, community and government contracted agencies, not government interventions focussed on broader systemic issues, are best able to provide individualised solutions to the problem of foundation skills.

2 A History of the Future of Foundation Skills

As should be apparent at this point, our genealogical research was a way of using these key policy moments to provoke a rethinking of values, to direct a destabilising light on the 'history of the present' of the problem of foundation skills by denormalising current identities, institutions and patterns of thought and action, and to transform this reality by opening up new possibilities for thought and action (Foucault, 1981). At this point, having done this work, we want to *speculate* on the ways in which this genealogy can inform community, academic and policy understandings of the possibilities and limitations of the governmental ambitions of the neoliberal foundation skills apparatus.

We want to do this, a little provocatively, by seeking to write a limited version of the 'history of the future' of foundation skills by projecting forward the work we have done so far. Our intent here is to identify, discuss and problematise a limited number of future 'events' that are *likely* to continue to shape the foundation skills apparatus – even if these possible futures will be uncertain, unpredictable, disruptive, discontinuous and non-teleological.

In engaging in these forms of 'speculative projection', we want to revisit, briefly, the work we introduced in Chapter 4, where we described how 'reflexive governance' can be understood as a mechanism for the ongoing reconfigurations of the urgent needs, elements, and strategic relations that give an apparatus its particular character. At that point, our understanding of reflexive processes in the apparatus was more in the sense of 'reflex' than 'reflection', in which change, development, and novel interventions emerge as a reflex to previous decisions or activities, which may lead to unintended or even surprising consequences (Aiken, 2000). In neoliberal arts of government, when consequences of policy actions may result in the market failing to produce efficient or equitable outcomes, various agencies and governments can decide whether and how to intervene and mobilise processes of reorganisation, reform, review, consultation and audit.

In the foundation skills apparatus, processes of reflexive governance have allowed national, state, regional, and more global discussions on what foundation skills policy and program structures should look like to find a footing. These reflexive processes have allowed stakeholders to enter the conversation in ways that may have been closed at other times. They have also enabled the ongoing generation and review of data, evaluations, and discursive positions that have highlighted, quite markedly, the diverse competing and contradictory positions that structure the foundation skills field. However, there are concerns that forms of neoliberal reflexive governance have become compromised neoliberal rationalities and technologies of government (Leonard & Lidskog, 2021). Our analysis of Zoellner's (2011) study of the reflexive governance of the Australian VET system is an example of this concern. Feindt and Weiland (2018, p. 661) also argue that reflexive government can become entangled with 'unavoidable politics; the influence of broader discursive systems that shape actor's strategic interests; and structural and deliberate limitations to the range of admitted epistemological understandings, normative perspectives and material practices'.

Government, in this sense, is an ongoing, always 'failing' project characterised by the recurring reconfigurations of the urgent needs, elements, and strategic relations that give an apparatus its particular character. In the speculative thinking that closes this book, we want to engage with a number of recent, and even foreseeable, 'future' events and episodes – some global, some more local to Australia. A number of these events and episodes have already had significant impacts on such things as labour markets, processes of globalisation and digital innovation. Some are about to occur and, given the work we have done, we can suggest that they will have significant influence on the ways in which the 'problem of foundation skills' will be re-imagined in Australia and other economies around the globe – in the near and more distant future.

A key challenge associated with thinking about the 'history of the future' of foundation skills is the problem that futures – as unknowable, 'counterfactuals' that have yet to happen, and which may not happen – pose for examining the entanglements of the pasts-presents-futures (Kelly et al., 2023). Agencies and organisations such as the World Economic Forum, UNESCO, the OECD, the International Monetary Fund, the World Bank, the European Commission, and corporations such as the 'big 4' consulting firms (Deloitte Touche Tohmatsu, KPMG International, PricewaterhouseCoopers [PwC], and Ernst & Young), have few qualms in creating particular scenarios about the future of work, the emergences of new technologies, and the sorts of skills people will need in order to be, become, and remain employable in these futures. Indeed, in many of these instances, this forecasting and scenario building commodifies and monetises these imaginings of the future.

Norbert Elias, in his 1987 paper *The Retreat of Sociologists into the Present*, argued that 'much of current social science, especially sociology, has turned away from historical critique'. For Elias (1987, p. 224):

> the immediate present into which [we] are retreating... constitutes just one small momentary phase within the vast stream of humanity's development, which, coming from the past, debouches into the present and thrusts ahead toward possible futures.

So, while our work to this point has been about developing a 'history of the present' of foundation skills – work that has been framed by the importance of historical critique of the present – in thinking about conducting 'speculative projections' about the 'history of the future' of foundation skills, we are confronted with dilemmas about the scale and scope, the time and space, that we want to work with. What futures are we talking about? 2030? 2050? Net Zero Futures? The 21st century? The AI Armageddon? At this moment, we are not engaged in scenario planning for what, for example, the world of work will look like in 2030. Our projections, in part, are about having done the work we have done, and in being witness to a number of events and emergences, what projections can we make that can inform thinking in the present about the complex entanglements of these futures with pasts and presents?

2.1 *The Pandemic and Its Aftermath: A Skills-led Economic Recovery?*

In a recent book, we (Brown et al., 2024) have undertaken a detailed analysis of how, at the start of the 21st century, globalising 'modernisation' processes condemn billions of people to live lives on the margins of these processes in largely unregulated economies and forms of labour that offer few protections, and/or the rights and privileges afforded workers in more regulated economies and labour markets (Bauman, 2004). Our primary purpose there is to present an overview of key dimensions of the challenges and opportunities that were, and that continue to be, amplified by the social, cultural, economic and political consequences of the COVID-19 pandemic as these continue to echo through, and shape, the informal economies and the experiences of informal workers, of Latin America and the Caribbean, the Middle East and North Africa, Sub Saharan Africa, Central and Eastern Europe, and the Asia-Pacific. We have framed this discussion through an engagement with the ways in which skills, education and training, and contested ideas about lifelong learning are understood as being central to the problem of 'informality', and as the 'panacea' to this problem.

That book also seeks to highlight historical and contemporary characteristics of informality in these different regions, including the ways in which the COVID-19 pandemic, and the public health, social, and economic policy responses to the pandemic, have impacted informal workers in different regions in different ways. A report from the International Labour Organization (2021b, p. 19), for example, points to the fact that 70 percent of the global working-age population (4 billion people) have little or no safety net, leaving only 30 percent 'legally covered by comprehensive social security systems... with women's coverage lagging behind men's' (International Labour Organization, 2021b, p. 19). There are significant challenges across and within regions 'with coverage rates in Europe and Central Asia (83.9 percent) and the Americas (64.3 percent) above the global average, while Asia and the Pacific (44.1 percent), the Arab States (40.0 percent) and Africa (17.4 percent) have far more marked coverage gaps'.

The COVID-19 pandemic, as a profound disruption to social, economic and political processes and lives, has impacted how we live, work, and study, even if we acknowledge that these impacts and their consequences have been unevenly, and inequitably, distributed – locally, nationally and globally. In this sense, in speculating on the history of the future of foundation skills, we can imagine the pandemic as a major 'event' that has, and will continue to, impact on the ways in which the 'problem of foundation skills' will be re-imagined in Australia and other economies around the globe.

In Australia, as elsewhere, there is evidence that the burden of the COVID-19 crisis has fallen disproportionately on already vulnerable groups (OECD, 2021b). A review at the end of the first year of the pandemic by The Australia Institute: Centre for Future Work claimed that workers in casual jobs lost employment eight times faster than those in permanent positions. Part-time workers suffered job losses three times worse than full-time workers. Young workers, women and workers who did not work in offices also suffered disproportionate job losses during the initial shutdowns (Nahum & Stanford, 2020). The World Health Organisation (2021, para. 2) also predicted that the stress from lockdowns would impact many people's usual activities, routines or livelihoods with 'levels of loneliness, depression, harmful alcohol and drug use, and self-harm or suicidal behaviour… expected to rise'.

In Chapter Two, we discussed how Australia was understood to be facing a skills challenge with the evolution of automation, AI and new digitally enabled technologies transforming the world of work. A report by PwC Australia (2022) claimed that the pandemic made that challenge more complex and more urgent, necessitating immediate interventions. Their survey of global businesses indicated that just over a half were planning to make remote work a permanent option and accelerate automation and digital ways of working to recover from the impacts of the pandemic. According to EY Global (2020), the realisation of such forecasts are likely to place increasing demands on digital and network resources. The infrastructure required for automation and digitisation – artificial intelligence, autonomous vehicles, robots, augmented and virtual reality that is unprecedentedly lifelike and autonomous – will also critically rely on the development of five technologies: 5G technologies, edge computing, next generation batteries, precision sensors and quantum computing.

During the period from 2020 to 2022 – the more acute time frame of COVID-19 infections, ongoing public health lockdowns, and the emergence of new, often more virulent strains of the virus – a number of agencies suggested that a post-pandemic economic and social environment characterised by an accelerated digitalisation of business may have broader implications for society, exacerbating the digital divide and making it increasingly difficult for individuals to overcome barriers to access, affordability and digital capabilities (PwC Australia, 2022). There were fears that people would be affected by volatile market conditions caused by the effects of the pandemic if they worked in industries that were being reconfigured by new technologies (World Economic Forum, 2021). For example, older workers, particularly blue-collar workers, were imagined as likely to face specific challenges in bouncing back in terms of time to re-employment and earnings loss after being displaced from their jobs (OECD, 2021a). Individuals unemployed for a significant time frame might face financial hardship and mental stress, and according to the OECD (2021a, p. 39), a 'scarring' that can impede future job prospects, making future jobs harder to find, less lucrative and more unstable. Workers who have the opportunity to upskill and improve their digital capabilities 'on-the-job' were likely to have a significant advantage over those who do not (PwC Australia, 2022). The need for digital literacy led Digital Skills Organisation CEO Patrick Kidd (cited in *The Australian*, 2022, para. 1) to claim that 'digital skills are now as important as reading and writing'.

To meet these demands, there have been claims, such as those from the World Economic Forum (2021, p. 4), that 'there is an enormous opportunity to reconfigure the world of work at this critical juncture and embark on an upskilling revolution that will give people across the world the ability to participate fully in the future of work, whatever that might be'. The World Economic Forum (2021, p. 3) added that half of all employees worldwide will need reskilling by 2025. From an Australian perspective, PwC Australia (2022, para. 1) argued that 'inaction is not an option. What Australia needs now is a business-led recovery that's built on upskilling and supported by government initiatives'. Similarly, peak national employer organisation, the Australian Industry Group, claimed that the severity of growing skills shortages and labour mismatches requires 'all sides of politics to go on a war footing to tackle what is one of the biggest barriers to our COVID-19 economic recovery and to the resumption of real income growth' (Lilly, 2021, para. 3). The Australian Chamber of Commerce and Industry (2022, para. 4) argued that 'we have a once in a generation opportunity to introduce landmark policy reform to help businesses access the skills and labour they need to power the economy forward'.

During this period (2020–2022), a Heads of Agreement between the Commonwealth, States and Territories recognised that Australia's adult education system should play a critical role in supporting Australia's economic recovery from the pandemic. The agreement emphasised how the system needed to immediately provide additional support to job seekers to enable them to reskill and upskill, ensure that all school leavers had access to training, and that businesses could get the skilled workers where and when they needed them (Australian Government, 2020d). One action area from this agreement was the development of a new *National Skills Agreement*[1] that prioritised:

- a national VET system that provides high-quality, responsive and accessible education and training to boost productivity;
- support for Australians to obtain the skills and capabilities they need to obtain well-paid, secure jobs; and,

- ensuring Australia has the skilled workforce it needs now and into the future, with TAFE at the heart of the VET sector (Australian Government, 2023b).

In September 2022, the Jobs and Skills Summit hosted by the Albanese Labor Government, four months after it was elected in May 2022, brought together governments, industry, unions and civil society to address the economic challenges that were amplified and energised by the pandemic. The summit focussed on a wide range of issues including unemployment, boosting productivity, sustainable wage growth, creating opportunities for the disadvantaged, addressing skills shortages, promoting jobs in renewable energy, and enhancing equal opportunities for women and migrants. The theme and the outcomes of the Summit informed the development of an *Employment White Paper* that was meant to provide a roadmap for:

> ensuring more Australians are the beneficiaries of the big shifts underway in the economy and our society over the coming decades. It crystallises our ambition for a dynamic and inclusive labour market in which Australians have the opportunity for secure, well-paid jobs in a country where workers, employers and communities can thrive and adapt. (Australian Government, 2023c, p. v)

In the *White Paper,* the Albanese Labor Government argued that future policy design for foundation skills was dependent on collaboration between all levels of government. The *National Skills Agreement* and an investigation titled the *Foundation Skills Study* were positioned as the ways to shape national coordination and build practical policies to lift the foundation skill levels for adult Australians (Australian Government, 2023a). The commitment to foundation skills was identified as 'part of the Government's broader approach to lifting human capital across the workforce, starting in the compulsory education system and continuing throughout people's lives' (Australian Government, 2023a, p. 213).

In these and other respects, the skills-led response to the pandemic is likely to form a significant episode and event in the history of the future of foundation skills. The 'promise' of pandemic recovery positions the foundation skills apparatus at a similar juncture to the 'skills crisis', used as a justification for the development of the *National Strategy* in 2012. It is already provoking similar 'skills' debates to those that we revealed in our genealogical analysis of this period, and which problematised the human capital purpose of education to supply skilled labour for the labour market. Our work has attempted to trouble the assumptions that an increase in a person's foundation skills produces a linear and a seamless pathway to 'a good job, better pay and the potential for promotion, the capacity to participate fully in society and with the right kind of skills, the ability to move jobs and careers and engage in personal transformation' (Wheelahan et al., 2022, p. 475). Wheelahan et al. (2022, p. 475) claim that the 'COVID recovery' skills discourse follows a similar logic. They label the COVID-19 response as a 'skills fetish' focusing on how education can configure the 'right kind of skills' (Wheelahan et al., 2022, p. 475). They suggest that these 'right kind' of skills, understood in one way as 'digital skills', are a critical component of the gig economy. While many 'gigsters' might be able to use 'technology to attract aligned gigs... work out what their skills are and use technology to cherry pick the gigs that suit them... have a better life rather than just working 9–5' (Brandet, 2021, para. 17), these jobs are also precarious, informal and attract fewer rights such as minimum wage, superannuation, workers compensation, paid leave and the monitoring of dangerous work conditions.

With these kinds of work conditions in mind, Wheelahan et al. (2022, p. 475) argue that the 'fetishization' of skills degrades education, work and social life. They, along with Brown et al. (2020), argue that a 'skills fetish' repeatedly fails to deliver its promise of high-skilled jobs in a highly skilled economy. The main failure of this fetishisation is that 'the fundamental problem is not that there is a shortage of the relevant skills that employers demand but that there is a lack of good-quality jobs' (Brown et al., 2020, p. 133). Allais and Wedekind (2020, p. 336) warn that on a global scale, unrealistic target settings and expectations for foundation skills and technical vocational education and training (TVET) sectors can lead to:

> vastly inflated ideas of what TVET can and should do, and by expecting too much from TVET we make it very difficult for it to do almost anything. Governments take fragile institutions and give them impossible tasks, and then create the illusion that the reasons for the failure of TVET systems are reformable by changing TVET policy.

These concerns connect with other provocations in relation to how a 'skills recovery' can succeed. Yerby and Page-Tickell (2020), for example, question if the current crisis will propel a response from stakeholder groups – gig-based work platforms, governments, individuals, and trade unions – to change the trajectory and precarity inherent in the labour market. In a similar vein, Matilla-Santander et al. (2021) argue that in order to mitigate the impact of this pandemic, and respond to future ones, a legislative transformation of a new social contract of recognition, protection and security is needed.

Walsh et al. (2021) argue that discourse that reimagines 'careers' as a discrete and linear pathway is problematic. They claim that an 'assemblage' of roles, perceptions and attitudes towards work and life across time – 'a process, not a destination' – is more reflective of contemporary career identities (Walsh et al., 2021, p. 32). To facilitate a shift in thinking of what constitutes a career identity, Walsh et al. (2021, p. 32) stress that lifelong learning is now a 'necessity', not a 'desirable' activity, with 'learning how to learn', work-based learning opportunities, social interaction and communication all critical components of any policy response. Yet Mason (2020, para. 13–29) predicts that governments and policymakers will continue to design responses limited to 'V-shaped' recoveries and seek to restore a neoliberal system that has just 'broken down'. It is likely, though not inevitable, that governments will continue their 'neoliberal herd thinking' (Sparkle & Williams, 2022, p. 27).

2.2 *The Programme for the International Assessment of Adult Competencies (PIAAC) and the 'Politics' of the Future of Foundation Skills*

In engaging in speculative projections about the history of the future of foundation skills, it is difficult to ignore the impending results from the second cycle of the OECD's *Programme for the International Assessment of Adult Competencies (PIAAC)* survey due to be released in late 2024. As we outlined in Chapters One and Three, these surveys – conducted in 1996, 2006 and 2012 – have been defining events in global foundation skills policy discussion and making processes. They have also been central to the ways in which the urgent problem, diverse elements, and strategic relations characteristic of Australia's neoliberal foundation skills apparatus have taken the form that they have. They have revealed the 'urgent need' that processes of reflexive governance, and the apparatus, rely upon to organise and regulate populations with low foundation skills. Criticisms that the surveys are not reliable in producing meaningful comparisons between countries and understanding the relationship between literacy and economic indicators of wealth and well-being have largely been set aside (Hamilton & Barton, 2000). As we briefly problematise the impacts of the surveys in this section, we are not only illustrating another 'event' in the genealogy of foundation skills, but we argue, the potential reoccurrence of a 'social practice or institution we take for granted' (Foucault, cited in Gordon, 2000, p. XXXIV).

For Australia, the upcoming PIAAC surveys have been mired in what can be understood as a political contest, conducted in a complex and often competing bureaucratic form. As part of the ten-year *National Strategy*, the surveys were to provide the evaluative benchmark for its 'aspirational' target: 'by 2022, two-thirds of working-age Australians will have literacy and numeracy skills at Level 3 or above' (SCOTESE, 2012, p. 10). SCOTESE (2012, p. 2) claimed that to meet this target, a significant shift would be needed from the 2012 PIAAC results, which suggested that approximately 56 percent of Australia's working-age population would demonstrate foundation skills at level 3; that is, the level needed to meet the complex demands of work and life in modern economies (Australian Bureau of Statistics, 2013). In 2020, the Australian Council for Adult Literacy (2020) announced that they had been contacted by the Morrison Liberal-National Coalition government to consult on the development of a new national framework for foundation skills. Australian Council for Adult Literacy disclosed that the framework would build on the *National Strategy* by reviewing what had changed, and what could be enhanced and renewed. In March 2022, as a precursor to a new framework, the Coalition government released their inquiry – titled *Don't take it as read* – into adult literacy and its social, cultural and economic importance. The inquiry disclosed that a scoping study was being undertaken to consider the currency of the *National Strategy*. It acknowledged the *National Strategy's* aspirational target, but commented that it was necessary to draw on additional data on need, demand, success, and current funding, 'so that we have a more fulsome picture' (Parliament of the Commonwealth of Australia, 2022, pp. 7–8). This readjustment of focus was, perhaps, the key reason, despite Australia's participation in the previous three OECD surveys in 1996, 2006 and 2012, that it was not listed as a participating country for the second cycle (OECD, 2022).

The 2022 Jobs and Skills Summit convened by the Albanese Labor Government resulted in a commitment to reinvigorating foundation skills policy and programs, in partnership with states and territories, and stakeholders (Australian Government, 2023c). As a response, in December, the government released a draft of the *National Foundation Skills Framework 2022–2032* (Australian Government, 2022a). The new framework was similar to the *National Strategy*, in that it set a ten-year target of positive change, and recognised the critical role foundation skills play in equipping Australian adults to participate confidently in the community, the workplace, and in education and training (Australian Government, 2022a). It is unclear if the draft framework was a remnant of work that was carried over from their conservative Coalition predecessors, an expedited draft developed by the new government, or both. Months prior the Coalition was considering the currency of the *National Strategy* and the use of the OECD surveys as an evaluative tool, which could explain its absence of any discussion of the *National Strategy* or reference of the PIAAC surveys in the new framework. The framework shifted from the singular OECD measurement and, alternatively, adopted a raft of outcomes-based measures such as:

- levels of satisfaction of learners with when, where and how training is delivered;
- number of completions of recognised foundation skills units of competency;
- changes in proficiency levels of students;
- self-reported rating of readiness for further training or employment;
- number of enrolments in accredited training; and,
- qualitative reporting of information outlining whole-of-government investment in promotion and outreach for foundation skills at a national level (Australian Government, 2022a).

In October 2022, a new government advisory body named Jobs and Skills Australia was formed to provide expert advice on the current, emerging, and future skills and human capital needs of the economy, and on the effectiveness of the national skills system in meeting these needs (Australian Government, 2024c). One part of the responsibilities of Jobs and Skills Australia was to lead the development of a national study on adult literacy, numeracy and digital literacy skills named the *Foundation Skills Study*. In a similar manner to the objectives of the OECD surveys the study would survey Australian adults to assess their current skills levels. Also, the study would include a feasibility study into how best to assess the literacy, numeracy, and digital literacy levels of First Nations people; and an analysis of Commonwealth administrative and other data to 'drill down' into the results for priority groups. To facilitate the *Foundation Skills Study,* in April 2023, Jobs and Skills Australia released a discussion paper to determine the intent and desired outputs of the study (Australian Government, 2023a). The discussion paper drew on the *Don't take it as read* report to contextualise its existing data sets, however, there was no reference to the draft *National Foundation Skills Framework 2022–2032*. The framework was also not mentioned in the press release from the then Minister for Skills and Training, Brendan O'Connor, who announced Australia would rejoin the second cycle of the PIAAC surveys in 2024. Framing the return as a way to 'make up for a lost decade when foundation skills didn't get the attention they deserved' (Ministers of the Employment and Workplace Relations Portfolio, 2024, para. 19), Minister O'Connor also explained that the survey data would complement, not replace, the *Foundation Skills Study,* to help create a national evidence base to assist governments, policymakers and program managers in improving foundation skills access and delivery.

While this is likely another policy event in the evolving, shifting, complexity of Australia's foundation skills apparatus, it is also a key event in our speculative projection of the history of the future of foundation skills. The concept of reflexive governance suggests that within the Commonwealth's policy discussions, a change in perspective, or a self-critical questioning, could be evident in how the policy apparatus is managing populations with low foundation skills. Indeed, Feindt and Weiland (2018, p. 662) observe that the effects of different problem conceptualisations can promote the 'opening up' of the policy space. But in this event, we suggest that these deliberations could well signal a 'closing down' of the space. A closing down in which the norms, beliefs and assumptions are largely predetermined in two significant ways. First, the Commonwealth has seemingly deferred its policy response through the 2022 framework – that advocated for an outcomes-based measurement of success and not OECD data – to one of developing a further evidence base of survey data to (re)inform its direction. The *National Strategy* of 2012 was largely driven by the 2006 OECD data results, and the next policy direction may follow a similar approach. We liken this approach to our earlier discussions that drew on examples from Black et al. (2013), who identified some foundation skills discourses to be understood as 'common sense', accepted as standard, and rarely contested. Second, we draw on Foucault's (2008, p. 132) assertion that neoliberalism should not be 'be identified with laissez-faire, but rather with permanent vigilance, activity, and intervention'. The neoliberal processes of individualisation and responsibilisation that were rigorously advocated and promoted in the *National Strategy* are not clearly evident in the new framework or discussion paper proposal, in so far as these processes are now an accepted way of acting and thinking in the apparatus.

The second PIAAC results are likely to be heavily scrutinised in relation to the 'reality' that since 1996, global results have remained relatively fixed. It is possible that policy debates that emerged from the 2013 PIAAC results in many OECD countries could resurface or continue to be amplified. For example, adult literacy in the United States has remained stagnant across the survey series with twenty-one percent (43 million) of US adults finding it difficult to compare and contrast information, paraphrase, or make low-level inferences (National Centre for Education Statistics, 2021). There were concerns that the nation's approach to adult education had effectively become a high-school equivalency credentialing program, prioritising more advanced students, at the expense of those with greater literacy needs (Waldan et al., 2022). In Canada, the percentage of adults (48 percent) assessed as having inadequate literacy skills for contemporary forms of work had increased notably over the previous decade (OECD, 2013). This 'inadequacy' was identified, in part, as being connected to such things as: the situation that many jobs in the past had not required the daily use of reading comprehension and information synthesis skills (Chin, 2021); and the COVID-19 pandemic exacerbating increasing levels of precarity, instability and inequality in many households (Cooper &

Dixit, 2021). In this context, there have been calls for policy movements on adult training opportunities for those at higher risk of skills depreciation (Mahboubi, 2018), which, according to Elfert and Walker (2020, p. 121), 'have fallen out of favour in Canada'. In the United Kingdom, governments were alarmed by results that indicated that their youngest adult age group was near the bottom of OECD performance tables (The Centre for Literacy, 2013). The PIAAC results have been one factor in the reform of adult education and skills policy called the *Skills for Jobs: Lifelong Learning for Opportunity and Growth* which seeks to increase access to education and training. One part of this reform is to increase English, maths, and digital skills by encouraging '16- 19-year-old students without an approved intermediate level (level 2) in English and maths to continue studying these subjects' (Department for Education, 2021, p. 25).

Reflexive governance seeks to enable action and find specific solutions to problems. Yet if there is no significant improvement in the PIAAC results, processes of reflexive governance will encounter difficulties in managing the diversity of diagnoses and prognoses from the range of education, industry and policy stakeholders, and negotiating the legitimacy of these, or similar types of truth claims. Situated in this contentious space, there can be attempts to offer solutions or breakthrough arguments to explain a problem that should be understood as 'complex'. In contrast to a problem characterised by traditional 'cause and effect' or 'simplistic linear thinking', a problem is 'complex' in-so-much as it is made up of 'nonlinear, complex and multidimensional processes' (Miles, 2009, p. 140), and contains 'a large number of parts that interact in a non-simple way' (Herbert, 1962, p. 468). As a problem gets more complex, the ability to understand every aspect of the system is diminished (Bacal, 2019). Understanding foundation skills as a 'complex' problem can illuminate the difficulties in predicting how a solution in one part of the system may affect how well the system works, or a process may yield some favourable results, yet, have unintended consequences that are not favourable (Bacal, 2019). In this sense, tensions, contradictions, ambiguities and uncertainties are inevitable outcomes of complex interactions and need not be seen as things to resolve. The complex system can be productive in ways that are not entirely predictable. This tension and unpredictability results in the phenomenon of 'continually emerging novel behavior' (Kelly, 2013, p. 129).

In framing foundation skills as a 'complex' problem through a 'reflexive government' lens, we argue that government agencies, businesses and other groups must not avoid or seek to simplify complexity, but to 'honour complexity' (Cochran-Smith, 2003, p. 5). Within a reflexive response, this includes processes that are 'as simple as possible, but no simpler', avoiding the design of metrics that are inadequate for understanding and supporting the complexity of education and lowering the expectations of neat conclusions (Cochran-Smith, 2003, p. 5). Cochran-Smith (2003) claims that there needs to be a balance between being responsible and responsive to the public's concerns, acknowledging the demands of public policy, and preserving complexity in the press for accountability. This includes reconciling the need for policy to service the varied and often competing ends of the millions of individuals dispersed throughout an advanced economy, and simultaneously avoiding one-size-fits-all solutions to promote diverse individual outcomes (Meadowcroft, 2010). In accepting that there are no pre-determined 'correct' solutions or 'right' outcomes (Meadowcroft, 2010), there should be recognition that: solutions may emerge spontaneously in complex interactions; unforeseen and unexpected outcomes will emerge; and new ways of doing things will be discovered, all of which may be contrary to the preferences of government, policymakers, academics, professional groups, RTOs and industry.

2.3 *Artificial Intelligence and the Futures of Work and (Foundation) Skills*

Peter

'Tech-bro' is a term often used to describe a particular type of person who works in the fields of digital technologies, their applications, and the opportunities for profit that these developments provide – often with, it seems, little regard for the consequences, intended or otherwise, that flow from these developments. There are many attempts at defining this type of person. Provide a detailed definition of the term 'tech-bro' that captures what might be considered the positive and negative attributes of such a person.

ChatGPT

The term "tech-bro" is a colloquial and often pejorative label used to describe a certain archetype within the technology industry. This term encapsulates a blend of positive and negative attributes that are frequently observed in individuals who embody this stereotype. Here's a detailed definition that aims to capture the multifaceted nature of a "tech-bro":

Positive Attributes:

1. *Innovative and Forward-Thinking*:
   - *Visionary*: Often has grand ideas about the potential of technology to change the world.
   - *Risk-Taker*: Willing to take significant financial and personal risks to bring new ideas to market.

2. *Technologically Skilled*:
   - *Proficient*: Possesses a deep understanding of technology and its applications.
   - *Problem-Solver*: Capable of identifying and solving complex technical problems with innovative solutions.
3. *Entrepreneurial Spirit*:
   - *Ambitious*: Driven by a strong desire to build successful companies and products.
   - *Resourceful*: Adept at leveraging limited resources to achieve significant outcomes.
4. *Charismatic Leadership*:
   - *Influential*: Often charismatic and able to inspire teams and investors with their vision.
   - *Networked*: Well-connected within the tech industry, often having access to influential people and resources.

Negative Attributes:

1. *Overly Competitive and Aggressive*:
   - *Cutthroat*: May prioritize winning and personal success over collaboration and ethical considerations.
   - *Arrogant*: Displays a sense of superiority and dismissiveness towards those with differing viewpoints or less technical knowledge.
2. *Ethically Ambiguous*:
   - *Disregard for Consequences*: Often accused of ignoring or underestimating the social, environmental, and ethical implications of their innovations.
   - *Profit-Driven*: Primarily motivated by financial gain, sometimes at the expense of broader societal well-being.
3. *Lack of Diversity Awareness*:
   - *Homogeneous Culture*: Contributes to a monoculture within tech companies, often dominated by similar demographic and socio-economic backgrounds.
   - *Exclusivity*: May unconsciously or consciously create environments that are unwelcoming to women, minorities, and other underrepresented groups in tech.
4. *Work-Life Imbalance*:
   - *Burnout Culture*: Promotes a culture of overwork, valuing long hours and constant availability over personal well-being and balance.
   - *Unsustainable Practices*: Encourages unsustainable work habits that can lead to high employee turnover and long-term mental health issues.

Conclusion:
A "tech-bro" is often a complex individual characterized by a blend of entrepreneurial zeal and technical acumen, coupled with a tendency towards competitive, sometimes ethically questionable behavior. While they can be innovative and transformative figures within the tech industry, their approach can also perpetuate exclusionary practices and overlook the broader impact of technological advancement.

Ray Kurzweil is the best-selling author of *The Singularity Is Near* (2005), which predicted that 'computers would reach human-level intelligence by 2029 and that we would merge with computers and become superhuman around 2045', and is currently described as a 'computer scientist and techno-optimist' who is also the 'principal researcher and AI visionary at Google' (Corbyn, 2024). In a recent interview with Zoë Corbyn (2024) in *The Guardian* to mark the publication of *The Singularity Is Nearer* (Kurzweil, 2024), Kurzweil outlined what we would call his 'speculative projections' for the near and more distant futures of the evolution and development of both 'human-level' machine intelligence and for 'artificial general intelligence (AGI)'. Corbyn's identification of Kurzweil as a 'techno-optimist' and 'AI visionary at Google' is important to the structure of the interview as published, and what it is that we want to highlight at this time.

Corbyn (2024) observes that Kurzweil's projections and predictions in the two books have remained largely consistent – a point Kurzweil acknowledges by claiming that 'I'm really the only person that predicted the tremendous AI interest that we're seeing today. In 1999 people thought that would take a century or more. I said 30 years and look what we have'. This self-congratulatory tone is matched by his 'techno-optimism' and becomes more evident as he provides detail on how he sees these developments occurring, and in what time frames these developments will occur:

> So 2029, both for human-level intelligence and for artificial general intelligence (AGI) – which is a little bit different. Human-level intelligence generally means AI that has reached the ability of the most skilled humans in a particular domain and by 2029 that will be achieved in most respects... AGI means AI that can do everything that any human can do, but to a superior level. AGI sounds more difficult, but it's coming at the same time. And my five-year-out estimate is actually conservative: Elon Musk recently said it is going to happen in two years. (Corbyn, 2024, para. 3)

The main reasons for Kurzweil's continued 'optimism' about the veracity of his projections, and why we should 'believe' him, is related to his suggestion that the 'most important driver' of the development of forms of machine intelligences is the 'exponential growth in the amount of computing power for the price in constant dollars. We are doubling price-performance every 15 months. LLMs [Large Language Models] just began to work two years ago because of the increase in computation' (Corbyn, 2024). With these increases in computational capabilities, Kurzweil, in response to a series of questions from Corbyn (2024) about such things as the employment replacing impacts of machine and artificial intelligences, the 'existential' threats to humankind of the capabilities and consequences of developing and deploying these technologies, and the social, cultural and political impacts of these developments, embodies many of the characteristics of what others identify as a 'tech-bro':

The Singularity: 'will occur when we merge our brain with the cloud. We're going to be a combination of our natural intelligence and our cybernetic intelligence, and it's all going to be rolled into one. Making it possible will be brain-computer interfaces, which ultimately will be nanobots – robots the size of molecules – that will go noninvasively into our brains through the capillaries. We are going to expand intelligence a millionfold by 2045, and it is going to deepen our awareness and consciousness'.

A phone in your brain: 'Think of it like having your phone, but in your brain. If you ask a question your brain will be able to go out to the cloud for an answer similar to the way you do on your phone now – only it will be instant, there won't be any input or output issues, and you won't realise it has been done (the answer will just appear). People do say, "I don't want that": they thought they didn't want phones either!'

The existential threat to humanity: 'I have a chapter on perils. I've been involved with trying to find the best way to move forward and I helped to develop the Asilomar AI Principles [a 2017 non-legally binding set of guidelines for responsible AI development]. We do have to be aware of the potential here and monitor what AI is doing. But just being against it is not sensible: the advantages are so profound. All the major companies are putting more effort into making sure their systems are safe and align with human values than they are into creating new advances, which is positive'.

Should we be afraid of the 'job killing' potentials of AI?: 'Yes, and no. Certain types of jobs will be automated and people will be affected. But new capabilities also create new jobs. A job like "social media influencer" didn't make sense, even 10 years ago… Universal basic income will start in the 2030s, which will help cushion the harms of job disruptions. It won't be adequate at that point but over time it will become so'.

There is much else that is interesting in Corbyn's questioning of Kurzweil, including his observations on 'human' forms of intelligence, and the 'value proposition' that machine intelligences bring to relations and practices where the limits and possibilities of the 'human' appear as 'self-evident' to 'tech-optimists' such as Kurzweil. Here, the human future – for those who can afford it – is a future that is augmented, even merged into a techno-human hybrid that promises forms of 'physical and digital immortality'. Suggesting that many 'people will be sceptical of your predictions about physical and digital immortality', Corbyn (2024) reminds Kurzweil of his speculation that 'medical nanobots arriving in the 2030s… will be able to enter our bodies and carry out repairs so we can remain alive indefinitely', and that he foresees the advent of 'after life' technologies by 'the 2040s that will allow us to upload our minds so they can be restored – even put into convincing androids – if we experience biological death'. Kurzweil's response is interesting as a further example of a particular form of 'techno-optimism' about what human futures will look, and feel, like:

> Everything is progressing exponentially: not only computing power but our understanding of biology and our ability to engineer at far smaller scales. In the early 2030s we can expect to reach longevity escape velocity where every year of life we lose through ageing we get back from scientific progress. And as we move past that we'll actually get back more years. It isn't a solid guarantee of living for ever – there are still accidents – but your probability of dying won't increase year to year. The capability to bring back departed humans digitally will bring up some interesting societal and legal questions. (Corbyn, 2024, para. 15)

Absent from this sort of techno-optimism is any sense of the massive disparities and inequalities in relation to access to medical care, especially in the US which lacks many of the publicly-funded health care systems and services of other high-income economies – let alone any recognition of the cavernous health inequalities between high-income, and medium- and low-income economies. Also absent is any sense that the 'interesting societal and legal questions' that Kurzweil hints at, might, in reality, be more *existentially devastating* than 'interesting'. But this lack of recognition doesn't stop Kurzweil. Indeed, in his response to Corbyn's (2024) query about his 'own plan for immortality', Kurzweil provides a clear insight into the thoughts and actions of one 'tech-bro' on what it takes to transcend the corporeal limits of what it means, at this time, be a 'biocultural creature' (Frost, 2016):

> My first plan is to stay alive, therefore reaching longevity escape velocity. I take about 80 pills a day to help keep me healthy. Cryogenic freezing is the fallback. I'm also intending to create a replicant of myself [an afterlife AI avatar], which is an option I think we'll all have in the late 2020s. I did something like that with my father, collecting everything that he had written in his life, and it was a little bit like talking to him. [My replicant] will be able to draw on more material and so represent my personality more faithfully. (Corbyn, 2024, para. 16)

In our own more limited, possibly more pragmatic, 'speculative projections' about the emergences of forms of machine and artificial Intelligences, and the possible impacts and consequences of these emergences for the futures of work and foundation skills, we want to return to our earlier reference to the Australian Federal government's policy work in the aftermath of the pandemic which resulted in the *National Skills Agreement*, an *Employment White Paper* and the *Draft National Foundation Skills Framework 2022 to 2032*. There is also a form of 'techno-optimism' evident in these policy documents and the ways in which they imagine 'robotics and artificial intelligence' facilitating the automation of more mundane work practices and processes. In a short section dedicated to 'robotics and artificial intelligence', the framers of the *Employment White Paper* claim that:

> In addition to changing where and when people work, new technologies are changing the tasks jobs require, and how people work with technology. As robotics and artificial intelligence become capable of automating a growing share of routine tasks, there will be greater opportunities for businesses to leverage technology to make their workplaces safer and reduce administrative tasks for workers, and provide workers better access to information and decision-making tools. In these ways, effective adoption of technology can boost labour productivity. (Australian Government, 2023c, p. 9)

In this particular form of 'techno-optimism', governments focus on what they imagine to be the benefits to business, to workers, to regions, and to the economy more broadly:

> We are already witnessing businesses beginning to make this transformation. Since 2013 there has been considerable growth in demand in the Australian labour market for advanced digital skills related to artificial intelligence (AI), IT automation and the internet-connected physical infrastructure which makes up the internet of things... Notably, these

> technologies can be applied in ways that enhance the capabilities of workers or automate repetitive or time-consuming tasks, rather than replace jobs. This will allow workers to focus on activities with significantly higher value add such as problem-solving, interpersonal and other non-routine tasks. They also improve connectivity between regions, providing opportunities for collaboration and knowledge spillovers regardless of location. (Australian Government, 2023c, p. 81)

In a similar way, the *Draft National Foundation Skills Framework* briefly discusses the digitalisation and automation of the labour market – which it identifies as being amplified by the pandemic. In this context, the *Framework* identifies a need for workers to develop and increase their digital skills:

> The need to develop new skills has been highlighted during the COVID-19 pandemic, which accelerated changes already transforming the workplace such as digitalisation and automation. In the longer term the effect of the pandemic will likely interact with existing structural changes and our ageing population to increase demand for digital skills in a variety of sectors. (Australian Government, 2022a, p. 4)

In this form of 'techno-optimism', these policy documents warn of the dangers of not building what are identified as 'digital skills'. The *Draft National Foundation Skills Framework* warns that people with low literacy, numeracy and digital skills are less likely to be employed, or more likely to be employed in low-skilled, insecure occupations with a higher risk of being offshored or automated, and are at greater risk of redundancy (Australian Government, 2022a). The *Employment White Paper* identifies that:

> These routine tasks are more prevalent in lower-skill occupations which have seen slower employment growth over the last few decades. However, technological advancements like automation are expected to disrupt some tasks of most occupations, rather than automating entire roles. (Australian Government, 2023c, p. 87)

The World Economic Forum (Ekelund, 2024), which has played a leading role in advocating for the economic and employment upsides of what it has long called the Fourth Industrial Revolution, and which continues to be a significant organisational actant in the foundation skills apparatus in Australia, and in many other economies, remains optimistic in its investigation of *Why there will be plenty of jobs in the future – even with artificial intelligence*. Citing a long history of pessimistic projections about the employment replacing tendencies of previous industrial revolutions, Henrik Ekelund (2024, para. 4), who is identified as the Founder and Chairman of the BTS Group, and the recipient of the Swedish Entrepreneur of the Year award in 2011, observes that:

> Over the last 200 years, predictions of fewer jobs in the future have generally proven to be false. The pessimists have been wrong repeatedly. But make no mistake – hundreds of millions of jobs have been destroyed. First, agricultural technology replaced millions of farming jobs, while the industrial revolution moved people into factories. Then automation moved them back out of the factories, giving rise to an economy of services.

Central to this observation, which is shared by many other entrepreneurs, business people and tech-optimists, is Ekelund's (2024) suggestion that these 'revolutions' are enabled by, and are part of, successive 'waves' of 'creative destruction'. The implication here is that 'disruption' and 'breaking things' are, in the end, 'creative' – at least for those who might reap any benefits that flow from these forces. At the same time, Ekelund (2024, para. 6–15) recognises that things might 'be different this time because AI is different'. Indeed, technology 'will not always support people in doing their jobs, it will primarily replace jobs. New types of jobs will emerge, however'. This *benignly optimistic* assessment acknowledges that creative destruction 'stemming from tech development may lead to hard times and new challenges for many people, as well as for whole cities and regions'. In glossing over the material realities, precarity, and insecurity for hundreds of millions of people of these 'hard times and new challenges', Ekelund (2024) ignores the social, cultural, economic and political realities produced by 'breaking things', the consequences of which can be seen in the rise of extremism, populism, and forms of racism and xenophobia that characterise large parts of the local and more global social, cultural and political landscapes of the first quarter of the 21st century. The solutions imagined by Ekelund (2024, para. 15) revolve around governments fixing the things that are 'broken' by forces of creative destruction: 'Governments can play an important role in alleviating this by providing opportunities or support programmes for reskilling, as well as unemployment benefits and other forms of transitional safety nets'.

In a number of different spaces, these opportunities and challenges are similarly imagined in benignly optimistic ways. The US-based National Bureau of Economic Research describes itself as undertaking 'economic research' that is 'supported by grants from government agencies or private foundations, by corporation and individual contributions'.[2] In a National Bureau of Economic Research Working Paper – *Generative AI at Work* – Erik Brynjolfsson, Danielle Li and Lindsey Raymond (2023) suggest that inexperienced workers can benefit most from the use of generative AI in different work processes and tasks. Their investigation of US-based contact centre agents claims to reveal a 14 percent increase in the productivity of lower-skilled workers who benefitted from access to an LLM conversational assistant such as ChatGPT. The OECD (2023) also claims that forms of machine and artificial intelligence can be a helpful tool to promote inclusiveness in labour markets, such as complementing the work of people with low literacy skills or disabilities through text generation and translation tools. Bronwyn Hemsley (2023, para. 11) makes a similar observation, pointing to how newer versions of ChatGPT are likely to be more inclusive of diversity by being able to:

> understand poorly written commands, or sentences with several grammar or spelling errors. It can reportedly "read" poorly structured input, re-write and improve imperfect writing, and simplify complex texts into simpler summaries for early-stage readers. ChatGPT could be considered an "assistive technology" if it assists people with communication disability to get their message across more efficiently or effectively.

The emergence of these different applications of forms of machine and artificial intelligence assistance, named as being more 'inclusive' and as promoting labour market participation and productivity, raise further questions about the relationships between LLMs and literacy. Daniel Fitzpatrick (2024, para. 10), for example, in a blogpost – *Why Literacy Skills are Key to Success in the AI Era* – that targets literacy teachers, suggests that 'the false dichotomy of literacy versus AI is a red herring. Both are now intimately connected'. Fitzpatrick (2024) argues that unless people have high literacy skills to start with, their use of AI will be limited. However, he identifies AI and education as opportunities for people to simultaneously increase their literacy levels while developing their AI skills.

In a number of these policy and practice observations of the present, and their projections of the future consequences of the emergence of forms of machine and artificial intelligence, there is both a benign optimism in relation to these developments, and a narrow time horizon for when these effects will manifest themselves. In effect, these narrow time horizons produce this benign optimism. If, for example, governments in the assemblages we have defined and analysed were capable of imagining and projecting into wider time horizons, then the benign optimism they exhibit might take on a different character. In making this observation, our intention here is not to engage with, and indulge in, dystopian speculations about these possible futures. That would mean wandering into the domain of science fiction, and is likely as problematic as 'techno-optimism'. At the same time, as we have indicated, there are any number of emerging observations and analyses which include the possibilities that this machine and artificial intelligence revolution (which has long been a trope in science fiction) will be 'employment replacing' in ways unwitnessed in earlier 'industrial revolutions' that were themselves marked by automaton like machine-driven processes of mass production and automation. Georgios Petropoulos (2018), for example, suggests that past industrial revolutions have produced short-term job displacement, but that new industries also emerged, with a net positive impact on employment. Referencing the example of how the introduction of automobiles in daily life led to a decline in horse-related jobs, the productivity effects of the emergence of these machine technologies and processes tended to have a positive impact on employment overall, and new occupations and jobs emerged to replace those lost. In suggesting that *this time things might be different,* Petropoulos (2018, p. 122), citing work from Dobbs et al. (2015), estimates that the disruption of society caused by machine and artificial intelligences is happening ten times faster, at 300 times the scale, and 3,000 times the impact of the industrial revolution of the late 18th and early 19th centuries. In these contemporary emergences, 'machines are trained to be intelligent, which can have additional implications for the workforce'.

Speculative projections about the history of the future of foundation skills, as this future will be transformed by machine and artificial intelligences, must acknowledge the likely profound disruptions and discontinuities, as well as the histories and continuities that are bequeathed as legacies of the past and present. In this sense, the release of ChatGPT into the wild on November 30th, 2022, will likely, at some point in the near and/or more distant future, be positioned as a significant 'event' in the history of the present of the 'problem' of foundation skills at that moment in time. That genealogy, that history of that present, would need to unearth a number of things, including, importantly, the silences, absences and lack of concern for the life chances, life choices, and life courses that characterise what it means to be alive for more than 99 percent of the human population of the planet that arise in an encounter with various forms of 'techno-optimism' and 'visionary' accounts of the futures of human-machine-intelligence-assemblages (Montero & Kelly, 2021).

In a recent essay, Naomi Klein (2023) examines what she calls the 'hallucinations' of the 'tech-bros' who are disrupting and 'breaking things' in their pursuit of the profits that they imagine will flow from the forms of exploitation and extraction that drive these emergences – including the 'hoovering up' (the theft?) of all that humanity has produced to this point to 'feed' various forms of machine and artificial intelligence. A number of her observations about these hallucinations are instructive as we close this history of the future of foundation skills. In that essay, Klein (2023) plays on the use of the concept of 'hallucination' – that tendency for some forms of machine and artificial intelligence, such as ChatGPT, to just make things up when they are unable to provide a credible answer to a prompt/input. She argues that it is not these LLMs that are prone to hallucination: 'Warped hallucinations are indeed afoot in the world of AI… but it's not the bots that are having them; it's the tech CEOs who unleashed them, along with a phalanx of their fans, who are in the grips of wild hallucinations, both individually and collectively'. Here, 'hallucination' has a different meaning: 'These folks are just tripping: seeing, or at least claiming to see, evidence that is not there at all, even conjuring entire worlds that will put their products to use for our universal elevation and education'. Klein's (2023) first two of four 'hallucinations' – *AI will solve the climate crisis*, and *AI will deliver wise governance* – rest on the proposition that machine and artificial intelligences will provide the data, the tools, and the strategies to deal with problems that humans have created, but apparently cannot solve – because 'we' don't yet have access to these data, tools, and strategies. The hallucinatory state here ignores, as she observes, that the 'problem' is not 'due to a deficit of smarts':

> Never mind that smart people, heavy with PhDs and Nobel prizes, have been telling our governments for decades what needs to happen to get out of this mess: slash our emissions, leave carbon in the ground, tackle the overconsumption of the rich and the underconsumption of the poor because no energy source is free of ecological costs. (Klein, 2023, para. 19)

In her third hallucination – *Tech giants can be trusted not to break the world* – Klein (2023) addresses the sorts of techno-optimism that is a characteristic of so many tech-bros. Here, she references Sam Altman, the CEO of OpenAI, and his reply to concerns about the many adverse possibilities that arise in the release of machine and artificial intelligences energised by the motivation for profit and shareholder value. At one level, Altman acknowledges these concerns, however, in the interview she cites, he observes that: '"Hopefully it will all work out". Of his fellow tech CEOs – the ones competing to rush out their rival chatbots – he said: "I think the better angels are going to win out"'. As an indignant Klein (2023) suggests:

> Better angels? At Google? I'm pretty sure the company fired most of those because they were publishing critical papers about AI, or calling the company out on racism and sexual harassment in the workplace. More "better angels" have quit in alarm… That's because, contrary to the hallucinations of the people profiting most from AI, Google does not make decisions based on what's best for the world – it makes decisions based on what's best for Alphabet's shareholders, who do not want to miss the latest bubble, not when Microsoft, Meta and Apple are already all in.

All of these hallucinations are important for understanding the context of extractive and exploitative capitalism that has been the driver for so many of the elements of these novel developments in machine and artificial intelligences. And the ways in which these characteristics are so little discussed and/or acknowledged in benignly optimistic accounts of these emergences, and the futures they portend. More so in the particular accounts of the ways in which these intelligences promise to 'disrupt', even 'break' futures of work, to reconfigure the character of those 'skills' that are imagined as being essential for participating in different labour markets in these futures, and/or what these developments will mean for those hundreds of millions of people who are likely to be most vulnerable as a consequence of these disruptions and breakages.

Klein's (2023) final hallucination – *AI will liberate us from drudgery* – canvasses these concerns and provides a point on which we can conclude this speculative projection on the history of the future of foundation skills. As she observes, the suggestions that machine and artificial intelligences will free us from 'work as toil and drudgery' (Kelly, 2013), comes from a 'playbook' with a long history:

> Many lives and sectors have been decimated by earlier iterations of this playbook, from taxi drivers to rental markets to local newspapers. With the AI revolution, these kinds of losses could look like rounding errors, with teachers, coders, visual artists, journalists, translators, musicians, care workers and so many others facing the prospect of having their incomes replaced by glitchy code. (Klein, 2023, para. 31)

In these benignly optimistic accounts that reference a long history of imagining a post-work order of leisure and more creative pursuits by humans freed from the obligation to earn a living, we are told by these techno-optimists not to be concerned: 'Don't worry, the AI enthusiasts hallucinate – it will be wonderful. Who likes work anyway? Generative AI won't be the end of employment, we are told, only "boring work" – with chatbots helpfully doing all the soul-destroying, repetitive tasks and humans merely supervising them'. Again, Sam Altman imagines a 'future where work "can be a broader concept, not something you have to do to be able to eat, but something you do as a creative expression and a way to find fulfillment and happiness"' (Klein, 2023, para. 32).

Peter
Given these attributes [of a 'tech bro'] define a Silicon Valley cosmology or view of how the world functions, or could be imagined as functioning, and the roles that technology and tech-bros play in bringing this cosmology into view.

ChatGPT
Silicon Valley Cosmology: An Imaginative Framework. The Silicon Valley cosmology is a worldview shaped by the unique blend of values, beliefs, and practices prevalent in the technology epicenter. It envisions a world fundamentally transformed by technological innovation, where the roles of technology and tech-bros are pivotal in shaping the future. This cosmology is characterized by several core elements:

Core Beliefs and Values
1. *Technological Determinism*:
   - *Belief*: Technology is the primary driver of societal change and progress.
   - *Implication*: Advancements in technology will inherently lead to improvements in the quality of life, efficiency, and problem-solving.
2. *Disruption as Progress*:
   - *Belief*: Established systems and industries are often inefficient and ripe for disruption.
   - *Implication*: Challenging and replacing these systems with innovative solutions is essential for progress.
3. *Meritocracy:*
   - *Belief*: Success is primarily determined by individual talent, effort, and innovation.
   - *Implication*: Anyone with the right skills and mindset can achieve significant success, regardless of background.

4. *Optimism and Utopianism*:
   - *Belief*: Technology can solve most of humanity's problems, leading to a utopian future.
   - *Implication*: Investing in and developing new technologies is the best path toward a better world.

Imagined Functions of the World

1. *Hyper-Connectivity*:
   - *Vision*: A world where everyone and everything is interconnected through seamless communication networks.
   - *Role of Technology*: The internet, IoT (Internet of Things), and advanced communication platforms enable real-time, global interaction.
2. *Automation and AI*:
   - *Vision*: A society where mundane, repetitive tasks are handled by intelligent machines, freeing humans for more creative and strategic roles.
   - *Role of Technology*: AI and robotics are at the forefront, driving efficiency and innovation in every sector.
3. *Decentralization:*
   - *Vision*: Power and resources are distributed across a network rather than concentrated in centralized entities.
   - *Role of Technology*: Blockchain and decentralized technologies empower individuals and communities, reducing reliance on traditional power structures.
4. *Personalization:*
   - *Vision*: Services and products are tailored to individual preferences and needs, creating highly customized experiences.
   - *Role of Technology*: Big data, machine learning, and advanced analytics enable companies to understand and anticipate consumer desires.

Roles of Technology and Tech-Bros

1. *Innovators and Visionaries*:
   - *Function*: Tech-bros are seen as the driving force behind technological breakthroughs.
   - *Impact*: Their willingness to take risks and push boundaries leads to new products, services, and industries.
2. *Disruptors and Reformers*:
   - *Function*: By challenging existing norms and industries, tech-bros create opportunities for new, more efficient systems.
   - *Impact*: This disruption can lead to economic growth and societal change, although it may also cause upheaval and displacement.

3. *Evangelists and Influencers*:
   - *Function*: Tech-bros often act as public figures who promote the benefits and potential of technology.
   - *Impact*: Their charisma and influence can attract talent, investment, and public support for technological initiatives.
4. *Investors and Mentors*:
   - *Function*: Successful tech-bros often reinvest their wealth into new startups and mentor the next generation of entrepreneurs.
   - *Impact*: This cycle of investment and mentorship fuels ongoing innovation and growth within the tech ecosystem.

Potential Consequences and Critiques

1. *Ethical Blind Spots*:
   - *Issue*: The relentless pursuit of innovation can lead to ethical oversights and unintended negative consequences.
   - *Critique*: This can result in privacy violations, job displacement, and increased inequality.
2. *Exclusivity and Monoculture*:
   - *Issue*: The Silicon Valley culture can be insular and unwelcoming to those outside its typical demographic.
   - *Critique*: This lack of diversity can stifle different perspectives and lead to a narrow focus on certain types of problems and solutions.
3. *Short-Term Focus*:
   - *Issue*: The pressure to achieve rapid success and returns can prioritize short-term gains over long-term sustainability.
   - *Critique*: This approach may neglect the broader societal and environmental impacts of technological development.

Conclusion

The Silicon Valley cosmology envisions a world where technology is the primary agent of change, driven by the innovative and entrepreneurial spirit of tech-bros. While this worldview champions progress and optimism, it also faces significant challenges and critiques, particularly regarding ethics, diversity, and sustainability. The role of technology and tech-bros in this cosmology is both transformative and contentious, reflecting the complex interplay between innovation and its broader societal implications.

This Silicon Valley cosmology is reflective of a particular location in time and space, of a particular history of the experience of 'work', and of a particular lack of a sense of what it means to have to toil in contexts in which the concept and materiality of 'choice' in relation to labour is not the same as for those who occupy different cosmologies. As Klein (2023, para. 29) indicates:

> That's an exciting vision of a more beautiful, leisurely life, one many leftists share... But we leftists also know that if earning money is to no longer be life's driving imperative, then there must be other ways to meet our creaturely needs for shelter and sustenance. A world without crappy jobs means that rent has to be free, and healthcare has to be free, and every person has to have inalienable economic rights. And then suddenly we aren't talking about AI at all – we're talking about socialism.

In this sense, any speculative projection about the history of the future of foundation skills needs to recognise, and account for the reality – which is not an accidental by-product of their emergence – that the primary reason for the current rush to develop, evolve, and deploy machine and artificial intelligences 'never was to solve climate change or make our governments more responsible or our daily lives more leisurely. It was always to profit off mass immiseration, which, under capitalism, is the glaring and logical consequence of replacing human functions with bots' (Klein, 2023, para. 39). As Klein (2023, para. 33) observes, 'we do not live in the Star Trek-inspired rational, humanist world that Altman seems to be hallucinating'. Rather, in the material reality of 21st century, neoliberal, globalising forms of capitalism, 'the effects of flooding the market with technologies that can plausibly perform the economic tasks of countless working people is not that those people are suddenly free to become philosophers and artists. It means that those people will find themselves staring into the abyss' (Klein, 2023, para. 31). An abyss in which these people will continue to be imagined, for the foreseeable future, as choice-making, rational consumers of those foundation skills products and services that agencies, governments, and businesses promise will equip them with the skills deemed necessary for securing participation in these futures of work.

Notes

1 The *National Agreement for Skills and Workforce Development* was first established in 2012. It identifies the long-term objectives of the Commonwealth, State and Territory governments in the areas of skills and workforce development to support a VET system that enables all working age Australians to develop the skills and qualifications needed to participate effectively in the labour market and contribute to Australia's economic future (Australian Government, 2019c).

2 https://www.nber.org/about-nber/support-funding

Bibliography

Abbott, T. (2004). Church, civil society and politics. In F. Sullivan & S. Leppert (Eds.), *Church and Civil Society* (pp. 1–5). ATF Press.

ABC Melbourne. (2012). *Analysis of TAFE cuts shows more women affected*. Retrieved February 14, 2022, from https://www.abc.net.au/local/audio/2012/09/26/3598242.htm?site=gippsland

ABC News. (2018). *Insecure work the 'new norm' as full-time job rate hits record low: report*. Retrieved November 7, 2021, from http://www.abc.net.au/news/2018-06-07/full-time-job-rate-hits-new-low-as-casual-work-takes-over-report/9840064

Acharya, M. (2018, March 7). Australian Citizenship: Migrants to face tougher English language test. *SBS News*. https://www.sbs.com.au/language/english/australian-citizenship-migrants-to-face-tougher-english-language-test

ACIL Allen Consulting. (2015a). *AMEP & SEE Programme Allignment Report: Final Report to the Department of Education & Training*. ACIL Allen Consulting.

ACIL Allen Consulting. (2015b). *AMEP Evaluation: Final Report to the Department of Education & Training*. ACIL Allen Consulting.

ACIL Allen Consulting. (2015c). *SEE Programme Evaluation: Final Report to the Department of Education & Training*. ACIL Allen Consulting.

Adult Learning Australia. (2011). *Let's Get Serious About Adult Literacy and Numeracy*. Adult Learning Australia and Australian Education Union.

Adult Literacy Information Office. (1990). *ALIO Update No.16*. Adult Literacy Information Office.

Adult Literacy Information Office. (1999). *Defining Adult Literacy – Again. Literacy Discussion Paper*. New South Wales Department of TAFE.

Agamben, G. (2009). *What is an apparatus? and other essays*. Stanford University Press.

Ager, A., & Strang, A. (2008). Understanding Integration: A Conceptual Framework. *Journal of Refugee Studies, 21*(2), 166–191. https://doi.org/10.1093/jrs/fen016

Aiken, M. (2000). Reflexive modernisation and the social economy. *Studies in Social and Political Thought, 2*(3), 3–21.

Alla-Mensah, J., Fakoush, H., McGrath, S., & Wedekind, V. (2019). Migrants in the labor market: Implications for TVET. In S. McGrath, M. Mulder, J. Papier, & R. Suart (Eds.), *Handbook of Vocational Education and Training. Developments in the Changing World of Work* (pp. 159–176). Springer.

Allais, S., & Wedekind, V. (2020). Targets, TVET and transformation. In A. Wulff (Ed.), *Grading Goal Four: Tensions, Threats, and Opportunities in the Sustainable Development Goal on Quality Education* (pp. 322–338). Brill Sense.

Allen, A. (2011). Foucault and the politics of our selves. *History of the Human Sciences, 24*(4), 43–59. https://doi.org/10.1177/0952695111411623

Andrews, K. (2017a). *Address to AMEP and SEE Provider Forum*. Ministers for the Department of Education and Training Media Centre. Retrieved May 22, 2019, from https://ministers.education.gov.au/andrews/address-amep-and-see-provider-forum

Andrews, K. (2017b). *Improving Learning Opportunities for Migrants and Job Seekers, 18 April 2017 Media Release.*

Antcliff, S. (1988). Behind the rhetoric: A closer look at the New Right. *Australian Quarterly, 1*(Autumn), 63–69.

Appleby, Y., & Barton, D. (2008). *Responding to people's lives. Developing adult teaching and learning: Practitioner guides*. National Institute of Adult Continuing Education.

Arup, T. (2012, June 16). Angry protests as Baillieu defends TAFE cuts in times of uncertainty. *The Age*.

Australia Council of TESOL Associations. (2014). *AMEP and Skills for Education and Employment Evaluation: Submission from The Australia Council of TESOL Associations*. Australia Council of TESOL Associations.

Australia Council of TESOL Associations. (2019). *The Evaluation of the Adult Migrant English Program (AMEP) "New Business Model"*. Australia Council of TESOL Associations.

Australian Bureau of Statistics. (1996). *Aspects of Literacy: Assessed Skill Levels Australia*. Canberra, ACT: Australian Government Publishing Service.

Australian Bureau of Statistics. (2001). *Australian schools: Participation and Funding 1901 to 2000*. Australian Bureau of Statistics.

Australian Bureau of Statistics. (2006). *Adult Literacy and Life Skills Survey – Summary Results*. Australian Government Publishing Service.

Australian Bureau of Statistics. (2013). *Programme for the International Assessment of Adult Competencies, Australia, 2011–2012*. Australian Bureau of Statistics.

Australian Chamber of Commerce and Industry. (2022). *Media release: ACCI releases blueprint to tackle labour and skills crisis*. Australian Chamber of Commerce and Industry. Retrieved April 24, 2022, from https://www.australianchamber.com.au/news/acci-releases-blueprint-to-tackle-labour-and-skills-crisis/

Australian Competition & Consumer Commission. (2021a). *Compliance & enforcement policy & priorities*. Australian Competition & Consumer Commission. Retrieved August 19, 2021, from https://www.accc.gov.au/about-us/australian-competition-consumer-commission/compliance-enforcement-policy-priorities

Australian Competition & Consumer Commission. (2021b). *Fines & penalties*. Australian Competition & Consumer Commission. Retrieved August 19, 2021, from https://www.accc.gov.au/business/business-rights-protections/fines-penalties

Australian Council for Adult Literacy. (2001). *A Literate Australia: National Position Paper on the Future Adult Literacy and Numeracy Needs of Australia*. Australian Council for Adult Literacy.

Australian Council for Adult Literacy. (2020). *New Foundation Skills framework planned.* Australian Council for Adult Literacy. Retrieved July 31, 2021, from https://acal.edu.au/new-foundation-skills-framework/

Australian Council for Private Education and Training. (2013). *Education and Employment Committee Inquiry into TAFE.* Australian Council for Private Education and Training.

Australian Council of Social Service. (1997). *JobsPack, Information and Policy Paper, November 1997.* Australian Council of Social Service.

Australian Education Union. (2019). *New TAFE agreement puts teachers at the centre of rebuilding TAFE.* Australian Education Union – Victorian Branch. Retrieved May 9, 2020, from https://www.aeuvic.asn.au/new-tafe-agreement-puts-teachers-centre-rebuilding-tafe

Australian Government. (2012). *Australia in the Asian Century: White Paper.* Department of the Prime Minister and Cabinet.

Australian Government. (2013a). *Program Guidelines – Skills for Education and Employment (SEE) Program.* Department of Industry, Innovation, Climate Change, Science, Research and Tertiary Education.

Australian Government. (2013b). *Skills for Education and Employment (SEE) Program Changes.* Department of Education and Training.

Australian Government. (2015a). *Jobactive – Help For job seekers.* Department of the Prime Minister and Cabinet.

Australian Government. (2015b). *Users' Guide to the Standards for RTOs.* Australian Skills Quality Authority.

Australian Government. (2016). *Skills for Education and Employment (SEE) Program.* Department of Industry, Innovation, Climate Change, Science, Research and Tertiary Education. Retrieved April 10, 2017, from https://www.education.gov.au/skills-education-and-employment

Australian Government. (2017). *Revised Business Model for the Adult Migrant English Program.* Department of Education and Training.

Australian Government. (2019a). *Changes to the Adult Migrant English Program (AMEP).* Department of Home Affairs. Retrieved May 19, 2020, from https://immi.homeaffairs.gov.au/settling-in-australia/amep/about-the-program/background

Australian Government. (2019b). *Jobactive Guideline: Performance Framework.* Department of the Prime Minister and Cabinet.

Australian Government. (2019c). *National Agreement for Skills and Workforce Development (NASWD).* Department of Education, Skills and Employment. Retrieved April 24, 2022, from https://www.dese.gov.au/skills-information-training-providers/national-agreement-skills-and-workforce-development

Australian Government. (2020a). *AMEP: Success Stories.* Department of Home Affairs. Retrieved May 19, 2020, from https://immi.homeaffairs.gov.au/settling-in-australia/amep/about-the-program/success-stories

Australian Government. (2020b). *Become an Australian citizen*. Department of Home Affairs. Retrieved July 19, 2020, from https://immi.homeaffairs.gov.au/citizenship/become-a-citizen

Australian Government. (2020c). *English Language: Proficient English*. Department of Home Affairs. Retrieved July 19, 2020, from https://immi.homeaffairs.gov.au/help-support/meeting-our-requirements/english-language/proficient-english

Australian Government. (2020d). *Heads of Agreement for Skills Reform*. Department of the Prime Minister and Cabinet.

Australian Government. (2021a). *How SEE helps job seekers*. Department of Education, Skills and Employment. Retrieved May 19, 2020, from https://www.dese.gov.au/skills-education-and-employment/job-seekers

Australian Government. (2021b). *Industry Groups*. Australian Government. Retrieved September 10, 2021, from https://info.australia.gov.au/information-and-services/business-and-industry/primary-industry/industry-groups

Australian Government. (2021c). *Reform of the Adult Migrant English Program (AMEP)*. Department of Home Affairs. Retrieved April 12, 2020, from https://immi.homeaffairs.gov.au/settling-in-australia/amep/about-the-program/background

Australian Government. (2022a). *Draft National Foundation Skills Framework 2022 to 2032*. Australian Government.

Australian Government. (2022b). *Medicare*. Department of Health. Retrieved May 25, 2022, from https://www.health.gov.au/health-topics/medicare

Australian Government. (2022c). *Superannuation*. Services Australia. Retrieved May 25, 2022, from https://www.servicesaustralia.gov.au/superannuation?context=22526

Australian Government. (2022d). *Sustainable Development Goals: Goal 4 Quality Education*. Department of Foreign Affairs and Trade. Retrieved May 25, 2022, from https://www.sdgdata.gov.au/goals/quality-education

Australian Government. (2022e, February 22). *What is a Unique Student Identifier (USI)?* Australian Government. Retrieved February 22, 2022, from www.usi.gov.au

Australian Government. (2023a). *Foundation Skills Discussion Paper*. Australian Government.

Australian Government. (2023b). *National Skills Agreement*. Australian Government. Retrieved July 11, 2024, from https://www.dewr.gov.au/skills-reform/national-skills-agreement

Australian Government. (2023c). *Working Future. The Australian Government's White Paper on Jobs and Opportunities Commonwealth of Australia*. Australian Government.

Australian Government. (2024a). *Adult Migrant English Program (AMEP): About the program*. Retrieved June 28, 2024, from https://immi.homeaffairs.gov.au/settling-in-australia/amep/about-the-program#:~:text=you%20can%20now%20access%20unlimited,until%20you%20reach%20vocational%20English.to

Australian Government. (2024b). *Agree to your Job Plan*. Retrieved June 28, 2024, from https://www.workforceaustralia.gov.au/individuals/obligations/learn/your-obligations/job-plan

Australian Government. (2024c). *Jobs and Skills Australia: About Us* Retrieved June 28, 2024, from https://www.jobsandskills.gov.au/engage/about

Australian Government. (2024d). *Workforce Australia Services Provider Performance Ratings*. Retrieved June 28, 2024, from https://www.dewr.gov.au/workforce-australia/workforce-australia-information-providers/workforce-australia-services-provider-performance-ratings

Australian Industry and Skills Committee. (2021). *Skills Service Organisations*. Department of Education, Skills and Employment. Retrieved September 10, 2021, from https://www.aisc.net.au/industry-reference-committees/skills-service-organisations

Australian Industry Group. (2010). *National Workforce Literacy Project: Report on Employer Views on Workplace Literacy and Numeracy Skills*. Australian Industry Group.

Australian Industry Group. (2011). *National Foundation Skills Strategy for Adults Consultation Paper*. Australian Industry Group.

Australian Industry Group. (2016). *Tackling Foundation Skills in the Workforce*. Australian Industry Group.

Australian Labor Party, & Australian Council of Trade Unions. (1983). *Statement of accord by the Australian Labor Party and the Australian Council of Trade Unions regarding economic policy*. Australian Council of Trade Unions.

Australian National Training Authority. (1994). *National Training Reform Agenda*. Australian National Training Authority.

Bacal, R. (2019). *The Laws of Complex Systems Applied To Real Life*. Bacal & Associates. Retrieved April 18, 2022, from http://work911.com/articles/complexity-first.htm

Bailey, P. (2013). The policy dispositif: historical formation and method. *Journal of Education Policy*, *28*(6), 807–827. https://doi.org/10.1080/02680939.2013.782512

Balatti, J., Black, S., & Falk, I. (2006). *Reframing adult literacy and numeracy course outcomes: A social capital perspective*. NCVER.

Balatti, J., Black, S., & Falk, I. (2009). *A New Social Capital Paradigm for Adult Literacy: Partnerships, Policy and Pedagogy. An Adult Literacy National Project Report*. NCVER.

Ball, K. (2005). *Funding and Financing Vocational Education and Training: Research Readings*. NCVER.

Ball, S. (2003). The teacher's soul and the terrors of performativity. *Journal of Education Policy*, *18*(2), 215–228.

Ball, S. (2004). *Education For Sale! The Commodification of Everything? King's Annual Education Lecture 2004*. London, UK.

Ball, S., & Youdell, D. (2008). *Hidden Privatisation in Public Education*. Education International.

Barrett, G. (2012). The return to cognitive skills in the Australian labour market. *Economic Record, 88*(280), 1–17. https://doi.org/10.1111/j.1475-4932.2011.00775.x

Barton, D. (2006). The significance of a social practice view of language, literacy and numeracy. In L. Tett, M. Hamilton, & Y. Hillier (Eds.), *Adult literacy, numeracy and language: Policy, practice and research* (pp. 21–30). Open University Press.

Bauman, Z. (2004). *Work, consumerism and the new poor*. McGraw-Hill Education (UK).

Beck, U. (2000). *The brave new world of work*. Polity Press.

Becker, G. (1963). *Human Capital: A Theoretical and Empirical Analysis with Special Reference to Education*. Columbia University Press.

Becker, G. (1992). Human capital and the economy. *Proceedings of the American Philosophical Society, 136*(1), 85–92. https://doi.org/10.2307/2138769

Beeson, M. (2015, 1 January). Cabinet papers 1989: The origins of Asian engagement. *The Conversation*. https://theconversation.com/cabinet-papers-1989-the-origins-of-asian-engagement-35691

Beeson, M., & Firth, A. (1998). Neoliberalism as a political rationality: Australian public policy since the 1980s. *Journal of Sociology, 3*(34), 215–231.

Behrent, M. (2013). Foucault and Technology. *History and Technology, 29*(1), 54–104. https://doi.org/10.1080/07341512.2013.780351

Belot, H. (2018, 7 March). New migrants living in 'cultural bubbles' need to improve their English skills, Government warns. *Australian Broadcasting Commision* (ABC). https://www.abc.net.au/news/2018-03-07/english-language-tests-need-to-be-tougher-government-warns/9522412

Benseman, J. (2014). *Adult Refugee Learners with Limited Literacy: Needs and Effective Responses*. AKO Aotearoa.

Biddle, N., Edwards, B., Gray, M., & McEachern, S. (2018). *Public attitudes towards data governance in Australia*. Australian National University.

Bieber, F., & Moggia, J. (2021). Risk shifts in the gig economy: The normative case for an insurance scheme against the effects of precarious work. *The Journal of Political Philosophy, 29*(3), 281–304.

Bjursell, C. (2016). When theories become practice – a metaphorical analysis of adult-education school-leaders' talk. *European Journal for Research on the Education and Learning of Adults, 7*(2), 191–205.

Black, S. (2002). *Whose Economic Wellbeing? A Challenge to Dominant Discourses on the Relationship Between Literacy and Numeracy Skills and (Un)employment*. Adult Literacy and Numeracy Australian Research Consortium.

Black, S., Balatti, J., & Falk, I. (2010). Reconnecting young people with learning: A social capital approach in VET. *International Journal of Training Research, 8*(2), 103–115. https://doi.org/10.5172/ijtr.8.2.103

Black, S., & Yasukawa, K. (2013). Beyond deficit models for integrating language, literacy and numeracy in Australian VET. *Journal of Further and Higher Education*, *37*(4), 574–590. https://doi.org/10.1080/0309877X.2011.645469

Black, S., & Yasukawa, K. (2014). The literacy myth continues: Adapting Graff's thesis to contemporary policy discourses on adult 'foundation skills' in Australia. *Critical Studies in Education*, *55*(2), 213–228. https://doi.org/10.1080/17508487.2014.904809

Black, S., Yasukawa, K., & Brown, T. (2013). The literacy and numeracy 'crisis' in Australian workplaces: Discursive rhetoric vs. production floor realities. *Journal of Education and Work*, *28*(6), 607–630. https://doi.org/10.1080/13639080.2013.854875

Boland, T. (2016). Seeking a role: Disciplining jobseekers as actors in the labour market. *Work, employment and society*, *30*(2), 334–351. https://doi.org/10.1177/0950017015594097

Bondi, L. (2005). Working the spaces of neoliberal subjectivity: Psychotherapeutic technologies, professionalisation and counselling. *Antipode*, *37*(3), 497–514. https://doi.org/10.1111/j.0066-4812.2005.00508.x

Borevi, K., Jensen, K., & Mouritsen, P. (2017). The civic turn of immigrant integration policies in the Scandinavian welfare states. *Comparative Migration Studies*, *5*(1), 1–14. https://doi.org/10.1186/s40878-017-0052-4

Bradshaw, D. (1998). What is a basic education? *Fine Print*, *1*(Spring), 3–5.

Braithwaite, V. (2018). *All Eyes on Quality: Review of the National Vocational Education and Training Regulator Act 2011 Report*. Australian Government.

Brancaleone, D., & O'Brien, S. (2011). Educational commodification and the (economic) sign value of learning outcomes. *British journal of sociology of education*, *32*(4), 501–519. https://doi.org/10.1080/01425692.2011.578435

Brandet, P. (2021, 16 September). Is the gig economy worthwhile to individuals as the industry booms during a pandemic? *ABC Far North*.

Brennan, J., & Jaworski, P. (2015). In defense of commodification. *Moral Philosophy and Politics*, *2*(2), 357–377. https://doi.org/10.1515/mopp-2015-0018

Brennan, J., & Jaworski, P. (2016). *Market Without Limits: Moral Virtues and Commercial Interests*. Routledge.

Brenner, N. (1994). Foucault's new functionalism. *Theory and Society*, *23*(5), 679–709. https://doi.org/10.2307/658092

Brindley, G. (1998). Outcomes-based assessment and reporting in language learning programmes: A review of the issues. *Language testing*, *15*(1), 45–85.

Brindley, G. (2000). *Studies in immigrant English language assessment – Volume 1*. National Centre for English Language Teaching and Research.

Brock, P. (1997). *Literacy Discussion Papers: Paper No. 1. Breaking some of the myths – again. Edited version of opening address: Refocus on Reding Conference, University of Wollongong, July 18–19, 1997*. NSW Department of Education and Training.

Brooker, A. (1999). Mandatory literacy training – a simplistic response to a complex problem? *Fine Print, 1*(Spring), 32–33.

Brough, M. (2007). *National emergency response to protect Aboriginal children in the NT, media release, 21 June 2007.*

Brown, P., Lauder, H., & Cheung, S. (2020). *The Death of Human Capital? In Its Failed Promise and How to Renew It in an Age of Disruption.* Oxford University Press.

Brown, S., Kelly, P., & Phillips, S. (2024). *Informal Workers and a Political Economy of Life Long Learning: Lessons from the Margins of Global Capitalism.* Palgrave.

Brown, W. (2005). Neoliberalism and the end of liberal democracy. In W. Brown (Ed.), *Edgework: Critical essays on knowledge and politics* (pp. 38–59). Princeton University Press.

Brynjolfsson, E., Li, D., & Raymond, L. (2023). *Generative AI at Work.* MIT Management Sloan School.

Buckingham, A. (2000). Welfare reform in Britain, Australia and the United States. In P. Saunders (Ed.), *Reforming the Australian welfare state* (pp. 72–89). Australian Institute of Family Studies.

Buckmaster, L. (2009). *Money for nothing? Australia in the global middle class welfare debate.* Parliament of Australia.

Burchell, G., Gordon, C., & Miller, P. (Eds.). (1991). *The Foucault Effect: Studies in Governmentality. Two Lectures by and an Interview with Michel Foucault.* University of Chicago Press.

Burgess, J., & Campbell, I. (1998). The nature and dimensions of precarious employment in Australia. *Labour & Industry, 8*(3), 5–21. https://doi.org/10.1080/10301763.1998.10669175

Cahill, D. (2009). Is neoliberalism history? *Social Alternatives, 28*(1), 12–16.

Carney, T., & Stanford, J. (2018). *The Dimensions of Insecure Work: A Factbook.* The Australia Institute.

Carter, R. (2006). Of things said and unsaid: Power, archival silences, and power in silence. *Archivaria, 6*(1), 215–233.

Castle, F. (2001). A farewell to Australia's welfare state. *International Journal of Health Services, 31*(3), 537–544.

Castles, S., Korac, M., Vasta, E., & Vertovec, S. (2001). *Integration: Mapping the Field. Report of a project carried out by the Centre for Migration and Policy Research and Refugee Studies Centre.* University of Oxford.

Castleton, G. (2001). (E)merging discourses at work: Bringing together new and old ways to account for workplace literacy policy. In J. Lo Bianco & R. Wickert (Eds.), *Australian Policy Activism in Language & Literacy* (pp. 163–177). Language Australia.

Catlaks, G., & Dekoning, M. (2009). Hidden privatization in public education. *International Journal of Labour Research, 1*(2), 149–157.

Chandler, D., & Reid, J. (2016). *The neoliberal subject: Resilience, adaptation and vulnerability*. Rowman & Littlefield.

Chaney, D. (1981). Public opinion and social change: The social rhetoric of documentary and the concept of news. In E. Katz & T. Szecsko (Eds.), *Mass Media and Social Change* (pp. 115–136). Sage.

Chin, F. (2021, 17 January). Nearly half of adult Canadians struggle with literacy – and that's bad for the economy. *CBC Radio*.

Clarke, S. (2005). The Neoliberal Theory of Society. In A. Saad-Filho & D. Johnston (Eds.), *Neoliberalism – A Critical Reader* (pp. 50–59). Pluto Press.

Coates, S. (1996). *A strategic and educationally sustainable response to government requirements for accountability of adult English language and literacy programs*. World Congress on Comparative Education Societies.

Coates, S., Fitzpatrick, L., McKenna, A., & Makin, A. (1994). *National Reporting System: A Mechanism for Reporting Outcomes of Adult English Language, Literacy and Numeracy Programs*. Language Australia Publications.

Cochran-Smith, M. (2003). The unforgiving complexity of teaching: Avoiding simplicity in the age of accountability. *Journal of Teacher Education, 54*(1), 3–5. https://doi.org/10.1177/0022487102238653

Collins, J. (2018, 13 August). Refugees are integrating just fine in regional Australia. *SBS News*. https://www.sbs.com.au/news/refugees-are-integrating-just-fine-in-regional-australia

Commonwealth of Australia. (1994). *Working Nation – The White Paper on Employment and Growth*. Commonwealth of Australia.

Commonwealth Ombudsman. (2002). *Social Security Breach Penalties – Issues of Administration*. Canberra, ACT.

Community Colleges Australia. (2019). *Submission to the Australian Government Expert Review of the VET Sector*. Community Colleges Australia.

Conway, L. (2016). Delivering on policy: Strategy influences on teaching, learning and formal assessment. *Fine Print, 39*(3), 14–18.

Cooper, C., & Dixit, A. (2021, 9 September). Opinion: Closing Canada's literacy gap in a pandemic. *The Gazette*.

Corbyn, Z. (2024, 30 June). AI scientist Ray Kurzweil: 'We are going to expand intelligence a millionfold by 2045'. *The Guardian*.

Coulombe, S., Tremblay, J., & Marchand, S. (2004). *Literacy Scores, Human Capital and Growth Across Fourteen OECD Countries*. Statistics Canada.

Crowther, J., Maclachlan, K., & Tett, L. (2010). Adult literacy, learning identities and pedagogic practice. *International Journal of Lifelong Education, 29*(6), 651–664.

Cruikshank, B. (1996). Revolutions Within: Self-government and Self-esteem. In A. Barry, T. Osborne, & N. Rose (Eds.), *Foucault and Political Reason. Liberalism, Neoliberalism and Rationalities of Government* (pp. 231–251). University of Chicago Press.

Csiszar, E., & Heidrich, G. (2006). The question of reputational risk: Perspectives from an industry. *The Geneva Papers on Risk and Insurance – Issues and Practice, 31*(3), 382–394. https://doi.org/10.1057/palgrave.gpp.2510096

Cunning, D. (2007). *Foundation Skills Explained.* The Learning Resources Group. Retrieved July 11, 2020, from https://tlrg.com.au/blogs/news/foundation-skills-explained?gclid=CjwKCAjwxqX4BRBhEiwAYtJX7THkEK--tVBhhDFy60oz4kDqP4XaUcOsw48xQ8t_AyXQdgOMo20ASRoCHnwQAvD_BwE

Davies, W. (2014a). *The Limits of Neoliberalism: Authority, Sovereignty & The Logic of Competition.* Sage.

Davies, W. (2014b). Neoliberalism: A bibliographic review. *Theory, Culture & Society, 31*(7–8), 309–317. https://doi.org/10.1177/0263276414546383

Dawkins, J. (1991). *Transcript of John Dawkins, Minister for Employment, Education and Training, Press Conference for Australia's Language: The Australian Language and Literacy Policy.* Department of Employment Education and Training (DEET)

Dawkins, J., & Holding, C. (1987). *Skills for Australia.* Australian Government Publishing Service.

Dawkins, P. (2000). Labour market issues in welfare reform. In P. Saunders (Ed.), *Reforming the Australian welfare state* (pp. 224–249). Australian Institute of Family Studies.

Deacon, D., & Golding, P. (1994). *Taxation and representation: The media, political communication and the poll tax.* John Libbey Publishing.

Dean, M. (1994). *Critical and Effective Histories: Foucault's Methods and Historical Sociology.* Routledge.

Dean, M. (1995). Governing the Unemployed Self in an Active Society. *Economy and Society, 24*(4), 559–583. https://doi.org/10.1080/03085149500000025

Dean, M. (1998). Risk, Calculable and Incalculable. *Soziale Welt, 49*(1), 25–42.

Dean, M. (1999). *Governmentality: Power and Rule in Modern Society.* SAGE Publications.

Dean, M. (2013). *The Signature of Power: Sovereignty, Governmentality and Biopolitics.* SAGE Publications.

DEET (Department of Employment Education and Training). (1990). *The language of Australia: Discussion paper on an Australian literacy and language policy for the 1990s.* DEET.

DEET (Department of Employment Education and Training). (1991). *Australia's Language. The Australian Language and Literacy Policy.* Australian Government Publishing Service.

DEET (Department of Employment Education and Training). (1993). *National Collaborative Adult English language and Literacy Strategy.* Adult Literacy Information Office.

DEETYA (Department of Education Employment Training and Youth Affairs). (1997). Literacy and numeracy training for young jobseekers. *Adult English Language and Literacy*, *7*(September/October), 8–9.

Deleuze, G. (1992a). *Foucault*. University of Minneapolis Press.

Deleuze, G. (1992b). What is a Dispositif? In T. Armstrong (Ed.), *Michel Foucault, Philosopher* (pp. 159–168). Routledge.

Department for Education. (2021). *Skills for Jobs: Lifelong Learning for Opportunity and Growth*. Department for Education.

Department of Education and Training. (2015). *Review of quality assurance in Victoria's VET system*. Department of Education and Training,

Department of Education and Training. (2016). *Certificates in General Education for Adults*. Department of Education and Training

Department of Home Affairs. (2021, November 12). *Adult Migrant English Program (AMEP)*. Australian Government. Retrieved January 4, 2022, from https://www.immi.gov.au/living-in-australia/help-with-english/amep/

Department of the Parliamentary Library. (1991). *Australian Labor Party: Record of Achievements 1983–1990*. Australian Government.

DIIRD (Department of Industry Innovation Regional Development). (2008). *Securing Jobs for Your Future. Skills for Victoria*. Victorian Government.

Dobbs, R., Manyika, J., & Woetzel, J. (2015). *The Four Global Forces Breaking all the Trends*. McKinsey Global Institute.

Dolfsma, W. (2013). *Government failure: Society, markets and rules*. Edward Elgar.

Dreyfus, H., & Rabinow, P. (1982). *Michel Foucault: Beyond Structuralism and Hermeneutics*. Harvester.

Drori, G. (2006). Governed by governance: The new prism for organizational change. In G. Drori, J. Meyer, & H. Hwang (Eds.), *Globalization and organization: World society and organizational change* (pp. 91–118). Oxford University Press.

Drucker, P. (2001, 3 November). The Next Society (A Survey Of The Near Future). *The Economist*.

Dunleavy, P., & Hood, C. (1994). From old public administration to new public management. *Public Money & Management*, *14*(3), 9–16. https://doi.org/10.1080/09540969409387823

Dyrenfurth, N. (2013, 28 December). Back to the future: 1983 and all that. *The Sydney Morning Herald*. https://www.smh.com.au/national/back-to-the-future-1983-and-all-that-20131227-2zzhl.html

Eastmond, M. (2007). Stories as lived experience: Narratives in forced migration research. *Journal of Refugee Studies*, *20*(2), 248–264. https://doi.org/10.1093/jrs/fem007

Eccles, R., Newquist, S., & Schlatz, R. (2007). *Reputation and its Risks*. Harvard Business Publishing.

Ekelund, H. (2024). *Why there will be plenty of jobs in the future – even with artificial intelligence*. World Economic Forum. Retrieved July 11, 2024, from https://www.weforum.org/agenda/2024/02/artificial-intelligence-ai-jobs-future/#:~:text=But%20the%20most%20recent%20World,about%20half%20being%20negatively%20impacted

Elfert, M., & Walker, J. (2020). The Rise and Fall of Adult Literacy: Policy Lessons from Canada. *European Journal for Research on the Education and Learning of Adults, 11*, 109–125. https://doi.org/10.3384/rela.2000-7426.rela9203

Elias, N. (1987). The Retreat of Sociologists into the Present. *Theory, Culture & Society, 4*(2–3), 223–247. https://doi.org/10.1177/026327687004002003

Endemol Shine Australia. (2021, September 22). In J. Maxwell, *Lost For Words*. SBS.

Ernst, J. (1998). A Competitive Future: The Industry Commission and the Welfare State. In P. Smyth & B. Cass (Eds.), *Contesting the Australian Way. States, Markets and Civil Society* (pp. 215–227). Cambridge University Press.

Essential Services Commission. (2011a). *VET Fee and Funding Review – Volume I: Blueprint for Change*. Essential Services Commission.

Essential Services Commission. (2011b). *VET Fee and Funding Review – Volume II: Technical Analysis*. Essential Services Commission.

EY Global. (2020). *Megatrends 2020 and beyond*. Ernst & Young Global Limited.

Fadyl, J., & Nicholls, D. (2013). Foucault, the subject and the research Interview: A critique of methods. *Nursing Inquiry*, 20(1), 23–29. https://doi.org/10.1111/nin.12011

Falk, I., & Millar, P. (2001). *Review of research: Literacy and numeracy in vocational education and training*. NCVER.

Feindt, P. H., & Weiland, S. (2018). Reflexive governance: exploring the concept and assessing its critical potential for sustainable development. Introduction to the special issue. *Journal of Environmental Policy & Planning*, 20(6), 661–674. https://doi.org/10.1080/1523908X.2018.1532562

Fejes, A., & Salling Olesen, H. (2016). Marketization and commodification of adult education. *European Journal for Research on the Education and Learning of Adults*, 7(2), 146–150.

Field, C. (2019, 7 August). VET regulation that's clear as mud. *The Australian*.

Field, J. (2005). *Social Capital and Lifelong Learning*. Policy Press.

Fitzpatrick, D. (2024). *Unlocking the Power of AI: Why Literacy Skills are Key to Success in the AI Era*. TeacherGoals Publishing. Retrieved July 4, 2024, from https://teachergoals.com/literacy-skills-and-ai/?v=6cc98ba2045f

Fleischacker, S. (2013). *What is Enlightenment?* Routledge.

Foley, G. (Ed.). (1995). *Understanding Adult Education and Training*. Allen & Unwin.

Forward, P. (2013). *TAFE: Privatising the future*. Australian Education Union.

Foucault, M. (1972). *The Archaeology of Knowledge* (A. Sheridan, Trans.). Tavistock.

Foucault, M. (1977a). *Discipline and Punish* (*trans. A. Sheridan*). Pantheon.

Foucault, M. (1977b). Nietzsche, Genealogy, History. In D. Bouchard (Ed.), *Language, Counter-Memory, Practice: Selected Essays and Interviews* (pp. 139–164). Cornell University Press.

Foucault, M. (1979). *The History of Sexuality. Vol 1, An Introduction.* Allen Lane.

Foucault, M. (1980a). The Confession of the Flesh (1977) Interview. In C. Gordon (Ed.), *Power/Knowledge. Selected interviews and other writings* (pp. 194–228). Harvester.

Foucault, M. (1980b). *Language, Counter-Memory, Practice: Selected Essays and Interviews.* Cornell University Press.

Foucault, M. (1980c). *Power/Knowledge: Selected Interviews and Other Writings, 1972–1977* (C. Gordon, L. Marshall, J. Mepham, & K. Soper, Trans.). Pantheon Books.

Foucault, M. (1980d). Truth and Power. In C. Gordon (Ed.), *Power/Knowledge: Selected Interviews and Other Writings, 1972–1977* (pp. 109–133). Pantheon Books.

Foucault, M. (1980e). Two Lectures. In C. Gordon (Ed.), *Power/Knowledge: Selected Interviews and Other Writings, 1972–1977* (pp. 78–108). Pantheon Books.

Foucault, M. (1981). The Order of Discourse. In R. Young (Ed.), *Untying the Text: A Post-Structuralist Reader* (pp. 48–78). Routledge & Kegan Paul.

Foucault, M. (1982). The Subject and the Power. In H. Dreyfus & P. Rabinow (Eds.), *Michel Foucault: Beyond Structuralism and Hermeneutics* (pp. 208–226). Harvester.

Foucault, M. (1987a). The Ethic of Care for the Self as a Practice of Freedom. In J. Bernauer & D. Rasmussen (Eds.), *The Final Foucault* (pp. 1–19). MIT Press. https://doi.org/10.1177/019145378701200202

Foucault, M. (1987b). The Ethics of the Concern for Self as a Practice of Freedom. In J. Bernauer & D. Rasmussen (Eds.), *The Final Foucault* (pp. 1–19). MIT Press.

Foucault, M. (1988). Truth, Power, Self. Interview by R. Martin recorded on October 25th, 1982. In L. Martin (Ed.), *Technologies of the Self* (pp. 9–15). University of Massachusetts Press.

Foucault, M. (1991a). Questions of Method. In G. Burchell, C. Gordon, & P. Miller (Eds.), *The Foucault Effect: Studies in Governmentality. With Two Lectures By And An Interview with Michel Foucault* (pp. 73–86). The University Of Chicago Press.

Foucault, M. (1991b). What Is Enlightenment? In P. Rabinow (Ed.), *The Foucault Reader – An Introduction to Foucault's Thought* (pp. 32–50). Penguin Books.

Foucault, M. (1993). About the beginning of the hermeneutics of the self. Two lectures at Dartmouth. *Political Theory, 21*(2), 198–227.

Foucault, M. (1996). Impossible Prison. In S. Lotringer, L. Hochroth, & J. Johnston (Eds.), *Foucault Live: Collected Interviews, 1961–1984* (pp. 275–286). MIT Press.

Foucault, M. (1997a). What is Enlightenment? In S. Lotringer (Ed.), *The Politics of Truth* (pp. 97–120). Semiotext(e).

Foucault, M. (1997b). What is Revolution? In S. Lotringer (Ed.), *The Politics of Truth* (pp. 83–96). Semiotext(e).

Foucault, M. (2000). Truth and Power. In J. Faubion (Ed.), *The Essential Works of Foucault Volume 3: Power* (pp. 111–153). The New Press.

Foucault, M. (2004). *Society Must Be Defended: Lectures at the Collège de France 1975–1976*. Penguin Books.

Foucault, M. (2005). *The History of Sexuality: Volume I*. Biblioteca.

Foucault, M. (2007). *Security, Territory, Population. Lectures at the Collège de France 1977–1978*. Palgrave Macmillan.

Foucault, M. (2008). *The Birth of Biopolitics: Lectures at the Collège de France, 1978–1979* (G. Burchell., Trans.). Palgrave Macmillan.

Foucault, M. (2013). *Politics, Philosophy, Culture: Interviews and Other Writings, 1977–1984*. Routledge.

Foucault, M., Ewald, F., Fontana, A., & Gros, F. (2006). *The hermeneutics of the subject: Lectures at the Collège de France, 1981–1982*. Picador.

Freebody, P. (1992, 9 October). *Assembling reading and writing: How institutions construct literate competencies* National Conference of the Australian Council for Adult Literacy, Sydney, NSW.

Frost, S. (2016). *Biocultural creatures: Toward a new theory of the human*. Duke University Press.

Frost, T. (2015). The dispositif between foucault and agamben. *Law, Culture and the Humanities*, *15*(1), 151–171. https://doi.org/10.1177/1743872115571697

Furlong, A., & Kelly, P. (2005). The Brazilianisation of youth transitions in Australia and the UK? *Australian Journal of Social Issues*, *40*(2), 207–225.

Garland, D. (1996). The limits of the sovereign state: Strategies of crime control in contemporary society. *The British Journal of Criminology*, *36*(4), 445–471.

Garnaut, R. (1989). *Australia and the Northeast Asian Ascendancy*. Canberra, ACT

Gaventa, J., & Pettit, J. (2011). *Foucault: Power is everywhere*. University of Sussex. Retrieved 21 January 2022 from https://www.powercube.net/other-forms-of-power/foucault-power-is-everywhere/

Gilbert, J. (2013). What kind of thing is neoliberalism? *New Formations, Autumn/Winter* (80–81), 7–22.

Gillard, J. (2010). *CEDA Leader Series: Address to CEDA Leader Series*. Committee for the Economic Development of Australia. Retrieved August 29, 2019, from https://www.ceda.com.au/Events/Library/Past-Events1/S100504

Golding, P. (1981). The missing dimensions: News media and the management of social change. In *Mass Media and Social Change* (pp. 63–81). Sage.

Goode, W. (1960). A Theory of Role Strain. *American Sociological Review*, *25*(4), 483–496. https://doi.org/10.2307/2092933

Gordon, C. (2000). Introduction. In J. Faubion (Ed.), *Michel Foucault: Power. Essential works of Foucault, 1954–1984* (pp. XI–XLI). The New Press.

Gorur, R. (2014). Towards a sociology of measurement in education policy. *European Educational Research Journal, 13*(1), 58–72.

Gottdiener, M. (2000). *New Forms of Consumption: Consumers, Culture, and Commodification.* Rowman & Littlefield.

Grant, B. (1990). The global context of Australian-Northeast Asian relations: Some comments on the Garnaut Report. *Australian International Affairs, 44*(1), 3–7. https://doi.org/10.1080/10357719008445014

Grebel, Y. (2004). *Entrepreneurship: A New Perspective.* Routledge.

Green, B., Hodgens, J., & Luke, A. (1997). Debating literacy in Australia: History lessons and popular f(r)ictions. *The Australian Journal of Language and Literacy, 20*(1), 6–24.

Gribble, H. (1994). *Useful Knowledge: A Brief History and Description of Adult, Community and Further Education in Victoria.* Adult Community and Further Education Board.

Habermas, J. (1994). Some Questions Concerning the Theory of Power: Foucault Again. In M. Kelly (Ed.), *Critique and Power: Recasting the Foucault/Habermas Debate* (pp. 79–108). MIT Press.

Hake, B. (2016). Regulatory governance of 'training markets', 'market failure', and 'quasi' markets: Historical dimensions of the post-initial training market in The Netherlands. *European Journal for Research on the Education and Learning of Adults, 7*(2), 171–190.

Hall, W. (1999). Research into Work and Training. In J. Keeves & K. Marjoribanks (Eds.), *Australian Education: Review of Research 1965–1998* (pp. 301–325). Australian Council for Educational Research.

Halse, C., Hartung, C., & Wright, J. (2017). Responsibility and responsibilisation in education. *Discourse: Studies in the Cultural Politics of Education, 38*(1), 1. https://doi.org/10.1080/01596306.2016.1169585

Hamilton, D., & Zufiaurre, B. (2014). *Blackboards and Bootstraps: Revisioning Education and Schooling.* Sense Publishers. https://doi.org/10.1007/978-94-6209-473-4

Hamilton, M. (2012). The effects of the literacy policy environment on local sites of learning. *Language and Education, 26*(2), 169–182. https://doi.org/10.1080/09500782.2011.642882

Hamilton, M., & Barton, D. (2000). The International Adult Literacy Survey: What Does It Really Measure? *International Review of Education, 46*(5), 377–389. http://www.jstor.org.ezproxy.lib.rmit.edu.au/stable/3445256

Harris, P. (2001). From relief to mutual obligation: Welfare rationalities and unemployment in 20th-century Australia. *Journal of Sociology, 37*(1), 5–26. https://doi.org/10.1177/144078301128756175

Harris, R., & Short, T. (2014). *Workforce development: Perspectives and issues.* Springer.

Hartley, R., & Horne, J. (2006). *Social and economic benefits of improved adult literacy: Towards a better understanding.* NCVER.

Harvey, D. (2005). *A Brief History Of Neoliberalism*. Oxford University Press.

Harvey, D. (2006). *Spaces Of Global Capitalism: A Theory Of Uneven Geographical Development*. Verso.

Hauenschild, H. (1990, June). *Adult Literacy: Responding to Change* State Adult Literacy Conference, Brisbane, Queensland.

Hawke, R. (1989). *Launch of the Garnaut Report: Australia and the Northeast Asia Ascendancy*. Australian Government Publishing Service.

Hayek, F. (1976). *The road to serfdom*. Routledge.

Healey, J. (2014). *The Australian Labour Market in 2013*. Flinders University.

Hearn, M., & Michelson, G. (2006). *Rethinking work: Time, space and discourse*. Cambridge University Press.

Heath, A. (2016, 21 September). *The Changing Nature of the Australian Workforce* CEDA – Future Skills: The Education and Training Pipeline, Brisbane, QLD.

Hekman, S. (1983). Weber's ideal type: A contemporary reassessment. *Polity, 16*(1), 119–137.

Hemsley, B. (2023, 19 January). Will AI tech like ChatGPT improve inclusion for people with communication disability? *The Guardian*.

Hendricks, C. (2008). Foucault's Kantian critique: Philosophy and the present. *Philosophy & Social Criticism, 34*(4), 357–382.

Herbert, S. (1962). The Architecture of Complexity. *Proceedings of the American Philosophical Society, 106*(6), 467–482.

Hilgartner, S. (1992). The social construction of risk objects: Or, how to pry open networks of risk. In J. Short & L. Clarke (Eds.), *Organizations, uncertainties and risk* (pp. 39–53). Westview.

Hilmer, F. (1993). *National Competition Policy*. Canberra, ACT: Australian Government Publishing Service

Hilsenrath, J. (2021, 11 June). When Americans Took to the Streets Over Inflation. *The Wall Street Journal*. https://www.wsj.com/articles/when-americans-took-to-the-streets-over-inflation-11623412801

Hodge, S. (2011). Learning to manage: Transformative outcomes of competency-based training. *Australian Journal of Adult Learning, 51*(3), 498–517.

Hodge, S. (2014). Transformative Learning as an "Inter-Practice" Phenomenon. *Adult Education Quarterly, 64*(2), 165–181.

Hodge, S., & Harris, R. (2012). Discipline, governmentality and 25 years of competency-based training. *Studies in the Education of Adults, 44*(2), 155–170.

Hollander, R. (2010). Rethinking overlap and duplication: Federalism and environmental assessment in Australia. *Publius: The Journal of Federalism, 40*(1), 136–170. https://doi.org/10.1093/publius/pjp028

Hood, C. (1990). A public management for all seasons? *Public Administration, 69*(1), 3–19.

Hossenfelder, S. (2018). *Lost in Math*. Basic Books.

Hossenfelder, S. (2022). *Existential Physics: A Scientist's Guide to Life's Biggest Questions*. Penguin.

Hossenfelder, S. (2024). *Rapid AI Progress Surprises Even Experts: Survey Just Out*. Basic Books. Retrieved June 12, 2024, from https://www.youtube.com/watch?v=gS_iSrmCH5c

Howard, D., & Buultjens, J. (2004). Did Labour Market Programs Reduce Unemployment in Australia's Regions? *Journal of Economic and Social Policy*, *8*(2), 1–10.

Howard, J. (1997a). *Commonwealth Parliamentary Debates*. Australian Government.

Howard, J. (1997b). *Transcript of the Prime Minister; The Hon John Howard MP Address at the official launch of Centrelink (Commonwealth Services Delivery Agency) The Great Hall, Parliament House, 24 September*. Australian Government

Howard, J. (1999, January 29). *Transcript of the Prime Minister, The Honorable John Howard with 3AW's Neil Mitchell* [Interview].

Howe, B., Biddington, J., Munro, P., & Charlesworth, S. (2012). *Lives on Hold: Unlocking the Potential of Australia's Workforce (Howe Report)*. Independent Inquiry into Insecure Work in Australia.

Huff, R. (2016). *Political Science – Governmentality* [Type](Report (Series Political Science – Governmentality, Issue). Encyclopedia Brittanica Inc.

Humphrys, E. (2019). *How Labour Built Neoliberalism: Australia's Accord, the Labour Movement and the Neoliberal Project*. Brill.

Hunt, A. (1999). *Governing Morals: A Social History of Moral Regulation*. Cambridge University Press.

Ilcan, S., & Basok, T. (2004). Community government: Voluntary agencies, social justice, and the responsibilization of citizens. *Citizenship studies*, *8*(2), 129–144.

Independent Broad-based Anti-Corruption Commission. (2017). *Operation Lansdowne*. Independent Broad-based Anti-Corruption Commission.

Industry Commission. (1995). *Charitable Organisations in Australia*. Australian Government Publishing Service.

Industry Commission. (1996). *Competitive Tendering and Contracting by Public Sector Agencies*. Australian Government Publishing Service.

Industry Skills Councils. (2011). *No More Excuses – An Industry Response to the Language Literacy and Numeracy Challenge*. Industry Skills Councils.

Ingram, D., & Wylie, E. (1979). *Australian Second Language Proficiency Ratings. Mimeograph*. Brisbane College of Advanced Education.

International Labour Organization. (2018). *Women and men in the informal economy: A statistical picture. Third edition*. International Labour Organization.

International Labour Organization. (2021a). *Informal economy in Asia and the Pacific*. https://www.ilo.org/asia/areas/informal-economy/lang--en/index.htm

International Labour Organization. (2021b). *World social protection report 2020–22: Social protection at the crossroads in pursuit of a better future*. International Labour Organization.

Jackson, N. (2005). Adult literacy policy: Mind the gap. In N. Bascia, A. Cumming, A. Datnow, K. Leithwood, & D. Livingstone (Eds.), *International handbook of educational policy* (pp. 763–778). Springer.

Jackson, N., & Slade, B. (2008). Hell on my face: The production of workplace illiteracy. In M. De Vault (Ed.), *People at work: Life, power and social inclusion in the new economy* (pp. 25–39). New York University Press.

Jacobson, E. (2020). The Lessons of the Churn: Adult Basic Education and Disciplining the Adult Learner. *Adult Literacy Education*, 2(Fall), 4–15. https://doi.org/10.35847/EJacobson.2.2.4

Jobs Australia. (2015). *Jobactive*. Jobs Australia. Retrieved September 14, 2016, from https://www.ja.com.au/policy-advocacy/policy/jobactive

Joint Standing Committee on Migration. (2017). *No one teaches you to become an Australian: Report of the inquiry into migrant settlement outcomes*. Parliament of the Commonwealth of Australia.

Jørgensen, M. (2016). Precariat – What it is and isn't – Towards an understanding of what it does. *Critical Sociology*, *42*(7–8), 959–974.

Junankar, P., & Kapuscinski, C. (1997). *Was Working Nation Working?* Australian National University.

Kain, J., Kuruppu, I., & Billing, R. (2001). *Australia's National Competition Policy*. Parliament of Australia. https://www.aph.gov.au/About_Parliament/Parliamentary_Departments/Parliamentary_Library/Publications_Archive/archive/ncpebrief

Kant, I. (2016). Dare to Know, from What is Enlightenment?, 1784. In C. Warman (Ed.), *Tolerance: The Beacon of the Enlightenment* (p. 35). Open Book Publishers.

Karmel, T. (2011). *Vocational Education and Skills Policy in Australia*. NCVER.

Karpin, D. (1995). *Enterprising nation: renewing Australia's managers to meet the challenges of the Asia-Pacific century: report of the Industry Task Force on Leadership and Management Skills*. Australian Government Publishing Service

Karpov, A. (2013). The commodification of education. *Russian Education & Society*, *55*(5), 75–90. https://doi.org/10.2753/RES1060-9393550506

Keating, P. (1986, 14 May). *Speaking to John Laws*. [Interview].

Kelly, P. (2013). *The Self as Enterprise*. Gower Publishing.

Kelly, P. (2017). Growing up after the GFC: Responsibilisation and mortgaged futures. *Discourse: Studies in the Cultural Politics of Education*, *38*(1), 57–69. https://doi.org/10.1080/01596306.2015.1104852

Kelly, P., Brown, S., & Goring, J. (2023). Young people and post-pandemic futures: scenario planning as a radical politics of hope. *Qualitative Research Journal*, *23*(4), 357–371. https://doi.org/https://doi.org/10.1108/QRJ-09-2022-0124

Kemp, D. (1996, 22 October). *Interview with Ross Sally. ABC AM Program* [Interview].

Kemp, D. (1997). *New Employment Services: Media Release. 27 November*. Department of Education, Training and Youth Affairs.

Kemp, D. (1998a). *Media release K63/98: Work for the Dole Scheme.*

Kemp, D. (1998b). *Unemployed young people to take responsibility for their future: Media Release. 28 January 1998*. Department of Education, Training and Youth Affairs.

Kester, Z., & Miller, R. (2020). *Let The Good Deed Go Unpunished: Avoiding Nonprofit Board Liability*. Charitable Allies. Retrieved 22 May 2021 from https://charitableallies.org/news/board-liability/

King, M. (2009). Clarifying the Foucault–Habermas debate: Morality, ethics and 'normative foundations'. *Philosophy & Social Criticism, 35*(3), 287–314.

Klein, N. (2023, 8 May). AI machines aren't 'hallucinating'. But their makers are. *The Guardian*. https://www.theguardian.com/commentisfree/2023/may/08/ai-machines-hallucinating-naomi-klein

Knowles, M. (1973). *The Adult Learner: A Neglected Species*. Gulf Publishing.

Koon, D. (2020). Education Policy Networks: The Co-Optation, Coordination, and Commodification of the School-to-Prison Pipeline Critique. *American Educational Research Journal, 57*(1), 371–410. https://doi.org/10.3102/0002831219855338

Köpsén, J. (2022). Employers placing orders and students as commodities: Swedish post-secondary vocational education and training policy. *Journal of Vocational Education & Training, 74*(2), 167–186. https://doi.org/10.1080/13636820.2020.1744695

Krug, G., Drasch, K., & Jungbauer-Gans, M. (2019). The social stigma of unemployment: Consequences of stigma consciousness on job search attitudes, behaviour and success. *Journal for Labour Market Research, 53*(1), 1–27. https://doi.org/10.1186/s12651-019-0261-4

Kurzweil, R. (2005). *The singularity is near: When Humans Transcend Biology*. Viking Press.

Kurzweil, R. (2024). *The Singularity Is Nearer: When We Merge with AI*. Random House.

Lambert, J. (2018, 13 May). Vocational education and training: Time to think more laterally and creatively. *Financial Review*. https://www.afr.com/policy/health-and-education/vocational-education-and-training-time-to-think-more-laterally-and-creatively-20180511-h0zyst

Laming, A. (2019). *Speech to House of Representatives (Federal Parliament) – ASQA*. Canberra, ACT: House of Representatives Employment, Education and Training Committee

Latham, B. (2020). *Australia falls behind on UN Sustainable Development Goals*. Australian Institute of International Affairs. Retrieved May 25, 2022, from https://www.internationalaffairs.org.au/news-item/australia-falls-behind-on-un-sustainable-development-goals/#:~:text=A%20lack%20of%20political%20interest,Whitlam%20Institute%20director%20Leanne%20Smith

le Grand, J. (1991). The Theory of Government Failure. *British Journal of Political Science, 21*(4), 423–442.

Lee, A., & Wickert, R. (1995). Reading the Discourses of Adult Basic Education Teaching. In G. Foley (Ed.), *Understanding Adult Education and Training* (pp. 134–150). Allen & Unwin.

Lemke, T. (2001). The birth of bio-politics – Michel Foucault's lecture at the Collège de France on neo-liberal governmentality. *Economy and Society, 30*(2), 190–207.

Lemke, T. (2002). Foucault, governmentality, and critique. *Rethinking Marxism, 14*(3), 49–64.

Leonard, L. (2021). *Scholarly Community Encyclopedia: Reflexive Governance.* Multidisciplinary Digital Publishing Institute. Retrieved January 22, 2022, from https://encyclopedia.pub/11073

Leonard, L., & Lidskog, R. (2021). Conditions and constrains for reflexive governance of industrial risks: The case of the South Durban Industrial Basin, South Africa. *Sustainability, 13*(10), 56–79. https://www.mdpi.com/2071-1050/13/10/5679

Liebenberg, L., Ungar, M., & Ikeda, J. (2013). Neo-Liberalism and responsibilisation in the discourse of social service workers. *The British Journal of Social Work, 45*(3), 1006–1021. https://doi.org/10.1093/bjsw/bct172

Lilly, M. (2021, 7 December). Response to skills shortages needs to be placed on a war footing. *Sydney Morning Herald.*

Lindgard, B., Porter, P., Bartlett, L., & Knight, J. (1995). Federal/state mediations in the Australian national education agenda: From the AEC to MCEETYA 1987–1993. *Australian Journal of Education, 39*(1), 41–66.

lo Bianco, J. (1987a). *Adult Literacy Under the National Policy of Language.* Australian Council for Adult Literacy.

lo Bianco, J. (1987b). *National Policy on Languages.* Australian Government Publishing Service.

lo Bianco, J. (1991). A review of some of the achievements of the National Policy on Languages. *Australian Review of Applied Linguistics, Series S*(8), 23–38.

lo Bianco, J. (1996). Public Policy and Literacy Research Data: Will Knowing Lead to Doing. In Australian Bureau of Statistics (Ed.), *Aspects of Literacy: Assessed Skill Levels Australia.* Australian Government Publishing Service.

lo Bianco, J., & Wickert, R. (Eds.). (2001). *Australian Policy Activism in Language & Literacy.* Language Australia.

Lonsdale, M., & McCurry, D. (2004). *Literacy in the New Millennium.* NCVER.

MacIntyre, C. (1999). From Entitlement to Obligation in the Australian Welfare State. *Australian Journal of Social Issues, 24*(2), 103–117.

Mackay, S., Burgoyne, U., Warwick, D., & Cipollone, J. (2006). *Current and future professional development needs of the language, literacy and numeracy workforce.* NCVER.

MacLachlan, K., & Cloonan, M. (2003). Three dimensional change? The relationship between theory, policy, and adults' understanding of literacies. *Research in Post-compulsory Education, 8*(1), 123–136.

Mahboubi, P. (2018, 10 December). Zeroing in on Canada's literacy and numeracy skills gap. *Policy Options Politiques.*

Major, J. (2018, 28 January). Is democracy now being stifled by its own virtues? *Financial Review*. https://www.afr.com/opinion/is-democracy-now-being-stifled-by-its-own-virtues-20180128-h0pf3y

Marantz, A. (2023, 13 February). It's Not Possible for Me to Feel or Be Creepy: An Interview with ChatGPT. *The New Yorker*. https://www.newyorker.com/news/the-new-yorker-interview/its-not-possible-for-me-to-feel-or-be-creepy-an-interview-with-chatgpt

Martell, L. (2010). *The Sociology of Globalization*. Polity Press.

Martin, S. (1998). *New Life New Language: The History of the Adult Migrant English Program*. National Centre for English Language Teaching and Research.

Mason, P. (2020, 3 April). Will coronavirus signal the end of capitalism? *Aljazeera*. https://www.aljazeera.com/opinions/2020/4/3/will-coronavirus-signal-the-end-of-capitalism

Matilla-Santander, N., Ahonen, E., Albin, M., Baron, S., Bolíbar, M., Bosmans, K., Burström, B., Cuervo, I., Davis, L., Gunn, V., Håkansta, C., Hemmingsson, T., Hogstedt, C., Jonsson, J., Julià, M., Kjellberg, K., Kreshpaj, B., Lewchuk, W., Muntaner, C., … Bodin, T. (2021). COVID-19 and Precarious Employment: Consequences of the Evolving Crisis. *International Journal of Health Services*, *51*(2), 226–228. https://doi.org/10.1177/0020731420986694

McGuiness, P. (1999, 30 January). *The Sydney Morning Herald*.

McHugh-Dillon, H. (2015). *'If they are genuine refugees, why?' Public attitudes to unauthorised arrivals in Australia*. Victorian Foundation for Survivors of Torture.

McHugh, M., Nevard, J., & Taylor, A. (2001). The melody changes but the dance goes on – tracking adult literacy education in western australia from "Learning for Life" to "Lifelong Learning": Policy impacts on practice 1973–1999. In J. Lo Bianco & R. Wickert (Eds.), *Australian policy activism in language & literacy* (pp. 181–202). Language Australia.

McKay, J. (1990). Australia and the Northeast Asian ascendancy: Some commentaries on the Garnaut report. *Australian International Affairs*, *44*(1), 1–2. https://doi.org/10.1080/10357719008445013

Meadowcroft, J. (2010). Markets, Discovery, and Social Problems. In M. White (Ed.), *Accepting the invisible hand* (pp. 23–41). Palgrave. https://doi.org/10.1057/9780230114319_2

Mendelovits, J. (2011, October 23–25). *A slow burn: The impact of IALS in Australia* IALS (International Adult Literacy Survey): Its meaning and impact for policy and practice, Banff, Canada.

Mendes, P. (1998). From Keynes to Hayek: The social welfare philosophy of the Liberal Party of Australia, 1983–1997. *Policy, Organisation and Society*, *15*(1), 65–87. https://doi.org/10.1080/10349952.1998.11876679

Mendes, P. (2007). *Australia's Welfare Wars Revisited: The Players, the Politics and the Ideologies*. UNSW Press.

Mendes, P. (2009). Retrenching or renovating the Australian welfare state: The paradox of the Howard government's neo-liberalism. *International Journal of Social Welfare, 18*(1), 102–110. https://doi.org/10.1111/j.1468-2397.2008.00569.x

Mikulec, B., & Krašovec, S. J. (2016). Marketising Slovene adult education policies and practices using mechanisms of the Europeanisation of education. *European Journal for Research on the Education and Learning of Adults, 7*(2), 151–170.

Miles, A. (2009). Complexity in medicine and healthcare: People and systems, theory and practice. *Journal of Evaluation in Clinical Practice, 15*(3), 409–410.

Miller, B. (2010). Skills for sale: What is being commodified in higher education? *Journal of Further and Higher Education, 34*(2), 199–206. https://doi.org/10.1080/03098771003695460

Miller, P., & Rose, N. (1990). Governing economic life. *Economy and Society, 19*(1), 1–31. https://doi.org/10.1080/03085149000000001

Miller, P., & Rose, N. (1993). Governing Economic Life. In M. Gane & T. Jognson (Eds.), *Foucault's New Domains* (pp. 75–105). Routledge.

Miller, P., & Rose, N. (2010). Political power beyond the state: Problematics of government. *The British Journal of Sociology, 43*(2), 272–302. https://doi.org/10.1111/j.1468-4446.2009.01247.x

Miltenyi, G. (1989). *English in the workplace: A shrewd economic investment.* Office of Multicultural Affairs.

Ministerial Council on Employment Education Training and Youth Affairs. (2001). *Performance Measurement and Reporting Taskforce.* Ministerial Council on Employment Education Training and Youth Affairs.

Ministers of the Employment and Workplace Relations Portfolio. (2024). *Key research bolsters drive to improve foundation skills.* Minister's Media Centre. Retrieved May 28, 2024, from https://ministers.dewr.gov.au/oconnor/key-research-bolsters-drive-improve-foundation-skills-0

Montero, K., & Kelly, P. (2021). Young people and the human-car-machine-assemblage: aesthetics, erotics and other lessons for school-based health education. *Discourse: Studies in the Cultural Politics of Education, 42*(6), 840–853. https://doi.org/10.1080/01596306.2020.1740916

Moore, H. (2002). Who will Guard the Guardians Themselves? National Interest Versus Factional Corruption in Policymaking for ESL in Australia. In J. Tollefson (Ed.), *Language Policies in Education* (pp. 111–135). Lawrence Erbaum Associates Publishers.

Mueller, C. (1973). *The politics of communication: A study in the political sociology of language, socialization, and legitimation.* Oxford University Press.

Murphy, D. (2014, 30 December). Cabinet papers 1988–89: Australia looks to Asia with Garnaut report. *The Sydney Morning Herald.*

Murray, C. (1986). Losing ground two years later. *Cato Journal, 6*(1), 19–29.

Nahum, D., & Stanford, J. (2020). *2020 Year-End Labour Market Review: Insecure Work and the Covid-19 Pandemic (Briefing Paper).* The Australia Institute: Centre for Future Work.

Narayan, D., & Petesch, P. (2007). Agency, Opportunity Structure and Poverty Escapes. In D. Narayan & P. Petesch (Eds.), *Moving Out of Poverty* (pp. 1–44). World Bank.

National Archives of Australia. (2019). *Paul Keating: Before office*. National Archives of Australia. Retrieved November 13, 2021, from https://www.naa.gov.au/explore-collection/australias-prime-ministers/paul-keating/before-office#treasurer-1983%E2%80%9391

National Centre for Education Statistics. (2021). *Fast facts: Adult literacy*. Institute of Education Sciences.

National Research and Development Centre. (2011). *A Literature Review of International Adult Literacy Policies*. Institute of Education.

National VET Equity Advisory Council. (2011). *NVEAC Equity Blueprint 2011–2016. Creating Futures: Achieving Potential through VET*. Ministerial Council for Tertiary Education and Employment.

NCVER (National Centre for Vocational Education Research). (2011). *Building the Foundations: Outcomes From the Adult Language, Literacy and Numeracy Search Conference*. NCVER.

Newman, M. (1995a). Adult Education and Social Action. In G. Foley (Ed.), *Understanding Adult Education and Training* (pp. 246–260). Allen & Unwin.

Newman, M. (1995b). Program development in adult education and training. In G. Foley (Ed.), *Understanding Adult Education and Training* (pp. 54–74). Allen & Unwin.

Newport, C. (2023, 13 April). What Kind of Mind Does ChatGPT Have? *The New Yorker*. https://www.newyorker.com/science/annals-of-artificial-intelligence/what-kind-of-mind-does-chatgpt-have

Noor, P. (2017, 23 February). Now a degree is a commodity, no wonder more students are cheating. *The Guardian*. https://www.theguardian.com/education/commentisfree/2017/feb/22/degree-commodity-university-funding-students-plagiarism

Norton, M. (1996). So – How Many People Can't Read? In Australian Bureau of Statistics (Ed.), *Aspects of Literacy: Assessed Skill Levels Australia*. Australian Government Publishing Service.

OECD (Organisation for Economic Co-operation and Development). (2000). *Literacy in the Information Age: Final Report of the International Adult Literacy Survey*. OECD Publishing.

OECD (Organisation for Economic Co-operation and Development). (2013). *OECD Skills Outlook 2013: First results From The Survey Of Adult Skills*.

OECD (Organisation for Economic Co-operation and Development). (2018). *Skills for the 21st century: Findings and policy lessons from the OECD survey of adult skills. OECD Education Working Papers No. 166*. OECD Publishing.

OECD (Organisation for Economic Co-operation and Development). (2019). *OECD Future of Education and Skills 2030. Conceptual learning framework. Learning Compass 2030*. OECD Publishing.

OECD (Organisation for Economic Co-operation and Development). (2021a). Labour market developments: The unfolding COVID-19 crisis. In *OECD Employment Outlook 2021: Navigating the COVID-19 Crisis and Recovery*. OECD Publishing.

OECD (Organisation for Economic Co-operation and Development). (2021b). *OECD Employment Outlook 2021: Navigating the COVID-19 Crisis and Recovery*. OECD Publishing.

OECD (Organisation for Economic Co-operation and Development). (2022). *Survey of Adult Skills: PIAAC 2nd Cycle*. OECD. Retrieved June 28, 2024, from https://www.oecd.org/skills/piaac/about/piaac2ndcycle/

OECD (Organisation for Economic Co-operation and Development). (2023). *Artificial intelligence and jobs: An urgent need to act. OECD Employment Outlook: Artificial Intelligence and the Labour Market.*

Olssen, M. (2003). Foucault and Critique: Kant, Humanism and the Human Sciences. In M. Peters, M. Olssen, & C. Lankshear (Eds.), *Futures of Critical Theory* (pp. 73–102).

Packard, M., & Bylund, P. (2021). From homo economicus to homo agens: Toward a subjective rationality for entrepreneurship. *Journal of Business Venturing, 36*(6), 106–159. https://doi.org/10.1016/j.jbusvent.2021.106159

Parliament of the Commonwealth of Australia. (2022). *Don't take it as read: Inquiry into adult literacy and its importance*. Parliament of the Commonwealth of Australia.

Parliamentary Library. (2005). *Disability Support Pensioners, 1984–2004*. Parliament of Australia.

Peeters, R. (2013). Responsibilisation on government's terms: New welfare and the governance of responsibility and solidarity. *Social Policy and Society, 12*(4), 583–595. https://doi.org/10.1017/S1474746413000018

Peetz, D. (2018, 3 August). Self-employment and casual work aren't increasing but so many jobs are insecure – what's going on? *The Conversation*. https://theconversation.com/self-employment-and-casual-work-arent-increasing-but-so-many-jobs-are-insecure-whats-going-on-100668

Peltonen, M. (2004). From discourse to "dispositif": Michel Foucault's two histories. *Historical Reflections 30*(2), 205–219.

Perkins, K. (2009). *Adult Literacy and Numeracy: Research and Future Strategy. An Adult Literacy National Project Report*. NCVER.

Peters, M. (2017). From State responsibility for education and welfare to self-responsibilisation in the market. *Discourse: Studies in the Cultural Politics of Education, 38*(1), 138–145. https://doi.org/10.1080/01596306.2016.1163854

Peters, M., & Humes, W. (2003). Education in the knowledge economy. *Policy Futures in Education, 1*(1), 1–19.

Petropoulos, G. (2018). The impact of artificial intelligence on employment In M. Neufeind, J. O'Reilly, & F. Ranft (Eds.), *Work in the Digital Age: Challenges of the Fourth Industrial Revolution* (pp. 119–132). Rowman & Littlefield International.

PhillipsKPA. (2015). *Department of State Development – Evaluation of the NFSS Project.* PhillipsKPA.

Pile, S., Mooney, G., & Brook, C. (1999). *Unruly Cities?: Order/disorder.* Routledge.

Pincus, J. (2010). *Commonwealth–State Financial Relations: The Case for Competitive Federalism.* Parliament of Australia. Retrieved May 8, 2021, from https://www.aph.gov.au/About_Parliament/Senate/Powers_practice_n_procedures/~/~/link.aspx?_id=9E988B12F96D40D2BBF6A3F7B0A9B0F9&_z=z

Ploger, J. (2008). Foucault's dispositif and the city. *Planning Theory, 7*(1), 51–70. https://doi.org/10.1177/1473095207085665

Power, M., Scheytt, T., Soin, K., & Sahlin, K. (2009). Reputational risk as a logic of organizing in late modernity. *Organization Studies, 30*(02 & 03), 301–324. https://doi.org/10.1177/0170840608101482

Preiss, B. (2013, 13 July). TAFEs accused of rorting system to boost funds. *The Age.* http://www.theage.com.au/victoria/tafes-accused-of-rorting-system-to-boost-funds-20130712-2pvov.html

Productivity Commission. (1999). *Impact of Competition Policy Reforms on Rural and Regional Australia, Inquiry Report no. 8, September.* AusInfo.

Productivity Commission. (2003). *From Industry Assistance to Productivity: 30 Years of 'The Commission'.* Productivity Commission.

Productivity Commission. (2017). *Shifting the Dial – Five Year Productivity Review.* Productivity Commission.

Promberger, K., & Rauskala, I. (2003). *New Public Management: An Introduction from the UK Perspective.* University of Innsbruck.

PwC (Pricewaterhouse Coopers) Australia. (2022). *Where next for skills?* PWC Australia. Retrieved March 22, 2022, from https://www.pwc.com.au/important-problems/where-next-for-skills-business-led-upskilling-for-productivity-growth.html

Quiggan, J. (1993). *The Industry Commission Approach to Public Sector Reform.* Evatt Foundation.

Rabinow, P. (Ed.). (1986). *The Foucault Reader.* Peregrine.

Rabinow, P. (2003). *Anthropos Today. Reflections on Modern Equipment.* Princeton University Press.

Raffnsøe, S., Gudmand-Høyer, M., & Thaning, M. (2014). *What is a dispositive?: Foucault's historical mappings of the networks of social reality.* Copenhagen Business School.

Ranson, S. (2003). Public accountability in the age of neo-liberal governance. *Journal of Education Policy, 18*(5), 459–480.

Raper, M. (2000). Examining the assumptions behind the welfare review. In P. Saunders (Ed.), *Reforming the Australian welfare state* (pp. 250–270). Australian Institute of Family Studies.

Ravenhill, J. (1994). Australia in the global economy. In S. Bell & B. Head (Eds.), *Economy and Public Policy in Australia* (pp. 75–97). Oxford University Press.

Rawling, M. (2015). Regulating precarious work in Australia. *Alternative Law Journal, 40*(4), 252–256. https://doi.org/10.1177/1037969x1504000408

Reder, S. (2013). Lifelong and life-wide adult literacy development. *Perspectives on Language and Literacy, 39*(2), 48–53.

Refugee Council of Australia. (2016). *Education and Training.* Refugee Council of Australia. Retrieved August 30, 2016, from http://www.refugeecouncil.org.au/getfacts/settlement/learninghere/education-and-training/

Refugee Council of Australia. (2019, 2 Feburary 2019). *What makes a good advocate?* Refugee Council of Australia. Retrieved April 14, 2021, from https://www.refugeecouncil.org.au/what-makes-a-good-advocate/

Rhodes, L. (2016). Smoke and Mirrors: Where are the Adult Literacy Students Now? *Fine Print, 39*(3), 30–32.

Rizvi, M., & Lingard, B. (2010). *Globalizing Education Policy.* Routledge.

Roberts, P. (2000). Knowledge, information and literacy. *International Review of Education, 46*(5), 433–453.

Robeyns, I. (2006). Three models of education: Rights, capabilities and human capital. *Theory and Research in Education, 4*(1), 69–84. https://doi.org/10.1177/1477878506060683

Rogers, A. (2003). *What is the difference: A new critique of adult learning and teaching.* NIACE.

Rogers, A. (2006). Escaping the slums or changing the slums? Lifelong learning and social transformation. *International Journal of Lifelong Education, 25*(2), 125–137. https://doi.org/10.1080/02601370500510736

Romaine, S. (1991). *Language in Australia.* Cambridge University Press.

Rome, A., & Smith, A. (2012, 24 December). Do we want for-profit schools in Australia? *The Conversation.* https://theconversation.com/do-we-want-for-profit-schools-in-australia-7015

Rose, N. (1996). The death of the social? Re-figuring the territory of government. *Economy and Society, 25*(3), 327–356. https://doi.org/10.1080/03085149600000018

Ross, R. (1977). Problems of Advocacy. *The Journal of Sociology & Social Welfare, 4*(8), 1246–1259.

Rubin, E. (2015). *Soul, Self, and Society: The New Morality and the Modern State.* Oxford University Press.

Samson, D. (2011). *Karpin Report Revisited: Leadership and Management Challenges in Australia.* Innovation & Business Skills Australia.

Sandhu, S. (2021). *The biggest threat to the education and training sector in Australia is bad regulation!* Compliance and Quality Assurance. Retrieved May 3, 2021, from https://caqa.com.au/blogs/news/the-biggest-threat-to-the-education-and-training-sector-in-australia-is-bad-regulation

Sarian, E. (2018). Rethinking neo/liberalism and the Australian citizenship test: A history of regulating difference. *Cultural Studies Review, 24*(1), 119–136. https://doi.org/10.5130/csr.v24i1.5455

Saunders, D., & Blanco Ramirez, G. (2017a). Against "teaching excellence": Ideology, commodification, and enabling the neoliberalization of postsecondary education. *Teaching in Higher Education*, 22(4), 396–407. https://doi.org/10.1080/13562517.2017.1301913

Saunders, D., & Blanco Ramirez, G. (2017b). Resisting the neoliberalization of higher education: A challenge to commonsensical understandings of commodities and consumption. *Cultural Studies Critical Methodologies*, 17(3), 189–196. https://doi.org/10.1177/1532708616669529

Saunders, P. (2013). *Re-moralising the welfare state*. Centre for Independent Studies.

Savage, A., & Bell, F. (2012, 12 September). Baillieu defends TAFE cuts. https://www.abc.net.au/news/2012-09-12/baillieu-defends-tafe-cuts/4257888

Scanlon Institute. (2019). *Australia's English Problem: How to renew our once celebrated Adult Migrant English Program*. S. F. R. Institute.

Schultz, T. (1961). Education and Economic Growth. In N. Henry (Ed.), *Social Forces Influencing American Education* (pp. 46–88). University of Chicago Press.

Schwartzman, R. (2013). Consequences of commodifying education. *Academic Exchange Quarterly*, 17(3), 1–7.

Schwella, E. (2014). Knowledge based governance, governance as learning: The leadership implications. *International Journal of Leadership in Public Services*, 10(2), 84–90. https://doi.org/10.1108/IJLPS-05-2014-0004

SCOTESE (Standing Council on Tertiary Education Skills & Employment). (2012). *National Foundation Skills Strategy for Adults*. Department of Tertiary Education, Skills, Science and Research.

Sembou, E. (2011, 16–17 June). *Foucault's Genealogy* International Social Theory Consortium, University College Cork, Ireland.

Sennett, R. (1998). *The Corrosion of Character: The Personal Consequences of Work in the New Capitalism*. WW Norton & Company.

Shah, C. (2017). *Skills and Knowledge*. NCVER. Retrieved January 3, 2022, from https://www.voced.edu.au/pod-skills-and-knowledge

Shergold, P., Benson, K., & Piper, M. (2019). *Investing in Refugees. Investing in Australia: The Findings of a Review into Integration, Employment and Settlement Outcomes for Refugees and Humanitarian Entrants in Australia*. Australian Government.

Slater, D., & Tonkiss, F. (2001). *Market Society*. Polity Press.

Sledd, A. (1988). Readin' not riotin': The politics of literacy. *College English*, 50(5), 495–508. https://doi.org/10.2307/377478

Sloman, J., & Norris, K. (1999). *Economics*. Addison-Wesley.

Smith, L., & Brolan, C. (2020, 23 June 2020). *The goals for Australia to do better*. Whitlam Institute within Western Sydney University. https://www.whitlam.org/publications/2020/6/17/no-one-left-behind-implementing-the-sustainable-development-goals-in-australia

Social Compass. (2019). *Evaluation of the Adult Migrant English Program New Business Model: For the Department of Home Affairs*. Department of Education and Training.

Sparkle, M., & Williams, O. (2022). Neoliberal disease: COVID-19, co-pathogenesis and global health insecurities. *EPA: Economy and Space*, *54*(1), 15–32.

Springer, S., Birch, K., & MacLeavy, J. (Eds.). (2016). *The Handbook of Neoliberalism*. Routledge.

Standing, G. (2011a). *The Precariat: The New Dangerous Class*. Bloomsbury Publishing.

Standing, G. (2011b, 2 June). Who Will be a Voice for the Emerging Precariat? *The Guardian*. https://www.theguardian.com/commentisfree/2011/jun/01/voice-for-emerging-precariat

State Government of Victoria. (2012). *Public Response to the Essential Services Commission's VET Fee and Funding Review Report and Recommendations*. Higher Education and Skills Group.

State Government of Victoria. (2013a). *Learn Local Focusing on the Future*. Department of Education and Training.

State Government of Victoria. (2013b). *Next Steps for Refocusing Vocational Training in Victoria – Supporting a Modern Workforce*. Higher Education and Skills Group Department of Education and Early Childhood Development.

State Government of Victoria. (2015). *VET Funding Review Issues Paper*. Victorian Government.

State Government of Victoria. (2016). *Skills First: Real training for real jobs*. Department of Education and Training.

State Government of Victoria. (2019). *Skills for Victoria's Growing Economy*. Department of Education and Training.

State Government of Victoria. (2020a). *Stories from Learners*. Adult, Community and Further Education Board. Retrieved May 19, 2020, from https://learnlocal.org.au/stories-from-learners/

State Government of Victoria. (2020b). *VET funding contracts*. Department of Education and Training. Retrieved May 19, 2020, from https://www.vic.gov.au/vet-funding-contracts

Stayner, T. (2020, 28 August). English language program for migrants set for overhaul amid concerns about proficiency. *SBS News*. https://www.sbs.com.au/news/english-language-program-for-migrants-set-for-overhaul-amid-concerns-about-proficiency

Stewart, J. (2005). Educational policy: Politics, markets and the decline of 'publicness'. *Policy and Politics*, *33*(3), 475–487. https://doi.org/10.1332/0305573054325693

Stewart, J., & Stoker, G. (1995). *Local Government in the 1990s*. Macmillan.

Stokes, A. (2004). *The Labour Market In Australia*. Australian Catholic University.

Street, B. (1984). *Literacy in Theory and Practice* (Vol. 9). Cambridge University Press.

Street, B. (2003). What's "new" in New Literacy Studies? Critical approaches to literacy in theory and practice. *Current Issues in Comparative Education, 5*(2), 77–91.

Sugarman, J. (2015). Neoliberalism and psychological ethics. *Journal of Theoretical and Philosophical Psychology, 35*(2), 103–116. https://doi.org/10.1037/a0038960

Tamboukou, M. (1999). Writing genealogies: An exploration of Foucault's strategies for doing research. *Discourse: Studies in the Cultural Politics of Education, 29*(2), 201–217. https://doi.org/10.1080/0159630990200202

Tamboukou, M. (2003). *Women, Education and the Self: A Foucauldian Perspective.* Palgrave.

Tanke, J. (2009). *Foucault's Philosophy of Art: A Genealogy of Modernity.* Continuum.

Taylor, S., Pham, L., Rivkin, I., & Armor, D. (1998). Harnessing the imagination: Mental simulation, self-regulation, and coping. *American Psychologist, 53*(4), 429–439. https://doi.org/10.1037/0003-066X.53.4.429

Tease, W. (1990). *The Balance of Payments in the 1980s.* Reserve Bank of Australia.

Teghtsoonian, K. (2009). Depression and mental health in neoliberal times: A critical analysis of policy and discourse. *Social Science & Medicine, 69*(1), 28–35.

Teicher, J., Holland, P., & Gough, R. (Eds.). (2013). *Australian Workplace Relations.* Cambridge University Press.

Tett, L., & Maclachlan, K. (2007). Adult literacy and numeracy, social capital, learner identities and self–confidence. *Studies in the Education of Adults, 39*(2), 150–167.

Thaler, R., & Sunstein, C. (2008). *Nudge: Improving Decisions about Health, Wealth and Happiness.* Penguin Books.

Thar, R. (1990). *International Literacy Year.* ERIC Digest.

The Allen Consulting Group. (2011). *Competitive tendering and contestable funding in VET: Approaches to supporting access and equity.* National VET Equity Advisory Council.

The Australian. (2022). *Digital skills are as important as reading and writing.* Retrieved April 3, 2022, from https://www.theaustralian.com.au/business/digital-skills-are-as-important-as-reading-and-writing/video/58d2a6ab42fc82e0d21474d7007f58e6

The Centre for Literacy. (2013). *Early analyses of response to PIAAC.* Montreal, Canada. Retrieved June 26, 2024, from https://www.centreforliteracy.qc.ca/news/early-analyses-responses-piaac%23cda

The Senate Education and Employment References Committee. (2019). *Jobactive: Failing those it is intended to serve.* Parliament of Australia.

Tomasevski, K. (2003). *Education Denied.* Zed Books.

Tomazin, F. (2015, 19 September). Stop the rorts: $30 million crackdown looms for vocational sector's dodgy training providers. *The Age.* https://www.theage.com.au/national/victoria/stop-the-rorts-30-million-crackdown-looms-for-vocational-sectors-dodgy-training-providers-20150919-gjqbuk.html

Training Costs Review Committee. (1990). *Training Costs of Award Restructuring.* Australian Government Publishing Service.

Travers, M., Rule, T., Syed, I., & Lawlor, D. (2018). *Training and Assessment – Theory and Practice*. Cengage.

Treasury Australia. (1988). *Budget statements 1988–89: Circulated by the Honourable P.J. Keating, M.P., Treasurer of the Commonwealth of Australia, and Senator the Honourable Peter Walsh, Minister for Finance.* Australian Government Publishing Service.

Turner, J. (2015). Being Young in the age of globalization: A look at recent literature on neoliberalism's effects on youth. *Social Justice, 41*(4), 8–22.

Turner, R. (2008). *Neo-Liberal Ideology: History, Concepts and Policies.* Edinburgh University Press.

UNESCO (United Nations Educational Scientific and Cultural Organization). (1978). *Revised Recommendation Concerning the International Standardization of Educational Statistics. Volume I: Resolutions.* UNESCO.

UNESCO (United Nations Educational Scientific and Cultural Organization). (1990). *International Literacy Year.* UNESCO Standing Committee.

UNESCO (United Nations Educational Scientific and Cultural Organization). (2006). *Education for All Global Monitoring Report – Understandings of Literacy.* UNESCO.

UNESCO (United Nations Educational Scientific and Cultural Organization). (2015). *The Sustainable Development Agenda.* UNESCO.

UNESCO Institute for Lifelong Learning. (2013). *Effective Literacy Practice – The Australian Language, Literacy and Numeracy Program* (*LLNP*). Retrieved February 2, 2016, from https://www.uil.unesco.org/en/litbase/australian-language-literacy-and-numeracy-programme-llnp-australia

United Nations. (2018). *Sustainable Development Goals Knowledge Platform: Australia. Voluntary National Review 2018.* Department of Economic and Social Affairs Sustainable Development. Retrieved May 25, 2022, from https://sustainable development.un.org/memberstates/australia

van Onselen, L. (2013). *Pros and cons of the casualised workforce.* Australian Economy MacroBusiness. Retrieved September 1, 2020, from https://www.macrobusiness.com.au/2013/11/pros-and-cons-of-the-casualised-workforce/

Vaughn, S., Bos, C., & Schumm, J. (2000). *Teaching exceptional, diverse, and at-risk students in the general education classroom.* Allyn & Bacon.

von Platz, J. (2017). Person to person: A note on the ethics of commodification. *The Journal of Value Inquiry, 51*(4), 647–653. https://doi.org/10.1007/s10790-017-9618-5

Vucetic, S. (2010). Genealogy as a Research Tool in International Relations. *Review of International Studies, 37*(3), 1295–1312.

Waldan, A., Swaby, A., Clark, A., & Santa Cruz, N. (2022, 14 December). A Fifth of American Adults Struggle to Read. Why Are We Failing to Teach Them? *ProPublica.*

Walker, J. (2009). The inclusion and construction of the worthy citizen through lifelong learning: A focus on the OECD. *Journal of Education Policy, 24*(3), 335–351. https://doi.org/10.1080/02680930802669276

Walsh, L., Gleeson, J., Magyar, B., & Gallo Cordoba, B. (2021). *Life, Disrupted: Young People, Education and Employment Before and After COVID-19*. Monash University.

Wanna, J. (2018). *Keating's Working Nation plan for jobs was hijacked by bureaucracy: Cabinet papers 1994–95*. Australia National University.

Waterhouse, P., & Virgona, C. (2004). *Two-dimensional work: Workplace literacy in the aged care and call centre industries*. NCVER.

Watts, G. (2021). Are you a neoliberal subject? On the uses and abuses of a concept. *European Journal of Social Theory*, 1–19. https://doi.org/10.1177/13684310211037205

Webb, S., Holford, J., Hodge, S., Milana, M., & Waller, R. (2017). Lifelong learning for quality education: Exploring the neglected aspect of sustainable development goal 4. *International Journal of Lifelong Education, 36*(5), 509–511.

Weller, S., & O'Neill, P. (2014). An argument with neoliberalism: Australia's place in a global imaginary. *Dialogues in Human Geography, 4*(2), 105–130. https://doi.org/10.1177/2043820614536334

Wheelahan, L. (2012, 30 May). Victorian TAFE chaos: A lesson in how not to reform vocational education. *The Conversation*. https://theconversation.com/victorian-tafe-chaos-a-lesson-in-how-not-to-reform-vocational-education-7296

Wheelahan, L., Moodie, G., & Doughney, J. (2022). Challenging the skills fetish. *British Journal of Sociology of Education, 43*(3), 475–494. https://doi.org/10.1080/01425692.2022.2045186

Whyte, A., & Crombie, A. (1995). Policy and provision in Australia adult education and training. In G. Foley (Ed.), *Understanding Adult Education and Training* (pp. 93–107). Allen & Unwin.

Wickert, R. (1989). *No Single Measure: A Survey of Australian Adult Literacy. Summary Report. A National Policy on Languages Initiative*. DEET.

Wickert, R., & Kevin, M. (1995). *No Single Measure: The Final Report*. Australian Government Publishing Service.

Wickert, R., & McGuirk, J. (2005). *Integrating literacies: Using partnerships to build literacy capabilities in communities*. NCVER.

Wignall, L. (2015). *Research to Identify and Qualify Professional Practice in Foundation Skills*. Louise Wignall Consulting Services.

Williams, A. (2005). *Genealogy as Methodology in the Philosophy of Michel Foucault*. London Foucault Circle.

Williams, S., Bradley, H., Devadson, R., & Erickson, M. (2013). *Globalization and Work*. Polity Press.

Willmott, H. (1995). Managing the academics: Commodification and control in the development of university education in the UK. *Human Relations, 48*(9), 993–1027.

World Economic Forum. (2021). *Upskilling for Shared Prosperity: Insight Report, January 2021*. World Economic Forum.

World Health Organization. (2021). *WHO Mental Health and COVID-19*. World Health Organization. Retrieved 22 April 2022 from https://www.who.int/teams/mental-health-and-substance-use/mental-health-and-covid-19

Wyse, L. (2008). *Australian Core Skills Framework*.

Yang, R. (2006). The Commodification of Education and Its Effects on Developing Countries: A Focus on China. *Journal für Entwicklungspolitik*, 22(4), 52–69. https://doi.org/10.20446/JEP-2414-3197-22-4-52

Yasukawa, K., & Black, S. (2016). *Beyond Economic Interests: Critical Perspectives on Adult Literacy and Numeracy in a Globalised World*. Sense Publishers.

Yeatman, A. (1994). *Postmodem Revisionings of the Political*. Routledge.

Yerby, E., & Page-Tickell, R. (2020). *Where next for the gig economy and precarious work post COVID-19?* London School of Economics and Political Science. Retrieved February 25, 2021, from https://blogs.lse.ac.uk/management/2020/05/01/where-next-for-the-gig-economy-and-precarious-work-post-covid-19/

Zacharakis, J., & Holloway, J. (2016). The murky waters of neoliberal marketization and commodification on the education of adults in the United States. *European Journal for Research on the Education and Learning of Adults*, 7(2), 223–236.

Zoellner, D. (2011). *Change and VET: Thinking the unthinkable*. Charles Darwin University.

Index

Printed in the United States
by Baker & Taylor Publisher Services